CAPTAIN GILL'S WALKING STICK

CAPTAIN GILL'S WALKING STICK

The True Story of the Sinai Murders

SAUL KELLY

I.B. TAURIS
LONDON • NEW YORK • OXFORD • NEW DELHI • SYDNEY

I.B. TAURIS
Bloomsbury Publishing Plc
50 Bedford Square, London, WC1B 3DP, UK
1385 Broadway, New York, NY 10018, USA

BLOOMSBURY, I.B. TAURIS and the I.B. Tauris logo are trademarks of
Bloomsbury Publishing Plc

First published in Great Britain 2019

Cover design by Irene Martinez Costa
Cover image: Camp in Wady ed Deir, at foot of Jebel Musa from Aaron's Hill,
courtesy of the Palestine Exploration Fund.

A catalogue record for this book is available from the British Library.

A catalog record for this book is available from the Library of Congress.

ISBN: HB: 978-1-7845-3341-0
ePDF: 978-1-7867-3615-4
eBook: 978-1-7867-2608-7

Typeset by Newgen KnowledgeWorks Pvt. Ltd., Chennai, India
Printed and bound in Great Britain

To find out more about our authors and books visit www.bloomsbury.com
and sign up for our newsletters.

In Memoriam
Steven John Fairbairn
1960–2016.

CONTENTS

PLATES

1. Portrait of William Gill (by T. G. Wirgman; frontispiece to Gill, *The River of Golden Sand*)

2. Lt. Charles William Wilson (from C. Watson, *The Life of Major-General Sir Charles William Wilson*)

3. Charles Warren's party in Jerusalem, 1867 (left to right, Warren, Barclay, Phillips and Easton; from Palestine Exploration Fund – PEF)

4. Panoramic view of Jerusalem from the Mount of Olives (from C. W. Wilson, *Survey of Jerusalem*, PEF)

5. Interior of Haram-ash-Sharif. Eastern view of the Platform from the Golden Gate (from Wilson, *Survey of Jerusalem*, PEF)

6. South entrance to the Kubbat-as-Sakhra (from Wilson, *Survey of Jerusalem*, PEF)

7. Interior of the Kubbat-as-Sakhra (from Wilson, *Survey of Jerusalem*, PEF)

8. Eastern face of the south-east angle of Temple Mount (from Wilson, *Survey of Jerusalem*, PEF)

9. Frontispiece of the *Ordnance Survey of the Peninsula of Sinai* (PEF P5114/P5116)

10. Members of the Sinai Survey (*OSS*, Vol. 2.1, PEF P5051)

11. Non-commissioned officers of the Royal Engineers on the Sinai Survey (OSS, Vol. 1.2, PEF P4992)

12. Camp in Wady ed Deir at foot of Jebel Musa from Aaron's Hill (*OSS*, Vol. 1.8, PEF 5008)

13. Convent of St. Katherine and steps leading up to Jebel Musa (*OSS*, Vol. 1.20, PEF 5010)

14. Interior of convent of St. Katherine, west wall (*OSS*, Vol. 1.23, PEF 5013)

15. Jebel Katherine from summit of Jebel Musa (*OSS*, Vol. 1.34, PEF 5024)

16. Plain of Er Rahah from cleft of Ras Sufsafeh (*OSS*, Vol. 1.41, PEF P5031)

17. Rock inscriptions in Wady Mukatteb (*OSS*, Vol. 2.54, PEF P5104)

18. Palmer sketch of inscription in Sinai (Palmer notebook, St John's College, Cambridge)

19. Group of Bedouin (*OSS*, Vol. 2.3, PEF P5053)

20. Entering the desert by Ayun Musa (*OSS*, Vol. 1.3, PEF P4993)

ACKNOWLEDGEMENTS

I am grateful to the staff of the following archives and libraries for their help in facilitating my research for this book: the British Library, St. Pancras, London; the Caird Library, National Maritime Museum, Greenwich, London; the Hampshire Records Office, Winchester, Hants.; St. John's College, Cambridge; the Fitzwilliam Museum, Cambridge; the JSCSC library, Shrivenham, Wilts.; the National Archives, Kew, London; the Palestine Exploration Fund, Marylebone, London; the Royal Geographical Society, London; the School of Oriental and African Studies library; St. Paul's Cathedral; University College, London, library and the University of London library, Senate House. I would like to thank Professor G.I. Davies of the University of Cambridge, who provided me with a copy of his unpublished conference paper on 'E.H. Palmer's copies of the Nabataean Inscriptions in the Sinai Peninsula.' For permission to reproduce some of the illustrations for this book, I would like to thank the Palestine Exploration Fund and St. John's College, Cambridge. I am grateful to Jo Godfrey and David Campbell at I.B. Tauris/Bloomsbury for their editorial help. The eagle-eyed Oliver Everett has, as ever, been a boon companion on this book.

I have dedicated this book to the memory of my old friend Steve Fairbairn in remembrance of those sunnier times playing endless games of lawn tennis, drinking beer besides the Cam, and dancing the night away with our girlfriends.

Map 1 Jerusalem, from A. L. Rawson's Map of Palestine and all Bible lands (1873)

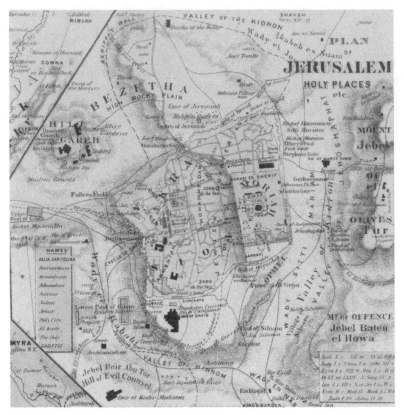

Map 2 Peninsula of Mt. Sinai, from A. L. Rawson's Map of Palestine and all Bible lands (1873)

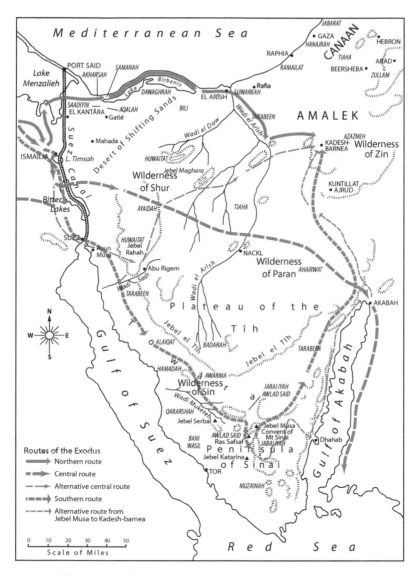

Map 3 The desert of the Exodus

1

Captain Gill's walking stick

On 27 September 2010 BBC News Edinburgh, Fife and East Scotland reported that a:

> walking stick used to bludgeon its spy owner to death more than a hundred years ago has fetched £1,400 at auction in Edinburgh. The intricately carved stick once belonged to William Gill, a British spy and multi-millionaire explorer. However, it was used by a Bedouin tribesman to murder Gill in the Sinai Desert in 1883. The 39-year-old adventurer was gathering intelligence for the British government at the time of his death. It was thought he was on his way to cut the telegraph line between Constantinople and Alexandria when he was killed.[1]

This short, evocative statement of the provenance surrounding an old walking stick was clearly intended by both BBC Scotland and the Edinburgh auction house to excite a general interest in this unusual sale of a murder weapon. It tapped into the abiding interest of the British public, fed by the media, in espionage, murder

and the net worth of the individuals concerned. If the murder of a rich spy happened in an exotic location, so much the better. In this respect we are not unlike our Victorian forebears. They were fed a steady diet of sensation, murder, mystery and mayhem by the early mass-circulation newspapers. The most famous case of this was the coverage of the 'Jack the Ripper' murders in Whitechapel in the East End of London in 1888. As this book will reveal, there is a direct and previously undetected connection between the Whitechapel murders and those that had taken place in the Sinai Desert six years earlier.

Who was this James Bond prototype spy and millionaire who was murdered in the Sinai in 1882 (not 1883, as the BBC mistakenly noted)?

Captain William Gill was a well-heeled Royal Engineer officer who sought adventure on the fringes of the British Empire from North Africa to China. He had a habit of popping up in the world's trouble spots: the borderlands of India, the Balkans, Turkey, Persia and Egypt. As a Royal Engineer, his skills as a surveyor meant that he could fill in the gaps on the existing maps of these places and also report on the prevailing political situation (usually unstable), which made him useful to the British government. Gill always travelled for a purpose: to 'spy out the land' and report to the Intelligence Department of the War Office in London on the suspicious and, occasionally, nefarious activities of the agents of Russia and France, Britain's two great power rivals in that arc of crisis stretching from China to North Africa. In the 1870s successive British governments had become concerned about Imperial Russia's rapid conquest of the khanates of Central Asia. This brought Russia's soldier-explorers to the uncharted borderlands of Persia and Afghanistan. Their movements were watched by Captain

Gill, among others, indulging in a spot of shooting leave in 1873 while busy mapping the mountain passes, rivers and routes of Khorasan in northeastern Persia. Some officials and politicians in Calcutta and London were alarmed about the effect Russia's presence at the gates of British India might have on potentially rebellious elements in India and on Britain's hold on the subcontinent.

A few years later (1876–77) Gill was in China, trying to enter Russian Central Asia from the northwestern province of Sinkiang (Xinjiang), but he was barred from entering due to the deteriorating state of Anglo-Russian relations. Recalled for another intelligence mission, Gill returned home via the great Yangtze River, eastern Tibet and the Irrawaddy in Burma (now Myanmar), mapping as he went. Gill's gaze was soon drawn towards Russian activities in Turkey. Russia's bite-and-chew approach to the Balkan and Caucasian territories of the Ottoman Empire resulted in the latter's defeat in war in 1877–8. To the British prime minister Benjamin Disraeli this seemed to presage the collapse of that empire, Russia's seizure of that great strategic prize, the Turkish Straits, and the ability to interdict British sea and land lines of communication with India. Russian pressure at Kabul and at Constantinople, the twin nerve points of the late nineteenth-century British Empire, caused a severe neuralgic spasm in London and Calcutta. In order to warn Russia off, Disraeli sent ships and men to the Eastern Mediterranean while his diplomats worked feverishly, and ultimately successfully, to thrash out a peace settlement which would contain Russia in the Balkans and the Caucasus. Again, Gill was among those British engineer-officers who argued with the Russians over where the boundaries of the new Balkan states should run. Soon after that in 1880, he was engaged in the British invasion and occupation of Afghanistan, intended to keep the Russians at bay. Gill's attempt to reach the Merv oasis in the Karakum desert ahead of the Russians was thwarted by the faintheartedness of the British Foreign Office, which was reluctant to to do anything which might prejudice relations with Russia.

Gill's further scouting adventures in Turkish Tripoli (now Libya) in 1881 were intended to monitor possible French designs on that province following France's annexation of Tunis (Tunisia). At that time Britain and France were rivals for paramountcy in Africa, especially in Egypt, which was still nominally part of the Ottoman Empire. In Egypt, the two nations shared a growing responsibility not only for restoring the country's fiscal health following its bankruptcy under the Khedive Ismail Pasha, but also for securing the routes through the Suez Canal to both the British and French eastern empires. It was an Islamo-nationalist revolt, led by the Egyptian Army officer Arabi Pasha, which threatened to undermine the Anglo-French position in Egypt. It led to the sole British military intervention in 1882 because the French baulked at the prospect at the last minute.

When Gill was murdered in the Sinai, he was again engaged in 'Secret Service' work. He was acting on behalf of the Admiralty, the lead department for much of the intelligence-gathering activity in the Mediterranean and Red Sea regions. He was accompanied by Edward Henry Palmer, the noted Cambridge University Lord Almoner's Professor of Arabic who was also an expert on the Sinai Bedouin. Palmer, rather than Gill, led the mission, which was given official imprimatur by the presence of a Royal Navy Lieutenant, Harold Charrington. Their mission was concerned with more than cutting telegraph wires and gathering intelligence. More ambitious aims were involved, as this book will show.

The murder of not only Gill, but Palmer and Charrington as well, was a *cause celebre* in England at the time. It received much attention in the press, leading to questions being asked in Parliament and resulted in the publication of two Command Papers for Parliament (known as 'Blue Books' because of the colour of their covers) of relevant official Admiralty and Foreign Office documents, with the names of British agents being carefully excised. The case drew the personal attention of two prominent Liberal cabinet ministers, the First Lord of the Admiralty, Lord Northbrook (of the Baring banking family) and the prime minister of the day, William Ewart Gladstone, the 'Grand Old Man' of British politics. Even Queen Victoria was swept up in the drama of the case and personally intervened at a key point. The resulting pressure on 'the men on the spot' in Egypt to find and 'deal with' the murderers of Gill, Palmer and Charrington lies at the heart of this story. It is a tale of first-class detective work in the desert by Lieutenant Colonel Charles Warren (another Royal Engineer officer), the man who was to be the commissioner of the Metropolitan Police at the time of the Jack the Ripper murders in London later that decade. It was Warren's impressive detective skills and sheer doggedness in pursuit of his quarry in the desert which resulted in his being made the chief policeman at Scotland Yard. He was headhunted by Hugh Childers, the then Home Secretary, and was chosen over four hundred other candidates because Childers knew of Warren's feat in the Sinai.

Why was Warren chosen to hunt for the killers of Gill, Palmer and Charrington in the Sinai? The simple reason is that Warren knew Palmer from their days working together in Jerusalem for the Palestine Exploration Fund. The latter body had from the late 1860s acted as an effective cover organization for British military surveying and intelligence-gathering activities in Palestine and the Sinai Desert. The French military intervention in Syria and the building of the Suez Canal in the 1860s, combined with Russian aggression against the Ottoman Empire in the 1870s, had raised British fears that these two revanchist powers were seeking to control the all-important imperial sea and land routes to India. To prevent this from happening, by force if necessary, Britain needed accurate maps of the approaches to Egypt from Palestine, especially down the Jordan Valley and across the Sinai. It fell to a select group of Royal Engineer officers led by Major Charles Wilson (later the first effective head of British Military Intelligence, which developed into MI5 and MI6) and including the likes of Warren and Horatio Herbert Kitchener to accomplish this task. They were joined by the quirky Cambridge professor of Arabic, Edward Palmer, who acted as interpreter and liaison with the Bedouin. As God-fearing Englishmen they readily adopted their garb as biblical archaeologists, searching for the likely routes taken by the Israelites on their Exodus from Pharaoh's Egypt, their forty years' wandering in the desert and their eventual arrival in the Promised Land of Canaan. In a twist of fate, Warren was to use these very same routes in his quest for the killers of Gill, Palmer and Charrington.

Warren had a rival in his murder hunt: Captain Sir Richard Burton, the famous explorer of the sources of the Nile. Burton knew Palmer well from their forays among the Bedouin tribes of Syria in the 1870s. Burton had also crossed the Sinai disguised as a Muslim on haj to Mecca and Medina and had searched for the legendary gold of the land of Midian. But Burton's search and rescue mission for Palmer in 1882 was to cause ructions both in Egypt and London. The involvement of two of the most prominent Oriental scholars of their day in the Sinai also raises a disturbing question with regard to late nineteenth-century Western conceptions of the Arabs and especially the Bedouin. It has been fashionable among certain academics for a generation now to decry the attempts of Western scholars to understand the Arabs, given an apparently innate even 'imperialist' bias, which seeks to denigrate 'the other'. The very opposite seems to be the case with the Sinai murders. It is one of the main contentions of this book that it was the romanticization, rather than an alleged vilification, of the Arabs and especially the Bedouin, by English travellers such as Palmer and Burton, that led to the deaths of Palmer and his colleagues in the desert. They and their political and military masters in London and on the spot laboured under a fatal illusion as to what could be achieved among the tribes of the Sinai during the British invasion of Egypt in 1882. This book is intended, therefore, as a cautionary tale, not only of intrigue, betrayal, murder and redemption, but also of a fatal illusion. The only man who did not share this illusion and showed a sure touch in his dealings with the Bedouin was Warren. At great personal risk to himself and his small hunting party, he forged a successful strategy of enquiry, based on impressive investigative skills, to discover the murderers and bring them to book in a foreign land. Above all, his quest for justice for those murdered in the Desert of the Exodus (the Sinai) was to lead to his becoming the commissioner of the Metropolitan Police at the time of the Jack the Ripper murders. His road to London started in the biblical lands of Sinai and Palestine.

2

Recovering Jerusalem

The modern British Secret Service can be said to have had its start in Palestine in 1864, for it was there that the 'father' of the service, Captain Charles Wilson, of the Royal Engineer (RE) corps (aka the Sappers) in the British army, carried out his survey of Jerusalem as a first step towards providing the city with a reliable freshwater supply. Wilson was to return to carry out more survey and secret intelligence work in western Palestine, and was to be followed by other Royal Engineer officers, Charles Warren, Claude Conder and Horatio Herbert Kitchener. The Sapper officers and their NCOs combined skills in surveying, which is essentially scientific observation and recording of the topography or terrain, with a talent for biblical archaeology. This combination provided the British military with the opportunity to build up a comprehensive intelligence picture of the strategically important land bridge between Asia and Africa: Palestine and the Sinai. As Warren later explained:

> The coast from Asia Minor to Egypt, from the Bay of Iskenderun to Port Said, running nearly north and south, with a slight inclination to west, and at a few miles (from twenty to thirty) inland there

exists a deep crack on the earth surface running nearly parallel to the shoreline, entirely cutting it off from Arabia ... the Peninsula of Sinai, Canaan and ancient Phoenicia are distinctly cut off from Asia, and form a sort of neutral ground between that continent and Africa.[1]

This 'neutral ground' was the traditional invasion route of armies heading north or south between Egypt and Constantinople, the heart of the Ottoman Empire. The perceived enfeeblement of that empire in the nineteenth century encouraged the rebellious pashas of Egypt, the Muhammad Ali dynasty, often with the encouragement of France, to seek independence from the Turkish sultan, while the sultan sought help wherever he could obtain it, whether from Russia, Britain or Germany.

In the early 1860s, France's Emperor Napoleon III sought to emulate his more infamous uncle and to expand his country's influence once again in the Ottoman Empire by backing Ferdinand de Lesseps's building of the Suez Canal, intervening in Lebanon and Syria to save the Maronite Christians from massacre by their Muslim Druze neighbours and sending military surveyors and archaeologists to Jerusalem. Napoleon III also despatched a secret emissary, the English Jesuit priest William Gifford Palgrave, on a mission to the tribal sheikhs of northern Arabia in pursuit of a plan to create a vast Arab kingdom under the defeated Algerian rebel leader, Abd al-Qadir, at that time in exile in Damascus, which would look to France for protection. To counter this growing French activity and influence in the Middle East[2] the British government encouraged Wilson's surveys of Jerusalem and Palestine and the subsequent despatch by the newly created Palestine Exploration Fund (PEF) of Charles Warren to engage in further archaeological and survey work in Jerusalem and Palestine.

The father of modern British intelligence

If intelligence work is done well, it is very hard to trace, both at the time and afterwards. It requires two essentials to work. First, it needs a good cover which, to be believable, must be a functioning activity in its own right and must act as an impermeable shield for the secret activity. Second, the 'story' to conceal this secret intelligence work must be sustainable to be credible and it must stand the test of time. Good intelligence work might well involve the destruction of incriminating material, and this may even be wilful, as it was in the case of Wilson. His detailed travel diaries, notebooks and letters to his wife (in which he recorded everything he did and saw when he was away 'on secret service') were destroyed after his death and his 'official' and very uninformative biography had been written by a fellow Sapper. Alternatively, it may be accidental, such as the destruction of the Ordnance Survey records at their headquarters in Southampton by the German Luftwaffe during World War II. Wilson's surveys of Jerusalem and the Sinai were carried out under the auspices of the Ordnance Survey (OS), which was responsible for scientific mapping, or cartography, for the British government at home and often overseas also. The OS worked closely with the War Office, which was interested in military mapping, and with the surveys of the Royal Engineers.

What has survived of Wilson's published and manuscript sources is intended to 'tell a tale' of selfless endeavour in the interests of pure science, humanitarian aid and biblical archaeology. This is a story in its own right, but it is also intended to cover up an inner story or a missing dimension. This was the struggle for influence in Palestine between the representatives, official and unofficial, of the great powers and Turkey, a struggle that involved secret service activity. This tactical battle on the ground centred on the custodianship of the religious shrines which are holy to three of the world's main religions, Judaism, Christianity and Islam. But that battle also had strategic implications, for whoever exerted the greatest influence on the ground would control the vital land bridge between Africa and Asia. It is possible to deduce this despite the paucity of direct sources by using the sort of intellectual triangulation techniques which would have found favour with the Royal Engineers themselves. However, as good intelligence officers, they might have been reluctant to admit it! There is enough extant material from other sources to reinterpret the activities of Wilson, Warren and the other Sapper officers. It is possible to show that in carrying out their survey and archaeological work they were also engaged in secret service activity, primarily intelligence gathering. This double role, public and secret, gives a mirage-like quality to many of their activities. In this hazy environment nothing is quite what it seems, and men and their motives seem to vanish into the desert air. Just as the mirage magnifies an object, there is a real risk of exaggerating and distorting events. For this reason, hard evidence will anchor everything that is said here about the activities of Wilson and Warren.

Throughout much of its history and by virtue of its holiness to Christendom, Judaism and Islam, Jerusalem has been a crucible of conflict between and within religions and later between nations. Revolutionary France had tried and failed twice, thwarted by the British, to secure control of Egypt and Palestine, once under Napoleon Bonaparte at the turn of the nineteenth century and again in the late 1830s under King Louis Philippe, who was backing the rebel pasha of Egypt, Muhammad Ali. But French military surveyors had been able to make topographical observations and draw up maps: Colonel Jacotin in 1799 (with his 1:100,000 map), Captain Gautier with his survey of the Palestine coast between 1816 and 1820 and Colonel Callier from 1832 to 1833 (with his 1:500,000 map of 1840, reissued by the French army in 1853). Callier also established the level of the Dead Sea, as did Count Jules de Berthou in 1838 (at 1,148 feet below the level of the Mediterranean). Moreover, the Egyptian occupation of Syria (which then included Palestine) from 1831 to 1840 provided the opportunity for Western scholars and clerics to travel to the Holy Land. By seeking scientific evidence for the accuracy of the Bible, these evangelical Christians aimed to counter the assaults on their faith by the new sciences, geology, anthropology and linguistics. However, the quest for 'scriptural geography' gave rise to its own problems. It led theologians in turn to disagree on the exact location of the sites mentioned in the Bible.

One of the most influential scriptural geographers was the American nonconformist missionary Professor Edward Robinson. After excursions to Egypt and Palestine in 1838 and 1852, he questioned the accepted site of Mount Sinai (see Map 2). He reasoned that the Israelite host could only have assembled on a plain 3 miles away and therefore could not possibly have heard Moses laying down the law from his mountain pulpit. Robinson capped this by declaring that every holy site in Jerusalem was a fake because the ancient city lay buried under its modern incarnation (see Map 1). He had noticed the skewback of a monumental arch near the southwestern corner of the Haram ash-Sharif ('the Noble Sanctuary'; 'Temple Mount' to Christians and Har ha-Bayit in Hebrew), known since as 'Robinson's Arch'. However, it was to be Charles Warren who correctly identified the arch as the arch of a monumental stairway to the Herodian Temple rather than the support of a 'great bridge' across the Tyropoean Valley. Another American missionary, Dr Barclay, discovered the lintel atop one of Herod's gates, which was thereafter dubbed 'Barclay's Gate'. Robinson had also sought to disparage the efforts of a party of British army and navy surveyors. At the request of Foreign Secretary Lord Palmerston, the surveyors had taken advantage of military operations against Egyptian forces to carry out a theodolite triangulation of the Syrian (Palestinian) coast in 1840 and 1841. In addition, they had fixed the levels of the Dead Sea (at 1,312.2 feet) and of Lake Tiberias. Inferior instruments meant that an inaccurate measurement was given for the level of Lake Tiberias (at 1,308 feet), which had led Robinson to question the value of the entire survey. But the American naval officer Lieutenant Lynch, during his 1848 expedition to the Dead Sea, substantiated the British survey party's level for that sea. Unfortunately, the work had been incorrectly incorporated into the final map, which was drawn up on a scale of 1:253,400 and privately printed in 1846 for the Foreign Office. Moreover, the cartographic information on Syria was sketchy and not fully reliable due to the survey having been carried out with pocket instruments. The surveyors had even managed in March 1841 to draw up a plan of Jerusalem on the scale of 1:4,800, a plan that was to prove controversial among biblical scholars and mapmakers because of an error of interpretation over the line of the western wall of the Haram ash-Sharif.[3] But the military surveyors did not enter the Haram ash-Sharif or the Citadel out of deference to their Ottoman allies. It fell to the next generation of military surveyors, Wilson and Warren, to resolve this dispute. The controversial findings of both Robinson and the military surveyors were to frame the debate among the evangelical fraternity, whether civil or military, for the next generation. This debate led to a veritable 'cavalcade of geographical missionaries' descending on Palestine to prove or disprove Robinson's theories, with each group publishing its own views, replete with illustrations. One prominent British clergyman, Arthur Penhryn Stanley, the Dean of Westminster, carried Robinson's book around in his pocket and wrote his own influential account of his travels. The result was that by the outbreak of the Crimean War, the 'Holy Land was better known than the English Lakes' to the British public.[4]

Catholic France and Orthodox Russia went to war in 1854, dragging in Protestant Britain and Muslim Turkey, in a dispute over control of the holy places in Palestine. The dispute did not end with Russia's defeat in what was known as the Crimean War (though it was fought on other fronts as well: in the Balkans, the Baltic, the Caucasus and the Far East). It continued over the holy places, with both sides trying to bolster their claims to controlling access to the shrines. The Russians tried to recoup their lost influence in the Levant by building a massive compound for their pilgrims on the approaches to Jerusalem. Meanwhile, the French Emperor in 1863 sent the well-known soldier, explorer, antiquarian and senator Felicien de Saulcy, and an Army Engineer officer, de Gelis, to survey Palestine and dig among the 'Tombs of the Hebrew Kings'. Three years earlier, Napoleon III had sent a French scientific expedition, led by the French philologist Ernest de Renan, to the Lebanon, one result of which was the publication of an accurate map of the country. De Saulcy had already made a name for himself on a previous expedition to Palestine in 1850–1 when he claimed to have discerned the outlines of the Cities of the Plain beneath the still waters of the Dead Sea. In 1853 he and de Gelis drew up the best map to date of that sea. This was surpassed a decade later by that of the French naval officer Vignes. Until then, the 1858 map by the Dutch naval officer van de Velde, based on his own and others' surveys, was the best map of Palestine. On his return to the Holy Land, de Saulcy was determined to make an equally startling and more tangible discovery in Jerusalem. This was to be among the supposed tombs of David and Solomon in the old mausoleum to the north of the Damascus Gate. De Saulcy was undeterred by the fact that it had been well ransacked of its funerary treasures over the centuries. He managed, through the spreading around of ample *bakshish*, to penetrate to the inner recesses of the tomb complex and returned to Paris with what he asserted was the sarcophagus of Seruyah, sister of King David. Closer examination by Parisian scholars of the attached inscription revealed that it was the last resting place of Queen Saddan. The mausoleum was that of her dynasty, and she had reigned some six hundred years after the kings of Judah. Unsurprisingly, French officials were reluctant to accede to and fund de Saulcy's proposal for his return to Palestine to undertake a grander and more detailed survey. The French Empire might have sought to strengthen its claims to the traditional shrines in Jerusalem and other Palestinian towns by claiming that France had scriptural authority based on the Bible. But the French Empire preferred to rely for this upon the lone and more economical efforts of French diplomats and officials, who pursued biblical archaeology in their spare time. It was to the great regret of both the French ambassador in Constantinople, Melchior de Vogues, and de Saulcy that it was to be the British rather than the French who were prepared to begin the semi-official survey of Palestine.

What piqued Britain's interest was the publication in 1864 of a two-volume, lavishly illustrated work entitled *Jerusalem Explored* by a Sardinian military engineer named Pierotti. He had dedicated the work to Napoleon III in gratitude for the latter's help in unifying Italy. Pierotti's skills had also come to the attention of the Ottoman governor of Jerusalem, Izzat Pasha. The latter had commissioned Pierotti to repair the water system of the Haram ash-Sharif (see Plate 5). In undertaking this work, Pierotti was the first European to undertake a thorough examination of the Al-Aqsa Mosque and of the Dome of the Rock (*Kubbetes-Sakhra*); this is where the rock (the *sakhra*) lies from which the Prophet Muhammad is said to have ascended to heaven (see Plates 6 and 7). He photographed them both and penetrated beneath the surface of the Haram ash-Sharif to discover, measure and sketch the gigantic water cisterns. It was here that Pierotti came across evidence of earlier remains of the temples of Herod and, he claimed, even the temple of Solomon.[5]

Pierotti's discoveries excited considerable interest in Christian Evangelical circles in England. For a generation there had been a growing interest in biblical archaeology and an increasingly bitter dispute over whether the traditional sites were, indeed, where key events from the Bible had occurred. Central to this dispute were two Victorian entrepreneurs and biblical scholars. They were the domineering wealthy indigo trader, architectural historian and archaeologist, James Fergusson, and the highly energetic and emotional lighthouse engineer and self-taught musician George Grove (the founder of the Royal Academy of Music and the *Dictionary of Music*). They had also both been instrumental in running the Crystal Palace as an attraction. Fergusson and Grove were convinced that the real site of Christ's tomb, the Holy Sepulchre, lay not in the existing church of that name, as the Catholic French and Russian Orthodox believed (and as did an English clergyman George Williams), but under the Dome of the Rock. Moreover, they believed that the temple of Solomon was in the southwest corner of the Haram. Orthodox Jews believe that the *sakhra* under the Dome of the Rock is the foundation stone of Solomon's Temple, where the Holy of Holies, the Ark of the Covenant, stood. It is the biblical Mount Moriah or Mount Zion, where Abraham offered to sacrifice his son Isaac.[6]

Fergusson's peculiar theory was expressed in several books and in an entry in Dr William Smith's *Dictionary of the Bible*, the essential reference work for mid-nineteenth-century antiquarians.[7] Only a scientific investigation could resolve this dispute. The opportunity presented itself with the decision of the Jerusalem Water Relief Society, consisting of the great and the good of mid-Victorian England and including the Dean of Westminster, Arthur Penrhyn Stanley, to enter the race with the French to provide clean water to the residents of the holy city. This was to protect them and pilgrims from waterborne diseases. In the summer 'a sort of miasma seems to rise up from the refuse' lurking at the bottom of the water cisterns from which the inhabitants of Jerusalem drew their drinking water.[8] The endeavour was also supported by the Syrian Improvement Committee and its prominent Jewish patron, Sir Moses Montefiore, dubbed 'the King of the Jews' by the English press. Before this noble goal could be achieved, however, the city and its subterranean water and drainage systems would have to be surveyed so that an accurate topographical map could be drawn that would show where corrective measures needed to be taken. Dean Stanley had been impressed by the large-scale map of London drawn up by the Ordnance Survey (OS) for the Metropolitan Sanitary Commission. Accordingly, through the good offices of the Earl de Grey and Ripon, Secretary of State for War, and Sir Henry James, the director of the OS, Dean Stanley secured the services of a Royal Engineer. This was one Captain Charles Wilson. The estimated cost of £500 would be borne by that paragon of Victorian philanthropy, Angela Burdett-Coutts, who had been on pilgrimage to Jerusalem in 1863. Protestant England had entered the lists in the Holy Land so that through scientific enquiry the British could discredit the respective claims of the Catholic French and the Orthodox Russians to be the true guardians of the holy places. In doing so, Britain was also making a bid to counter French and Russian political influence in Palestine. The chosen agent of British influence was the young British Sapper officer, Charles Wilson.

The 'official' biography of Wilson is singularly uninformative about his early life. He is shown in the book's frontispiece photograph, which is a conventional Victorian studio portrayal of a bemedalled and beribboned British major general. His neatly parted hair and full moustache, both flecked with grey, his straight tab eyebrows and nose complement his set expression. One is drawn to his dark eyes, above puffy lower lids. But they do not look directly into the camera; instead, they seem to be focused on some fixed point at the back of the studio, as if he is gazing at some distant mountain. Thus, we cannot look into his eyes and read his past. An early case of the gauze lens has resulted in a lack of lines on what must have been a weathered face. This prevents us from tracing the physical imprint of his experiences. We can only glean a few items from the official 'Life' which give us any sense of the formative influences on the young Wilson. He was a good scholar; he loved being outdoors and travelling, and he sought adventure. He rejected his Quaker roots and went into the army, being directly commissioned into the Royal Engineers during the Crimean War. He learnt his surveying and other skills of survival in wild country on the North American Boundary Commission from 1858 to 1862. It was here that photography had been first employed by the Royal Engineers to aid in the gathering of strategic knowledge on a key frontier along the 49th parallel between the United States and British Columbia. Fortunately, the official 'Life' has reproduced a revealing photograph of the young Wilson (see Plate 2). This shows a man in his mid-twenties, of probably medium height, with wavy dark hair and the shadow of a moustache and beard. He is standing outside a wooden hut on the frontier, a rifle ready at his side. He is dressed in off-duty clothes, a grey or white thigh-length frogged coat, with what looks like a tam-o'-shanter with a tassel set at a slightly jaunty angle on his head. This is offset, however, by his serious demeanour. His most distinguishing characteristic is the look of fixed determination in his eyes. Wilson was rather a loner, spending his spare time sailing when he was posted back to England to help build Palmerston's forts around Gosport and Portsmouth. Above all, he was very religious. This, and a yearning for adventure and an escape from garrison duty, resulted in his putting himself forward for the Jerusalem surveying job. He was helped by the fact that no one else wanted the job because the War Office would not cover personal expenses and there would be no extra pay. Wilson was regarded by his fellow officers as going on 'a fool's errand'.[9]

On landing in Palestine on 30 September 1864 and making his way to Jerusalem, Wilson was struck by 'the wild desolation' of the country. 'It is like nothing else on earth, and baffles all description; hills that were once covered with vineyards are nothing but a mass of rock and rubbish.' On reaching 'the summit of the last hill ... Jerusalem lay before us. I must say my feeling was one of disgust, for, right in front, and hiding a great part of the city from this point of view, the Russians have constructed an immense pile of ugly buildings, almost a town in itself, outside the walls (see Map 1 and Plate 4).'[10] Its location near the Jaffa Gate and close to the Church of the Holy Sepulchre had been deliberately chosen by the Tsar's elder brother, Grand Duke Konstantin Nicolayevich. The buildings were part of his strategy and that of his adviser Masurov and the Russian ambassador in Constantinople, Ignat'yev, to bolster Russian maritime, commercial, religious and political influence in Palestine and Syria. Comprising a hostel, apartments for visiting aristocrats, a hospital, a cathedral, a residence for the archimandrite and a consulate, the compound could help accommodate the large number of Eastern Orthodox pilgrims from Russia, the Balkans and the Ottoman Empire who were journeying to Palestine at this time.[11]

There were also large contingents of French Catholics as well as British and American Protestants making the pilgrimage to the Holy Land. Wilson got on well with Turkish governor of city, Izzat Pasha. The latter advised him to 'proceed with caution' amid the city's 'diversities of religions and population'. This may explain the Arabic signatures on the survey's notes on the interior of Jerusalem, which seem to indicate that Wilson and his assistants only surveyed streets and entered houses or properties after securing the permission of their inhabitants.[12]

As Wilson later related, with these permissions and an introduction from Montefiore to the Jewish community, he 'surveyed not only the city, but the Mosques and the Sacred Area ... I also made some experimental excavations to find the approximate depth of the rubbish, and to show that excavations could be made without arousing the fanaticism of the Moslems.'[13] He was able to explore, measure and sketch sixteen of the cisterns under the Haram ash-Sharif (including the 'Great Sea', al-Bahr al-Kabir, which could store 2 million gallons of rain water runoff from the Haram platform). This was no easy job:

> The cisterns were visited in December and January, before the fall of the later rains; the measurements were made with a rule when alone, with a tape in company, and the bearings taken with a prismatic or pocket compass; neither can be considered very exact, as it is no easy matter to work with a candle in one hand and up to his knees in water; it is very difficult in some cases to determine the character of the roof, and be certain that no conduits existed, as candles gave but a poor light in such large chambers, and before any magnesium wire could be obtained from England the winter rains had fallen and stopped further exploration. Three men were employed in visiting the cisterns, an interpreter and two porters; most of the descents were made with a rope ladder, but in some of the smaller cisterns the shaft was not large enough for this, and a rope tied around the breast was used, the arms being held well above the head to diminish the width of the shoulders as much as

possible; when the ladder was lowered one of the porters passed
his body through a rung, whilst the other held on to the spare
rope to prevent the first from being carried across the mouth of
the opening; the interpreter saw that all was right above ground
and lowered candles, etc, by a line kept for the purpose ... the only
trouble was in the ascending, as the ladder, which often hung free
in the air for 40 feet ... swayed and twisted in a very disagreeable
manner, and the wet clothes clinging to the legs prevented free
climbing action.[14]

Wilson came across evidence of the biblical period. In the tunnels
close to the Western Wall under the Gate of the Chain Street, he found
a monumental Herodian (or perhaps Umayyad or late Roman) arch
of the great bridge which crossed the Tyropoean Valley to the temple.
This was thenceforth known as 'Wilson's Arch' though it should really
be named after the Swiss physician, Titus Tobler, who had spotted it a
few years earlier. By the time Wilson's survey party left Jerusalem, the
surveyors were, according to him, 'looked upon as people who were
allowed to go anywhere or do anything, and they were considered to be
the friends of everyone. This was greatly due to the exceptionally good
conduct of the men, and the good management of the late Sergeant
James McDonald, afterwards Quarter-Master at Southampton' (the
HQ of the OS).[15] McDonald was also a master photographer, and his
evocative images of Jerusalem and its environs provided such accurate
imagery intelligence (IMINT) not only to the Jerusalem Water Relief
Society but also to the OS and the War Office. The Citadel, where
Ottoman troops were garrisoned, was mapped with notes on the
placement and poor condition of the small artillery pieces. Wilson

had completed detailed survey maps of Jerusalem and its environs (1:10,000), the walled city (1:2,500) and the Haram (1:5,000) plus plans of the Dome of the Rock and the Aqsa mosque. These were later published, along with a full description of the city and a separate volume of photographs, in a lavish edition intended for circulation not only to the great and the good but also to the well-heeled public. The need for such a survey and for the installation of a new, clean water system in Jerusalem was grimly emphasized a few months later, after Wilson had left the city. There was a cholera epidemic which killed 621 people, almost a tenth of the total population. As Wilson pointed out, 'the only way of affording a continual supply of good water to Jerusalem is to bring in the water from Solomon's pool either by constructing a new system of waterworks or by repairing the old ones, but the expense of this would be greater than seems likely at present to be incurred.'[16] On the basis of Wilson's survey, Burdett-Coutts offered to provide funds to improve the city's water supply. The Ottoman governor of Jerusalem was prepared to accept the funds but insisted that he should be the one to control how they were spent. Since there was no guarantee that the funds would be used for the purpose of improving the water supply, British philanthropists baulked at handing over the money. This standoff prevented any real improvements to the city's water supply for the next fifty years, a situation that was rectified only after the British military occupation of Jerusalem in 1917.[17]

Wilson had also run a levelling survey from Jaffa to Jerusalem and on to the Dead Sea. He proved that the latter was 1,292 feet below the Mediterranean. He was funded by the Royal Geographical Society (RGS), the Royal Society and the Syrian Improvement Committee.

They had asked him to run a level to Solomon's Pools, from which Jerusalem had in the past derived much of its freshwater via an old aqueduct.[18] His men suffered from the intense heat and polluted drinking water during this arduous and intense survey. But Wilson was building on the knowledge accumulated by the French surveyors and the American naval officer Lynch who had, in 1848, undertaken the first systematic exploration of the Jordan Valley and the Dead Sea. The extensive British newspaper coverage of Wilson's surveys of Jerusalem and Palestine excited the interest of the British public. Grove capitalized on this to set up the Palestine Exploration Fund (PEF) at a public meeting on 22 June 1865 for further scientific investigation of the Holy Land. The organization's preliminary meeting on 12 May was, appropriately enough, held in the 'Jerusalem' room of Westminster Abbey. The Archbishop of York, William Thomson, declared that the PEF should abstain from controversy, including religion. Yet, almost in the same breath, he stated that,

> this country of Palestine belongs to *you* and *me*. It is essentially ours. It was given to the Father of Israel in the words 'Walk through the land in the length of it and in the breadth of it, for I will give it unto thee.' *We* mean to walk through Palestine in the length and the breadth of it, because that land has been given unto us. It is the land whence comes news of our Redemption. It is the land to which we turn as the fountain of all our hopes: it is the land to which we look with as true a patriotism as we do this dear old England. I also think it is a sacred duty which we now undertake, to endeavour, by a new crusade, to rescue from darkness and oblivion much of the history of that country in which we all take so dear an interest.[19]

The PEF had, indeed, a truly national character since its operations were to be conducted by surveyors from the Royal Engineers. The archaeologist and parliamentary undersecretary of state at the Foreign Office, Lord Layard of Nineveh, wanted to use the PEF to counteract the expeditions of the French. As if to underline this point, Foreign Secretary Earl Russell joined the committee of the PEF and Queen Victoria became its patron, donating £150. This demonstrated that biblical archaeology was regarded by its practitioners and sponsors as another dimension of great power rivalry in the Near East.

Meanwhile squabbling broke out among various worthies as to who could claim credit for the foundation of the PEF. Reverend Henry Baker Tristram declared that it was as a result of his return from Palestine in 1864 and a talk with Grove and Dean Stanley that they approached the Archbishop of York, Thomson, with the idea. John Irwin Whitty, the hydraulic engineer who had toured Palestine with Stanley and the Prince of Wales in 1862, claimed that it was due to his research on how to provide clean water to Jerusalem that the Jewish Water Relief Society was set up, and that society in turn sent Wilson to Jerusalem and led to the PEF (there is a copy of Whitty's 1864 article in the *Journal of Sacred Literature* in the PEF archives, but this is not conclusive in itself). Then there was the chief hydrographer to the navy and former president of the Royal Geographical Society (RGS), Vice Admiral John Washington, who had launched a survey of the shores of the eastern Mediterranean from 1860 to 1863. He had proposed to the RGS an international effort to survey the Holy Land, linking with the findings of the 1840/1841 coastal survey, and he had urged geographers to complete the work of Dr Smith's *Dictionary of the Bible*. His exhortation had been passed on by Dean Stanley to Smith and

Grove. Washington had listed ten research themes which warranted investigation. These seem to have been reproduced as the nine points in the PEF's inaugural brochure, and this lends some credence to Washington being regarded as an unacknowledged founding father of the PEF. But there is much more evidence to suggest that it was George Grove, encouraged by James Fergusson and the artist David Roberts, who was the essential figure in galvanising support for the establishment of the PEF. Grove himself traced the origins of the PEF back to a conversation he had had with Fergusson during the construction of the Assyrian House at the Crystal Palace in 1853, in which the latter

> lamented that there was no complete concordance of the proper names of the Bible – Old Testament, Apocrypha, and New Testament. This was enough to lead to the production of a complete manuscript concordance, which again proved of most material service in the preparation of Dr W. Smith's 'Dictionary of the Bible', itself a remarkable monument of the movement; and it certainly was the discovery of the vague and casual state of our knowledge of the country by those who had most to do with that Dictionary that caused the actual formation of the Fund.[20]

Even before Wilson's return to England in July 1865, the newly founded PEF had decided that he should do an about-turn to Palestine forthwith to carry out a feasibility study regarding the further exploration of the Holy Land. At Russell's request, the sultan issued a *firman* (instruction) to his authorities in Syria granting Wilson free reign in his 'explorations and excavations'.[21] Wilson also wanted an honour to be bestowed on the pasha of Jerusalem, as had

been recently done for the bey of Tunis, to persuade him to accede
to Wilson's excavation of holy sites in Palestine.[22] Wilson returned
to Palestine in the winter of 1865, this time accompanied by another
Sapper officer, Lt. Anderson (who had been with him in Canada), and
a Sapper NCO, Corporal Phillips. They went via the Lebanon and
Syria, where French and Russian influence was thought by the British
to be paramount. They travelled to Beirut, Damascus, Banias (on the
northern limits of Palestine and near the sources of the Jordan River),
then to Tel Hum and Lake Galilee, Nablus and its environs before
arriving in Jerusalem.

The survey, completed in May 1866, can be said to have been a
qualified success, given the failure of various measuring instruments.
Anderson undertook most of the astronomical and trigonometrical
work, determining time and latitude, carried out at forty-nine
separate points between Beirut and Hebron and by a line of azimuths
(to determine longitude) from Banias to Jerusalem. This was done
in order to draw a series of maps, on the scale of 1 inch to the mile,
of the backbone or watershed of the country from north to south.
This map was later published by John Murray under George Grove's
supervision. Wilson mainly undertook the geological and botanical
observations. He also collected material for about fifty detailed
drawings of churches, synagogues, mosques and tombs. Anderson
carried out excavations at several sites. Both Anderson and Phillips
were skilled photographers and took some 166 photographs of sites,
architectural details and inscriptions. All this took place under
arduous weather conditions of winter rain, snow and cold. The
three men also encountered a Bedouin tribal war, suffered attacks
from robbers and dealt with aggressive Samaritans as well as with

untrustworthy servants and a shortage of forage and provisions due to a recent plague of locusts that had devastated the local crops.[23] Soon, the three men and their backers realized that a complete survey of Palestine would be a large, costly and time-consuming undertaking.

Although Wilson had exceeded his budget, he did some valuable preliminary work for future surveys, and he made what seemed to be new discoveries in Jerusalem. Worried about money, Grove recalled Wilson to England. Wilson returned to surveying duties with the Ordnance Survey in Scotland but became a member of the executive committee of the PEF. It was clear that, to survive financially, the PEF had to concentrate on 'the recovery of Jerusalem' because this was what appealed to the hearts, minds and, above all, to the purses of the Victorian charity-giver. Grove asked for another Royal Engineer officer to return to Jerusalem in order to confirm Fergusson's theory about the real location of the Holy Sepulchre in the Haram ash-Sharif. Accordingly, Fergusson was to help fund this expedition. Both the War Office and the Ordnance Survey acceded to this new request. But their proviso was that the officer appointed, Lt. Charles Warren, should also draw up a military reconnaissance map for the districts to the northeast and the southwest of the city, namely, on the approach routes to Jerusalem. This would add to the work already done by Wilson and Anderson.

'Jerusalem Warren'

We know more about the young Warren than we do about the young Wilson, despite the fact that Warren's son destroyed his father's papers, seemingly out of spite and dislike of him. What we know of the youthful Warren is primarily due to his self-revelatory speeches, recorded faithfully by his grandson. Warren gave these speeches in retirement with the purpose of using his stirring example to instil 'character' in a younger generation of boys at his old schools. These speeches resound with words such as 'duty' and 'glory', which may sound impossibly old-fashioned to later generations. But they reveal much about the man Warren was and about the beliefs that guided him through life. Those terms are important to an understanding of those qualities of character—and its limitations—that were to underlie his later conduct not only in Jerusalem in the late 1860s but also in the Sinai in the early 1880s.

Warren's family was an army family, so 'Charlie' was used to travelling from post to post in Britain and overseas—sadly, his three-year-old sister died during the family's crossing of the desert to Suez, probably from heatstroke. His family was religious (his grandfather was the Dean of Bangor Cathedral), and his father gathered his family together on Sunday nights to sing psalms and hymns.[24] Warren junior's favourite hymn was 'Glory to Thee, my God, this night'. His favourite psalm was Psalm 15, the 'gentleman's psalm', which was to be his 'guiding star through life, whose rays fell along paths of Purity, Truth, Honour, Humility, and Service for others—difficult paths to keep in'.[25] He was later to reflect that it was the best preparation for Jerusalem. He might have added that psalms and prayers had been recited in the Temple of Solomon. To guide and encourage him along the way, the young Warren had his father's favourite psalm, Psalm 91, 'Who so dwelleth under the defence of the most High shall abide under the shadow of the Almighty.' These firm religious beliefs were to give Warren great spiritual strength and guidance in the many adverse situations in which he later found himself. As a boy his favourite book was *The Arabian Nights Entertainment*; with its tales of Solomonic magic, it gave him a firm belief in an ever-present Providence, a belief that was to influence the way he interpreted the sights, sounds and smells of Jerusalem and later the Sinai. Warren later extolled the character-building virtues for boys and young men of 'the rough life'. He certainly experienced this at a succession of boarding schools and at 'The Shop', the Royal Military Academy at the Woolwich Arsenal, which produced generations of Royal Engineer, Artillery and Signals officers. Drafty dormitories and early morning bathing in ice-cold outdoor bathtubs were part of the Spartan regime. Short-sighted and sporting an eyeglass to compensate, Warren would not have passed the medical exam required for future generations, as he later admitted. But he more than made up for this ocular weakness with a real talent for mathematics and science. This ran in his family and enabled him to pass second in his year. He had no hesitation in applying for, and receiving, a commission in the Royal Engineers and proceeded to their base at Chatham Dockyard for two years of training. He finished just too late to join his father and elder brother in the Crimea, where his brother was killed and his father was wounded and decorated for leading the 55th Regiment of Foot to immortal glory at the battles of the Alma and Inkerman. Warren followed in his family's footsteps and began his career in January 1858 at Gibraltar, the celebrated rock fortress securing Britain's control of the western entrance to and exit from the Mediterranean. There Warren improved the gun batteries at Europa Point, and he scaled the dangerous rock face at Gibraltar (where the concrete water catchment now lies) to lay charges to blow away any crags and terraces where an enemy might get a hold. And he undertook the trigonometrical survey of the Rock on a scale of 1:600.

Warren also became a Freemason, thus presaging a long and distinguished career in that brotherhood. His father had been a Freemason, which entitled Charlie to be initiated into the Lodge of Friendship on 30 December 1859 at the early age of nineteen rather than the usual age of twenty-one (he was passed on 14 January and raised on 21 January 1860). Warren became a fervent advocate of Freemasonry, believing that it reinforced discipline in the army by binding together officers and men in common beliefs and sympathetic understanding. He joined the Royal Arch Chapter and Mark Lodge in October 1861 and two years later the Calpe Preceptory of the Knights Templar No.60. Templar traditions were carried on by the Freemasons. On joining the Inhabitants Lodge, Warren came under the strong influence of Brother (Bro.) Francis George Irwin, an Irish sergeant of the Royal Sappers and Miners (later the Royal Engineers). A zealous mason, Irwin was intent, through his lectures at lodge meetings, on interesting the new brethren in the search for the Temple of Solomon at Jerusalem. Its reconstruction was of central importance in Masonic thought. As a later Freemason and biographer of Warren explained: 'The allegory of the Temple itself is used in all Masonic meetings (Workings) as a symbol of mankind and the human body, in an esoteric sense, and the parallel of the construction activities and the tradesmen involved are reflected in the Masonic ceremonies worldwide.'[26] It seems to have been Irwin who inspired Warren to undertake 'a noble and masonic quest' to recover Solomon's Temple and the Ark of the Covenant, a quest that was not only for the benefit of the Masonic community, helping to explain its origins, legends and rituals, but also for the benefit of the world.[27] Of course, the Ark of the Covenant is said to contain Moses's Tablets of Stone with the Ten Commandments engraved upon them. For Freemasons, with their emphasis on allegory and symbolism, these tablets also assume great importance as containing primordial esoteric knowledge. Thus, Warren's hunt for the Ark of the Covenant was of major significance to the Freemasons, who trace their origins to a meeting on the porch of Solomon's Temple between the gigantic twin copper pillars of Jachin and Boaz. These guarded the entrance to the three chambers, which correspond to different degrees of Masonic initiation. Warren was supported in his quest by those prominent Freemasons who were also founding members of the PEF, namely, the liberal politician, Duke of Argyll, and the novelist Sir Walter Besant.[28] They shared with their fellow PEF founder the Earl of Shaftesbury, renowned Christian evangelist and social reformer, a desire to see the Jews return to Israel. For Shaftesbury this was 'God's will' in fulfilment of the prophecy, the conversion of the Jews and the Second Coming of Christ to signal the new Millennium. For Wilson, Warren, Kitchener and later for Conder, the return of the Jews was to the economic and strategic advantage of Britain.

Warren was instructed by the PEF to continue Wilson's work in Jerusalem and Palestine. In particular, he was to use his mining expertise to concentrate his excavations in and around the Haram ash-Sharif in order to find the exact location of the Solomonic and Herodian temples. Warren would have to contend with the local Turkish authorities who wanted to exclude European archaeologists. When Warren, accompanied by three Sapper corporals (Birtles, Phillips and Hancock), landed in Jaffa on 15 February 1867, he received help from his fellow Freemasons, among them the British vice consul, Bro. William Habib Hayat, the governor, Bro. Noureddin Effendi, and Bro. Howard, the hotelier at the Jaffa Gate in Jerusalem. The British vice consuls, Johnson and Beardsley, were also Masons. Warren also received limited assistance from the cautiously taciturn British consul in Jerusalem, the appropriately named Noel Temple Moore, who was concerned about Warren's plans and the diplomatic ructions that might ensue if Turkish Muslim sensibilities were offended. Warren's experiences in Jerusalem and Palestine mirrored passages from his favourite book, *An Arabian Nights' Entertainment.* He was waiting for a *firman* to arrive from the Porte in Constantinople and giving him the expected permission to conduct archaeological excavations in the Holy City. In the interim Warren received permission from the governor of Jerusalem to proceed. Warren began to dig beside the gigantic walls of the Haram ash-Sharif. He had a novel way of motivating his workforce:

> The difficulty for the Mussulmans is to keep up sufficient supervision, but, what with a quick dragoman, Jewish overseers, and parties of three each, working together, —one a Nubian, and the other two fellaheen from hostile villages, we create such a jealousy that anything going wrong very soon crops out.[29]

The military pasha could not understand why Warren wanted to dig around the Haram ash-Sharif. 'He could tell me what was under every stone. He then went through the several well-known legends regarding the sacred rock and the Sanctuary: winding up with the assurance that it lay on the top leaves of a palm tree, from the roots of which sprang all the rivers of the world: and that any attempt of a Frank

to explore them would only be followed by some fatal catastrophe.'[30]
Digging was soon suspended, however, following protests from the
Arab worshippers who rained stones down on Warren from the high
walls of the Haram ash-Sharif, angry that their devotions had been
disturbed by the noise of the excavations. Loath to lose any time,
Warren took off in April to explore Jericho and the Jordan Valley in
order to carry out a military and an archaeological survey. He called
on the PEF to send him Wilson's survey notes because he realized that
without a proper trigonometrical framework he would not be able to
carry out a topographical survey.

The new governor of Jerusalem, Nazif Pasha, and the military
pasha, were even more active in trying to thwart Warren's excavations
than their predecessor Izzat Pasha. When the *firman* arrived, it proved
disappointing and did not grant Warren the *carte blanche* to dig that
he had desired. Undaunted, he kept its contents secret and began
digging at various sites. The pashas called him 'the Mole', and they
took great pleasure in closing down Warren's sites soon after he had
opened them. They demanded bribes, *bakshish*, to reopen them, but
Warren refused to pay up. Nazif Pasha showed no sign of relenting.
So Warren went off to explore and survey the plain of Philistia as far
south as Gaza and the country to the southwest of Jerusalem, where
he visited the tightly guarded Sanctuary at Hebron. He had a notable
encounter with some villagers around Ashdod:

Many of them had been down south working on the Suez Canal,
and seeing our surveying instruments, they concluded that the
English were going to cut a rival canal through Philistia and the
Judean mountains to the Dead Sea, and to this they strongly

objected, as they considered that it would be the signal for our retaking possession of our inheritance; for they told me over and over again that they had taken the land from us, and that we should wrest it back from them again, but many of them added 'You will have to fight for it, we will not give it up without a struggle.'[31]

Warren explained:

They know quite well the differences between the English and French nations, and look upon them as the two powers of the world. About Jerusalem, on the contrary, the Governments of France and Russia are looked up to as supreme, and the prestige of Great Britain is only kept up by the individual independence of the British residents, for whom the inhabitants have the greatest respect, the common binding to a bargain in the market being 'on the word of an Englishman.'[32]

On his return to Jerusalem at the end of June, Warren sank shafts at the southeast corner of the Sanctuary wall. Thwarted again by the governor, he took off for the western shore of the Dead Sea, crossing the Jordan River to examine the Gilead hills and the Moab plains. This country had been little visited by European surveyors. 'Even Van de Velde's map, which was at that time the least imperfect of all, was hopelessly inaccurate … giving, as it did only an idea of what the country might be, whilst we wanted a sketch of what the country was.'[33] Warren was accompanied by some of his NCOs, who took photographs and drew plans of ancient ruins and existing buildings. There is a photograph of them, posing for the camera on the banks of a small stream or pond. With his close-cropped hair and full beard, lean torso and sun-burnt hands, Warren exudes mental determination and physical hardiness (see Plate 3). He needed it, for he and his companions were making a rapid reconnaissance and survey of new or only partially known country in a warzone where the Ottoman Turks had launched a punitive expedition against a recalcitrant Bedouin tribe. Warren later wrote about this in an article published in the journal of the RGS in which he laid out the principles upon which such a reconnaissance and survey should be conducted and the equipment needed. He made its military application clear when he stressed that a 'general's success in the field may depend much upon his knowledge gained from plans, and unless those plans are constructed by surveyors of experience, they are likely to fail in parts, and may be instrumental in the defeat of an army'.[34] It is clear that Warren saw his reconnaissance and survey of the country east of the Jordan as one of gathering military intelligence for future use by the War Office. It also took place under realistic warlike conditions. Warren and his men were out in the sun all day and devoted much of the night to reprising their day's findings. The temperature after sunset sometimes reached 110 degrees Fahrenheit. As Warren later recalled:

The Syrian climate is said to be one of the worst in the world; and certain it is, whether from undue exposure, malarious influences, or other causes, a considerable percentage of travellers in Palestine either suffer whilst in the country itself, or else carry back with them the seeds of illness, which develop often into lingering complaints. For my own part, during three and a half years it was my lot to serve in the Holy Land, I found health when encamped in the open, and sickness when housed in the towns, especially

Jerusalem; and I hailed with gladness the prospect of a month's reconnaissance of the hills of Gilead and plains of Moab, during that portion of the year when the fervid heat of the Syrian sun begins to influence all nature.[35]

As if to prove the point, one of Warren's NCOs, who was suffering from a bad bout of dysentery, made a full recovery while on survey.

However, the Bedouin band escorting them could not make up their minds as to whether 'it were better policy to be true or play us false'.[36] This was because they had taken Warren's money to act as guides to his party but had soon discovered that the Turks were engaged on a punitive expedition against their tribe (the Adwan) and desired to return to protect their granaries. They extracted a promise from Warren, 'on the word of an Englishman (a common form in Syria)' that he would protect them if they encountered the Turks. This did not prevent Warren from venturing near the Turkish army when his work required it.

The result of this was that we were sometimes left alone between the two armies, not knowing in the least whether we should have to defend our own lives against either party should we get into a skirmish. At one time we were within four hours of the Turkish army, their scouts being close on to us; we were deserted by the Bedouin, and were able to do a good day's work in Jerash in quietness. On that day, when climbing a hill, I came upon one of our Adwan acting as a scout, and passing signals from hill to hill as to the movements of the enemy, it being the desire to lure them into tangled woods about the River Jabbok, and there to slaughter them in detail. The Turks, however, were much too wary for this.[37]

The uncertain situation made it difficult to conduct the survey. Moreover, Goblan, the sheikh leading the escort party of Bedouin, had personal feuds all over the country. When the group came to the limits of Adwan territory, Goblan took 'ludicrous' precautions, 'sitting in a sleeping posture with his drawn sword in hand at the door of my tent'.[38] Despite this, Warren accomplished what he had set out to do. He had

already surveyed the eastern banks of the Jordan up to the hill country, joining on to Lieut. Anderson's survey, but [he] had failed to connect the plain with the hills from those on the west, and then those in the plain; the points on the east of the Jordan from the western hills, and those on the west from the eastern hills.[39]

Warren started from Jericho, crossed the Jordan at En Nwaimeh and camped at Kaferin on the plain. Of his few well-fixed points, Olivet was nearly due west and Gerizim could not be seen. Thus, for sketching he took bearings on points temporarily fixed in the plain. He also made rounds of angles with the theodolite with their true bearing and observations for latitude and time. He started hill-sketching and carried it forward to Arak-el-Amir, Kaferin, Nebbeh, and Mount Nebo. It was here that Warren completed a portion of the triangulation and fixed the points securely with reference to one another. He then continued the triangulation and sketching until he reached Jebel Husha above Es-Salt, where he connected his work with the hill country of Judea. Given the difficult conditions, this was quite a feat.

On his return to Jerusalem, Warren was increasingly convinced of the historical accuracy of the Bible. His dogged patience began to pay off from September on as he browbeat Nazif Pasha into submission. 'The Mole' sank shafts all around the walls of the Sanctuary to depths from 40 to 110 feet. He pioneered a new technology of using a series of wooden mining cases to support the sides of the shafts and then mining galleries towards the foundations of the walls. But wood was in short supply in Jerusalem and soon rotted in the local climate. It had to be imported from Malta and then from England. Warren and his faithful sidekick, Sergeant Birtles, were in constant nerve-fraying danger from repeated landslides caused by falling rubble or tools carelessly dropped down the shafts by Arab workmen, and they faced the threat of drowning in the narrow underground water channels. In November they cut their way through the walls of the Double Passage, one of the most secret Muslim places of pilgrimage in the Haram ash-Sharif and allegedly the site of Solomon's Palace. They had distracted the Nubian guards by sending them off on a hunt for the large lizards known as 'Warren' to the locals, presumably because he resembled a reptile crawling all over the Haram ash-Sharif. The most revolting job occurred on 28 October 1867 when the group was exploring the rock-cut passage running under the Convent of the Sisters of Zion and the military *serai*. This passage had been discovered by Pierotti and Wilson; it led to the double Struthion Pool, situated beyond the northwestern corner of the Haram and was permanently covered in several feet of sewage. Warren's description demonstrates the humour with which he cloaked his bravura:

> The passage is four feet wide, with smooth sides, and the sewage was from five to six feet deep, so that if we had fallen in there was no chance of our escaping with our lives. I, however, determined to

trace out this passage, and for this purpose got a few old planks and made a perilous voyage on the sewage to a distance of twelve feet … Finding the excessive danger of the planks, I procured three old doors … We laid the first door on the sewage, then one in front of it, taking care to keep ourselves each on a door; then taking up the hinder of the three it was passed to the front, and so we moved on. The sewage in some places was more liquid than in others, but in every case it sucked in the doors so that we had much difficulty in getting the hinder one up, while those we were on sunk down, first on one side and then on the other as we tried to keep our balance.[40]

They advanced like this for about 200 feet before the sewage became firm enough for them to walk on it, the roof all the time sloping down until they came to a dead end. This was hard up against the western wall of the Haram, which postdated the tunnel. They were close enough to the *serai* to 'hear voices and the tramping of feet overhead'.[41] It was only after Warren left Jerusalem that at his urging the *effendis* broke through the blocked up wall in the search for water.

Warren's excavations around the Haram ash-Sharif aroused the interest of the Jews, some of whom would sit by the shaft heads waiting for the discovery of a third underground spring of water. They held that this would presage the coming of the Messiah. Warren began to attract European visitors to Jerusalem, many of them on Cook's tours. He was quite prepared to show them around to gain good publicity and financial contributions to the PEF. He even lowered old ladies by basket-chair down into the shafts. In contrast, he tried to dissuade the local Ottoman officials from taking too great an interest in his 'diggings' by shaking the pulley ropes as they descended into the

stygian gloom of the shaft. But 'Jerusalem Warren', as he was coming
to be known, was increasingly short of funds despite his pleas for more
from the PEF and generous subventions from his fellow Freemasons
to the fund. He had to spend £1,000 of his own money. Although
it showed his cast-iron integrity, he had not helped his cause by
investigating and disproving Fergusson's theory about the original site
of the Church of the Holy Sepulchre being located under the Dome
of the Rock and Solomon's temple being in the southwest corner of
the Haram ash-Sharif.[42] With regard to the Dome of the Rock, he had
exploded the myth that the 'Well of the Souls' (the entrance to Hell for
Muslims) lay beneath the Cave of al-Maghara below the Holy Rock
(*es-Sakhra*) (see Plate 7). Moreover, it was not the entrance to a great
underground cavern which housed Solomon's treasure, including the
Ark of the Covenant. In fact, the hole in the floor of the cave leads
to a drain down to the valley of the Kedron. It may have been made
to carry off the blood of the animals sacrificed on the rock when it
was the altar of burnt offerings in the Temple. As his grandson later
related, the investigative methods employed by Warren in the Dome
of the Rock were bold in the extreme:

> Warren had heard of a curious opening somewhere on the surface
> of this rock, and so, with great secrecy and with the help of several
> accomplices who delayed the arrival of the officials and diverted
> the attention of onlookers, he paid an early morning visit to the
> spot. He vaulted over the railing and, as he put it, his 'unhallowed
> feet' touched the rock which could only be touched by mortal feet
> once a year; he scrambled up to a loose piece of flagging which he
> had previously observed, and tried to prise it up with a lever. In a

few minutes the stone began to loosen; but it was almost a square yard in area and three to four inches thick, and when he had raised it up halfway across the hole he wrenched his left shoulder and his arm hung powerless by his side. The stone was far too heavy to be held by the right arm only, and it fell with a crash into the hole below, right over the heads of the Mosque officials who were being detained in conversation by some English ladies who were party to the adventure.

Meanwhile Warren had dived down into the hole, taken measurements and made his observations (it was only 3 feet deep, 2 feet wide and 11 feet long), and he came out to find a Moslem friend of his keeping lookout behind a pillar (not, of course, on the rock itself), gesticulating to him in an agony of terror and urging him to make haste and come out before he got murdered. Warren wanted to try and put the stone back, but his friend became quite frantic at this and said, 'If you are found on the rock there is only one thing that can happen; but if only the stone is found displaced, who can suppose that you have done it? It is Allah who has thrown it down', upon which Warren asked, 'Will Allah get it up again tonight?' and the Moslem replied that he was sure he would. It is not known who Allah's human agents may have been, but in a few days' time the stone was observed to have been got up again and put in its place![43]

Outraged that Warren had contradicted his theories with actual archaeological evidence, Fergusson promptly withdrew his funding. Disturbed by the imminent loss of a rich patron, Grove and the PEF committee bowed to Fergusson's demand that Warren's written reports be minimized through censorship. Warren was obliged to return to

England in May 1868 to sort this out, leaving several of his men in their sickbeds suffering from dysentery and typhoid (one later died). He was disturbed to discover that Grove had also starved him of funds in order to ensure that Wilson had sufficient money for his survey of the Sinai Desert. Moreover, in 1869 the PEF had also given money it could ill afford to Edward Palmer, money that should have gone to Warren. The latter dubbed the PEF, 'the Debt'.[44] This introduced an element of rivalry between these two talented Sapper officers, Wilson and Warren. Warren seems to have been instrumental in forcing Grove to the sidelines and having him replaced first by the treasurer, Walter Morrison, MP, and later by Walter Besant. The latter was to play a role in later events in the Sinai (Warren and Wilson later filleted Grove's papers to remove any trace of this unpleasantness).[45] Under Besant's secretaryship, the PEF would in future rely for its funding on public subscription through the issuance of its 'Quarterly Statement' rather than on the whimsies and dictates of rich antiquarians.

For over two years Warren had successfully ignored the Ottoman *firmans* in order to dig around and explore within the Haram ash-Sharif. He had made valuable discoveries and had done prodigious work around the retaining walls of the Haram-ash-Sharif or Temple Mount; at Robinson's Arch (with its aqueducts, circular pools and subterranean canal), at Wilson's Arch (with its chambers and passages), the Pool of Bethesda and the Hill of Ophel. Above all, in November 1868 he thought he had found what he had been looking for all along, as did Emanuel Deutsche, a Semitic scholar at the British Museum (who was also the inspiration for George Eliot's Zionist novel *Daniel Deronda*). These were the red marks of the Phoenician masons on stones 90 feet below the surface of the southeast wall of the

Sanctuary (see Plate 8). He believed he was looking at the foundation stones of Solomon's Temple as they had been laid down by the masons of King Hiram of Tyre in the tenth century BC, thus establishing a symbolic link and tracing Freemasonry back to biblical times. The find was widely publicized in the press of the time. For example, the *Illustrated London News* had sent its correspondent, William 'Crimea' Simpson, who was covering the opening of the Suez Canal in 1869, hot-foot to Jerusalem to sketch the Masonic lettering. Warren took his fellow Freemason, Simpson, and the professional explorer John 'Rob Roy' MacGregor (who was then canoeing up the Jordan to its source) around the cisterns and tunnels of the Haram.[46] Subsequent archaeological work has, however, concluded that the stones are part of the retaining wall of the later Herodian Temple complex and that the red marks were graffiti left by Jewish masons. Warren had also explored and expertly recorded the dimensions of the great water cisterns, drains and conduits below the platform; these were the same ones Pierotti had partly chronicled. There was much speculation as to whether Warren had found Solomon's Stables, where the Knights Templars had stabled their horses during their occupation of Jerusalem. In fact, these vaulted cellars were built by Herod the Great to support the immense platform of the Temple Mount when he had extended and refurbished the Second Temple in the first century AD. Herod's platform survives as the Haram ash-Sharif. Nothing remains of Solomon's Temple, which was obliterated at least twice, cut down to bedrock and remodelled many times.

Warren believed that in King Solomon's Quarries (also known as Zedekiah's Cave) he had stumbled across a 'Masonic Hall', a large cavern with a domed roof, with a single pillar known as the apprentice pillar. The entrance was 150 metres east of the Damascus Gate and the cavern runs for five city blocks beneath the Muslim Quarter of Old Jerusalem. It was here on 13 May 1868, just before his return to London, that Warren had taken part in the first modern Freemasons' meeting in the Holy Land. It was attended by a past Grand Master of the Grand Lodge of Kentucky, Dr Robert Morris, the Prussian Consul Dr Henry Petermann, and officers on shore leave from HMS *Lord Clyde*.[47] Warren had also discovered a 14-metre vertical shaft, later named after him, from the Old City to near the Gihon Spring in the Kidron Valley. He believed he had stumbled upon Joab's secret route that had enabled David to capture Jerusalem from the Jebusites, as well as on the early water supply system for Jerusalem. It has since been shown by archaeologists to have been too narrow and the pool at its base too shallow to have been used to draw water. It is in fact a natural fissure in the rock which was breached by the original excavators when they were sinking a shaft to another pool much closer to the Gihon Spring. This pool was protected by a large tower outside the city walls as was Gihon Spring; the tower dates from the eighteenth century BC and was of Canaanite origin.[48] But Warren did find the Valley of the Cheesemakers (aka the Tyropoean Valley), which had been so filled up with the rock rubbish of centuries that it was only discernible as a shallow depression between the Temple Mount and the Upper City to the west. In the tunnels along the Western Wall, Warren discovered one of the main entrances to the Herodian Temple, appropriately known since as 'Warren's Gate'.[49] Warren became a prominent and influential figure in Jerusalem, to the extent that Christian, Muslim and Jewish city-dwellers approached him to intercede on their behalf with the Turkish authorities. He was regarded as the 'consul' for a mysterious country called the Palestine Exploration Fund, and in Jerusalem, as Warren put it, 'King Consul rules supreme!'[50] This was too much for the Ottoman sultan and the governor of Jerusalem, and in June 1869 the latter forbade further excavations anywhere near the Sanctuary.

Warren was soon caught up in the affair of the Moabite Stone, the only known written account of the history of the Holy Land as related in the Second Book of Kings in the Old Testament. It caused as much of a sensation at the time in Britain and Europe as the discovery of the tomb of Tutankhamen by Howard Carter and Lord Carnarvon did in 1922. The botched rescue of the Stone from total destruction by rival Bedouin tribesmen caused a furore among Prussian, French and British archaeologists. It was in connection with this affair that in early 1870 Warren met Edward Palmer, Lord Almoner's Professor of Arabic at Cambridge University who is to loom so large in this book.[51] Seeking revenge, Grove blamed Warren in *The Times* newspaper for not securing the Stone for the British Museum. Warren had, in fact, managed to get a set of 'squeezes', or impressions, of the broken pieces of the Stone and had a translation made. He and Palmer had also purchased some pieces; Warren later donated his to the Louvre in Paris, where the majority of pieces had been collected and deposited by the great French archaeologist Clermont-Ganneau. Outraged at Grove's treatment of him, Warren resigned from the PEF and returned to England via the Lebanon, where he found the time to conduct a survey.[52]

As a result of his crusade for the 'recovery of Jerusalem', Warren suffered from ill-health for some years. But the fever suddenly left him following a vigorous course of beagling, a heavy dose of Warburg's tincture (as recommended by Sir Richard Burton for tropical fevers) and a good sleep! He spent the next decade publishing his considerable archaeological findings as well as a valuable treatise on how to conduct a reconnaissance in new or only partially known territory.[53] 'Jerusalem Warren' had shown that it was possible to combine biblical archaeology with military intelligence gathering, the former acting as a legitimate cover for the latter, more secret activity. His survey work was to be continued and completed by Lt. Conder and Lt. Kitchener and was published as *The Survey of Western Palestine* (PEF, 1881–3). He had also demonstrated considerable perseverance, ingenuity and tact in the face of official obstruction from the local Turkish and British representatives. Moreover, he had overcome great physical and environmental difficulties to make real breakthroughs in the archaeological and topographical 'recovering [of] Jerusalem', the old rallying cry of the Crusaders, for Britain. As he reported to the PEF AGM on 16 May 1870: 'We have now advanced so far as to be able to lay down an approximate contoured plan of the city as it existed in olden times, and we have also examined round two-thirds of the Haram wall on the outside, some part of which is acknowledged by each theorist to have formed part of the outer court of Herod's Temple.'[54] For Freemasons, Warren's achievements in Jerusalem were due to 'his thirst to uncover a Masonic ideal which related to a physical object in the Temple of Solomon'.[55] Besant was certain that nothing would ever be done in the future to compare with what had been done by Warren: 'It was Warren who restored the ancient city to the world.'[56] He and Wilson had staked out Britain's claims in a number of fields and, as such, sought to exert British influence in that strategically important land bridge between Asia and Africa, the invasion route taken by all conquerors of Egypt and the Levant throughout the ages.

3

In the Desert of the Exodus

It is not surprising that the work of Wilson, Warren and the PEF in Jerusalem should have spurred others to call for modern survey and archaeological techniques to be applied in other fields of 'sacred geography' in an attempt to seek further scientific confirmation of the historical accuracy of the Bible. People sought to answer the question posed by Dean Stanley: 'Can such a connexion be traced between the scenery, the features, the boundaries, the situation of Sinai and of Palestine on the one hand, and the history of the Israelites on the other?'[1] By the late 1860s, a start had been made on the survey of Palestine, but only the coastline of the Sinai Peninsula seems to have been surveyed; that survey had been done by the Indian navy as part of its charting of the Red Sea.[2] There had been no systematic survey of the interior, nor was there any clear boundary between Egyptian and Turkish territory. The only data available for the compilation of books and maps was culled from travellers' accounts. These were not sufficient 'to judge of the general fitness of the land for the events recorded in the Sacred Narrative of the Exodus'.[3] However, a systematic survey of the Sinai was a major undertaking given that it covered about 11,600 square miles and thus was twice the size of Yorkshire. The peninsula was triangular in shape, situated between the two arms of the Red Sea, the Gulf of Suez and the Gulf of Akabah. At its southern end there rose the vastness of the Sinaitic Mountains. A belt of sandstone stretching across the middle of the peninsula from west to east separated the mountains from the plateau of the Tih, a drab desert which was drained by the Wadi el-Arish, the biblical River of Egypt. To the northeast of the Tih were the limestone hills of Judea, to the northwest, Egypt proper. It was an arid wilderness, suffering from drought, which had been known to the Romans as Arabia Petraea and was referred to by Christian Evangelicals as the Desert of the Exodus (see map 3). It was to the southern part of this wilderness of sand, gravel and granite, and a seemingly impenetrable maze of wadis that the sacred geographers and biblical history hunters turned in 1868.

Surveying Sinai

Encouraged by a Sapper officer, Captain Henry Spencer Palmer (who had served with Wilson on the British Columbia survey), the Reverend Pierce Butler, rector of Ulcombe in Kent, in 1867 set in train plans for a survey of 'the most interesting parts of the Sinaitic [or Sinai] Peninsula' (traversed by Butler in 1853).[4] The main intention was to answer the long-disputed questions over the location of the biblical Mount Sinai and the path of the Exodus of the Jews from captivity in Pharaoh's Egypt. This was followed by their Forty Years of Wandering in the Wilderness and their eventual arrival in the Promised Land of Canaan. As *The Times* put it, citing the Rev. George Williams:

The matters of chief topographical interest had become so overlain with conflicting statements and theories that it is impossible to say which was truth and which error. Even the best maps were sadly inaccurate and defective, and no fewer than five mountains in the Peninsula, with as many routes leading to them, had been 'identified, or at least suggested, by rival authorities as the true Sinai'. What we needed was to disinter the whole subject from all its superincumbent rubbish; to get at the exact facts; to subject the rugged heights of the Peninsula to the 'unreasoning though logical tests of theodolite and land-chain, of altitude and azimuth instruments, of the photographic camera, and the unerring evidence of the pole star and the sun'; and to have accurate plans and maps, sections, photographs, and models of the disputed places, with true native nomenclature collected by a competent Oriental scholar.[5]

Accordingly, the Rev. Butler set up the Sinai Survey Fund. This was well supported by his friends and other interested well-wishers. These included the Royal Geographical Society, and most important, Captain Palmer's uncle, Sir Henry James, the head of the Ordnance Survey (who reported to the Secretary of State for War). Unfortunately, before Butler could realize his ambition, he was struck down by a fatal illness. However, Palmer, James and Williams and the veteran Sinai explorer and honorary secretary of the PEF, the Rev. F.W. Holland, pushed the survey forward with the support of the Royal Society. The survey party was led by two Sapper officers. These were Captains Palmer and Wilson, with Wilson, the senior of the two, serving as the commanding officer. There were four Sapper NCOs, including the talented photographer Sgt. MacDonald, with Holland as guide.

There were also two academics: Mr Wyatt of Oxford was to study the natural history and collect specimens; the short, boggle-eyed, bearded and eccentric oriental scholar Edward Henry Palmer from Cambridge was known as the 'Pundit' to distinguish him from Capt. Palmer. The Pundit was to act as translator and collector of correct place-names from the Bedouin. He was also to examine the Sinaitic inscriptions, which some biblical scholars surmised had been carved on the rocks by the Israelites on their journey across the Sinai.[6] This was the Pundit's first visit to the Middle East. He had acquired his remarkable facility for Arabic, Hebrew and Persian while at the University of Cambridge, where he was a Fellow of St. John's College. According to his biographer, this short, slight, consumptive, plucky, scholar was 'always attracted by people who run shows, do things, act, deceive and in fact are interesting for any kind of cleverness'. Indeed, this was a good description of Palmer himself. There is a whiff of the mountebank about him. He concocted an elaborate story about his past, which he was keen to impress upon those who might be of use to him. He boasted that his friends were 'refugees, conspirators, gypsies, organ-grinders, fire kings and foreign sailors', from whom he had learned Romany, Italian and French. He was fascinated with the Theatre, and he claimed as a friend the budding thespian, Henry Irving. Palmer had dabbled in the then fashionable obsession with mesmerism and spiritualism, claiming that he could hypnotize people and commune with the spirits of the dead. In one of his more unguarded moments he admitted to a friend that this was all an illusion, but he had enjoyed perpetrating the deceit. This seemed to be his *modus operandi*. The truth about Palmer was far more mundane; his story was the classic tale of the poor Cambridge town boy who had rubbed shoulders with the undergraduates at his aunt's hotel on Bridge Street and had eventually adopted the gown. He seems to have impressed the dons of St. John's College with his knowledge of oriental languages, which he had picked up from various Indian exiles in Cambridge. For some odd reason this was enough to win him a succession of scholarships to read Classics at the university. Although he achieved only a third-class degree, he was made a fellow of his college due to the Master wanting to keep the job in-house. Palmer was a plausible operator who was assiduous in his cultivation of contacts in order to make his way in the world. He was also a risk-taker whose motto was: 'Let us try and see what may happen.'[7]

The Sinai survey party left Southampton on 24 October 1868, without the 'Pundit' who had gone ahead to conduct research in the colleges and libraries of the main mosques in Cairo. They arrived at Alexandria on 7 November, where they were sped through customs by order of the Khedive. This had been arranged at the request of the British consul-general in Cairo, Colonel Stanton, another Sapper officer. The survey party reached Suez by rail the next day. The surveyors were greeted by Holland's 'old acquaintances', two Arab sheikhs who between them could supply enough baggage and riding camels for the party. The Bedouin tribes of the southern Sinai were poor in camels, so hiring them for the Europeans had to be a collective effort by the sheikhs. The lengthy process of drawing up a contract for the hire of the camels was to be followed by a competition between the sheikhs for the lightest loads during the course of the survey. Departing Suez on 11 November, the caravan of thirty-two baggage camels and twelve riding dromedaries were sent around the head of the Gulf while the party crossed by boat to the far shore. As Palmer later related:

> The survey was a profound mystery to the Arabs, and at first the cause of no small suspicion ... on more than one occasion we received solemn deputations requesting to be informed whether we were not measuring the Peninsula with a view to purchasing it for the Christians, and ejecting the true believers from their patrimony. When we told them first we had no object but to establish the truth of the history of 'our Lord Moses and the Beni Israel', they accepted the explanation outwardly, for politeness's sake, but it was clear from their manner that they entertained no very exalted opinion of the intellectual capacity of those who could think it required any proof at all.[8]

The party had not been specifically instructed to fix the site of the Israelites' crossing of the Red Sea to Sinai, a question which remained 'vexed and vexatious', and they accepted the general opinion that it had been in the vicinity of Suez.[9] The oasis at Ayun Musa, which the party soon reached on the second day, was taken as the site of the Israelites' first camp in Asia from which they had then marched on to Sinai. Judging from a photograph of three European day-trippers snapped by the survey, Ayun Musa was within easy reach of Suez. The oasis is to loom large in this story, and one wonders whether the members of the survey party felt any sense of trepidation before they set out into the Sinai. There is a picture of some of them gathered on the beach, a solitary palm tree standing at their backs, on the fringe of the bay (see Plate 20). Their body language tells us much. Palmer radiates a debonair confidence, almost the man-about-the-desert in his white pith helmet and ducks and leaning on his cane. Lance Corporal Maling is the spitting image of a Victorian athlete, all in white, arms akimbo, legs apart, ready for all comers. The full-bearded Corporal Brigley stands slightly slouched with his favourite fez and tassel on his head, seemingly unfazed by his surroundings. There are two other pith-helmeted Europeans standing side-on to the camera, looking out to sea and perhaps thinking of home. But it is the Arab camel men, patiently squatting on the ground in the background who grab one's attention. They must have wondered what these infidels were doing in the desert.

The party continued on foot, as they did for the rest of the survey, to the Wadi Gharandel. Their way led along the desert strip between the wall-like Jebel Rahah and the sea. They identified it with the Wilderness of Shur (Shur in Hebrew means wall) and were intent on locating the stations mentioned in Exodus. Marah, which the Israelites reached on the third day, was placed either at Wadi Amarah or Ain Hawwarah, respectively 41 miles and 47 miles from Ayun Musa; the next station, Elim, at Wadi Gharandel or Wadi Useit, was 54 and 60 miles distant. The surveyors' camp by the sea was at the mouth of Wadi Taiyibeh, 75 miles on from Ayun Musa. At the head of this wadi, 4 miles from its mouth, two roads led to Jebel Musa, the preferred site for Mt. Sinai. There was considerable dispute among biblical scholars as to which route had been taken by the Israelites. One road, easier though longer, led down to the coast and then up the Wadi Feiran. The other turned inland and followed a more direct course through a series of lateral wadis. The survey party favoured the former route because its topographical features were consistent with the biblical narrative. It was the main highway through the peninsula.

The group reasoned that Moses, 'who knew the country well and was acting under divine Guidance', would have taken his people on the best route.[10] The surveyors identified El Markha, the coastal plain which ended 25 miles from Wadi Taiyibeh, as the Wilderness of Sin. Except for Rev. Holland, all considered Rephidim, where the Israelites met the Amelek in battle, to be at the mouth of Wadi Aleyat. This was near the ruins of Paran and below the Wadi Feiran and just north of Jebel Serbal. The surveyors pushed on by the shortest and most favourable road to Jebel Musa. They went via the wadis Kamlye, Burku and Berah, taking observations for a route sketch as they went. They passed the ruins of the temple to the Goddess Athor (the Egyptian Venus) at Serabit el Khadim, where the ancient Egyptians had mined turquoise and left an upright inscribed stone tablet or stela. In Wadi Berah they came across a large rock covered with Sinaitic inscriptions, a rock the Arabs believed to have been cleft in two by Moses to enable the Israelites to pass it. After traversing Wadi Akhdar, Wadi el Ush and Wadi el Shaikh, the survey party arrived at Jebel Musa on 21 November, ten days after having left Suez. They set up camp at the foot of Aaron's Hill, at the mouth of Wadi el Deir. Their little white tents were dwarfed by the massive mountain (see Plate 12), a humbling experience in itself. They visited St. Katherine's Convent and were welcomed by the monks, who offered them room and board. Although making use of a store room, the survey party preferred 'the independence of a tent life' (Holland had found on a previous journey that the monks had very little knowledge of the local topography). This is not surprising given the squalor in which the monks lived. As a photograph of the interior of the convent shows, their living quarters were very rudimentary and probably unhygienic.

A close look at the photograph of this four-square fortress shows two wooden outhouses stuck like limpets to the east wall, with their telltale tracks of droppings over a long time having stained and discoloured the brick.

The party's main task now was to identify the site of Mt. Sinai, the 'Mount of the Law', which involved surveying the cluster of mountains in the heart of the peninsula known as the Wilderness of Sinai. Holland described how the party set about its special survey of the most likely site, Jebel Musa (see Plate 13), for a map on a scale of 6 inches to the mile:

> A base was selected on the plain of er Rahah, and the limits of the survey having been settled, viz, the watershed of the plain of er Rahah on the north, Jebel Abu Aldi on the south, Wady Sebaiyeh on the east, and Wady Leja on the west, we all set to work to get the poling done, while the men were engaged in measuring the base and lower ground. The base was 69 chains 34 links in length, and the dimensions of the survey 4 miles by 4 1/2. The poling was a work of great labour. The monks supplied us with some good poles for the ends of the base, but all other stations we had to build cairns of stone, and whitewash them.
>
> There were twenty-nine stations, and, with the exception of four, their heights above our camp ranged from 800 feet, the lowest, to 2500 feet, the highest. But the height in feet does not give any idea of the difficulty of the climbing which had to be done. The necessity of carrying a pot of whitewash in one's hand, the upsetting of which would often have lost one a whole day's work, added much to the difficulty; and it had sometimes to be carried in the mouth

as we crawled along narrow ledges, overhanging precipices many hundred feet in height, or used each other by turns as ladders. Once Captain Palmer and I found ourselves on a ledge of rock on Jebel Musa from which it was impossible to proceed either up or down, but fortunately I had taken the precaution that day of taking with me a rope, and with it I lowered down Captain Palmer, and then, lying on my back, slid down as gently as I could, and he succeeded in breaking my fall at the bottom.

When the poling was completed we had again to visit most of the stations to take observations from them—a work which we could hardly have accomplished without the aid of some Arab ibex-hunters, whose bare feet, and experience in mountain work, enabled them to carry up the instruments without injury— and the calculation of the observations gave most satisfactory results. In the lower ground there were 31½ miles of traverse, not including offsets. The levelling, which amounted to 19¼ miles, was also a work of great difficulty, on account of the roughness of the watercourses and the great rises and falls crossing the watersheds.

Towards the end of December it grew so cold that hill-sketching was impossible on the higher mountains, and occasional snow-storms interfered much with the progress of the survey. Most of the highest peaks in the neighbourhood of Jebel Musa were, however, ascended, and true bearings were taken from Jebels Katharine, Ed Deir, Tinia (on the summit of which stands Abbas Pasha's half-built palace) and several other well-known mountains; and thus the position of most of the prominent peaks in this part of the Peninsula was fixed, and their altitudes determined by angles of elevation and depression. The altitudes of all peaks ascended were also determined by boiling point thermometers and aneroid barometers; but the latter we found could not be depended upon to 300 or 400 feet, at so great an altitude above the sea (5,000 feet).[11]

The party decamped on 1 January 1869 to conduct a special survey (again on a scale of 6 inches to the mile) of Jebel Serbal, a survey that presented nearly as many difficulties as that of Jebel Musa. Captain Palmer described it as follows:

In massive ruggedness, and in boldness of feature and outline, this mountain unquestionably presents an aspect unequalled by any other in the Peninsula, and, though not absolutely the highest, it has a greater command over the surrounding country than any we have yet seen. Unfortunately there is not a single point in the valleys near its base, which affords a comprehensive view of the mountain. It is only by ascending some of the neighbouring hills that the whole range of its magnificent peaks can be seen at once, and there is no plain anywhere in the vicinity suitable to the assembling of a large concourse of people in the sight of any one portion.[12]

This was regarded as crucial by the party in rejecting the claim by Karl Richard Lepsius, an earlier traveller and Egyptologist, that Jebel Serbal could have been the site of the giving of the Law by Moses. The assembled Israelites could neither have seen him nor heard him on the summit, which was really a 3-mile-long ridge with twelve main peaks.[13] This left Jebel Musa as the most likely site. The survey party rejected other possible mountains, Jebels Katherine, el-Ejmeh and

Umm Alawi, initially favoured by Holland.[14] As *The Times* put it, the survey had:

> The required topographical conditions, the chief of which are a commanding height, a plain or open space beneath it, well adapted for seeing or hearing, and capable of holding at least 2,000,000 spectators, and sufficient camping ground for them all in the immediate neighbourhood. Here a bold granite cliff, 2,000 feet high, forming the north-western end of the mountain block of Jebel Musa, confronts a smooth gravel plain about 400 acres in extent, which slopes down to the foot of the cliff in such a manner that spectators assembled on it would have been in the best position for seeing and hearing the sights and sounds described in the narrative of the law-giving. The whole cliff-front is called after its principal peak, the Ras Sufsafeh, and the plain is the plain of Er Rahah.... . The cliff, the plain and the adjacent heights thus form a great natural theatre, a scene which would at once rivet the attention.... . The acoustic properties of this vast theatre are very remarkable, the advantages offered by the physical formation being so heightened in effect by the desert stillness and the intense clearness of the air that sounds can be heard at astonishing distances.[15]

Moreover, the survey party found that the resources of Jebel Musa could provide the pasturage and water for the Israelites during their year's encampment 'before the mount'. But it was the sheer grandeur of this secluded spot which enhanced the scientific conviction of the party that it was worthy of the epic scene that had unfolded there many centuries before. Like Dean Stanley and others before him, Captain Palmer marvelled that the prospect from the plain of Er Rahah is so impressive and sublime that no beholder can fail to be attracted by it. There is nothing else like in this or any other part of the Peninsula ... In gazing on that noble cliff [Ras Safsabeh, the 'brow of Sinai'] and the spacious plain at its base [Er Rahah], it needs no effort or enthusiasm to recognize their peculiar fitness for the events described in Scripture as having attended the Promulgation of the Law.[16]

For *The Times*, in reviewing the lavishly illustrated three-volume findings of the survey, 'the superior claims of the Ras Sufsafeh and Er Rahab as a site for the Proclamation of the Law are conclusively proved' (see Plates 9 and 16).[17] They followed the survey in dismissing the alternative, the actual peak named Jebel Musa that was favoured by the monks of St. Katherine and the Bedouin. Although they conceded that it may have been the site of the Burning Bush and the delivery of the Law to Moses and of the instructions for the Tabernacle from God.[18]

As Holland pointed out, the special surveys of Jebel Musa and Jebel Serbal had taken up so much time that the survey party could not complete a general survey, 'on the scale of two inches to the mile, of the country between Suez, the ranges of Jebels Rahar and Tih, the plain of Senned, Jebel Abu Ma'sud, Jebel Umm Shaumer, Tor, and the Red Sea, *i.e.* the district through which the children of Israel must have marched, if either Jebels Serbal or Musa, or any mountain south of the Tih range, be the real Mount Sinai.'[19] But all the wadis which formed the possible routes had been traversed by the survey party: 91 miles of traversing and 45 of levelling over rough ground, comprising rocks, gravel and boulders in the wadis, which wore away the surveyors' boots. All told, the Sinai survey covered some 3,600 miles, an area the size of Kent in England, from whence the suggestion for the survey had fittingly come. All the essential features had been recorded, involving 800 miles of route surveying, reconnaissance sketches, 282 determinations of altitudes, 300 sets of astronomical observations fixing, along with a triangulation, 84 points in the Peninsula.

While Captains Wilson and Palmer conducted the survey work, Edward Palmer 'the Pundit', helped by Holland, examined and collected nearly 3,000 Sinaitic inscriptions, especially in the Wadis Mokatteb and Sidri. There is a photograph of Palmer looking quizzically through his half-moon spectacles at a rock at his feet, head cocked at a birdlike angle, as he tries to decipher the inscription for the camera (see Plate 17). It is the pose of an actor who wants to convey a moment of careful scientific enquiry. There is an even stranger photograph of him sitting in the middle of the survey group. The men are at rest in camp, no doubt after the end of long, tiring day among the rocks. The Pundit looks very much the pasha, about to puff on a *nargileh* or *hookah*, the water pipe for smoking scented tobacco or cannabis. But he is the odd one out in the group. The others have bored and slightly peeved expressions, as if they are having to put up with the Pundit's playacting. In particular Wilson, who has Palmer's *nargileh* hosepipe draped across his knees, seems to be fed up with this scene (see Plate 10). Was this to do with the quality of the Pundit's work? Palmer and Holland had taken impressions in paper and by photograph of what seemed to be the most important Sinaitic inscriptions (see Plate 18). But how important were they? Palmer never published an account of them, contrary to what had originally been intended. This may well have been due to Palmer losing interest in the project because the inscriptions did not cast any light on the route of the Exodus. Palmer admitted soon afterwards:

> In a philological point of view they do possess a certain interest, but otherwise the 'Sinaitic inscriptions' are as worthless and unimportant as the Arab, Greek and European graffiti with which they are interspersed. The language employed is Aramaean [Aramaic], the Semitic dialect which in the earlier centuries of our era held throughout the East the place now occupied by the modern Arabic, and the character differs little from the Nabathaean alphabet used in the inscriptions of Idumaea and Central Syria.[20]

Palmer surmised that they were largely made by 'a commercial people, trader, carrier and settler' travelling through the wadis.[21] The surveyors discovered twelve inscriptions in which the Greek and Sinaitic occur together. This enabled the Pundit to work out the value of every letter of the Sinaitic alphabet, perhaps his most important achievement. He collected Arab traditions and stories from the Towarah (the collective name for the Bedouin of the southern Sinai, who numbered about 4,000 men at that time). He ascertained the correct names of places by interviewing selected tribesmen around the campfire at night and examining the monks' manuscripts in the convent library. His two chapters written for the published survey entitled 'The Bedouin and their Traditions' and 'Mohammedan History of the Exodus' are as revealing about Edward Palmer as they are about the subject matter. He asserted that unlike other desert dwellers, the Towarah of the Sinai were law-abiding. 'Theft and fraud are absolutely unknown in the Sinai. In striking up a bargain, an Arab will not hesitate to lie and

over-reach you by every means in his power; but, when the terms are
once agreed upon, you may be perfectly assured that his word is his
bond.'[22] Yet, he also observed that the Bedouin 'resent any attempt to
enter their country without an escort from their own number, which
simply means hiring the necessary camels from their tribe.'[23] These
observations about the Towarah were to come back to haunt Palmer
some twenty years later. Although Palmer did some useful work in
debunking various travellers' theories about the Exodus based on
errors in names, the Arab traditions did not throw much light on the
route of the Israelites. The local Arabs associated nearly every notable
feature, including the markings and indentations in the rocks, with
Moses. 'The superstition that all saints and holy personages had the
faculty of leaving the impressions of their forms upon the hardest
rocks is by no means confined to the Bedawin, and may possibly
have had its origins in some vague intuitive conception of geological
phenomenon.'[24]

In addition to his many other duties, Wilson also compiled
accounts of the archaeological finds for the published survey volumes;
these finds included some strange circular beehive-shaped stone
huts, much like those he had seen while surveying near Inverness
in Scotland. The Arabs called them *nuamis* (mosquitoes) on the
grounds that they had been erected by the monks to ward off the
attentions of the insect of that name. They are found throughout
southern Sinai and seem to have been used initially as dwelling places
and later as burial chambers. Holland believed that they were built
by the Amelekites, the contemporaries of the Israelites, and this
theory raised in some minds speculation as to whether the structures
provided shelter for the Israelites during the plague of mosquitoes

at the time of the Exodus. By early 1869 Wilson and his party had surveyed the previously uncharted territory of the southern Sinai and its routes on the southern approaches to Suez. Wilson's biographer concluded that: 'Just as Wilson's survey of Jerusalem has been the basis of all subsequent exploration of that city, so his survey of the Sinai Peninsula is the foundation of scientific examination of the wandering of the Israelites.'[25]

There is no questioning the worth of the scientific surveying of the southern Sinai, which produced the first accurate map of the peninsula. But the surveyors, especially Wilson and Palmer, were heavily influenced by their evangelical Christian interpretation of the Bible. It is difficult to accept Captain Palmer's figure of two million Israelites trekking to Mt. Sinai. This figure was based on Exodus, xii, 37, which speaks of 'six hundred thousand men on foot, besides women and children' and thus points to a total of two million people. As Charles Doughty later surmised, this would have meant an Israelite convoy stretching for some six hundred miles![26] Modern scholarship is sceptical about the biblical account of the massive Israelite Exodus from Egypt and the Israelites' reception of the Law at Mt. Sinai in the books of Exodus, Leviticus, Numbers and Deuteronomy. Some scholars argue that there is no evidence from contemporary written or archaeological evidence for these occurrences in the thirteenth century BC. The sites in Sinai mentioned in the Exodus narrative are real, as the Wilson survey confirmed, but they were not occupied at the time they were meant to have played a part in the wandering of the Israelites in the wilderness. Some scholars have suggested that the narrative may reflect a later political conflict between Israel and Egypt in the seventh century BC, when the Exodus narrative reached its final form.[27]

But was this simply a survey expedition of biblical sites or a military mapping exercise as well? The Sinai was not only of religious interest to mid-Victorian Britain but also of military significance given the cutting of a canal through the isthmus of Suez by the French entrepreneurial engineer Ferdinand de Lesseps; he was a cousin of Empress Eugenie and was to open the canal to international shipping some eleven months after the completion of Wilson's survey. The British government had opposed the canal on the grounds that it would literally cut Egypt off from Ottoman control and place France, as guarantor of an independent Egypt, across Britain's short route to India. Fortunately for Britain, Egypt's protection of its own interests ensured the neutralization of the canal and prevented France from establishing a *place d'armes* along its banks and at Suez. British maritime supremacy in the Mediterranean and Red Sea would have made it difficult for France to control the canal. But it is a mark of Britain's nervousness at French intentions in Egypt that in addition to Wilson and Palmer, other Sapper officers were also sent to Egypt at this time to keep a watchful eye on the canal and the approaches to it. Colonel Stanton became consul-general in Cairo, Colonel Laffen investigated the financial position of the Suez Canal Company and Colonel Hamley attended the opening of the canal. In effect, the Sappers were acting as intelligence officers in Egypt, building up an accurate picture of the situation there, and their reports were thus vital for the decisions of their military and political masters in London.

With its close links with the War Office, Wilson's expedition, which was given considerable support by the Ordnance Survey, furthered the cause of biblical research, but it was also a believable cover for a military survey, mapping the southern approaches to the new Suez

Canal from Mt. Sinai to Suez, in case the peninsula became the scene of military operations in the future, either between Egypt and its Ottoman suzerains or between Britain and her traditional rivals in the Middle East: France and Russia. It was a natural step, therefore, for Wilson on his return to London to take charge of military mapping in the Topographical Department of the War Office and to turn that department into a nascent intelligence department within a few years.

In the desert of the wandering

While Wilson sought to forge a fully functioning intelligence department in Whitehall, he also continued to promote active intelligence-gathering operations in Ottoman territory. In lieu of a formal intelligence service, he could do this only under the auspices of the PEF. The latter body did not have the funds yet to sponsor a thorough survey of Western Palestine, which Wilson so earnestly desired in light of similar French activity in the Levant. However, the PEF was prepared to underwrite Wilson's plan of an expedition to explore the Desert of the Tih, the biblical 'Wilderness of the Forty Years' Wanderings of the Jewish tribes' after their Exodus from Egypt and before they entered Canaan, the Promised Land. Palmer later wrote:

> The desert of Et Tih is a limestone plateau of irregular surface, the southern portion of which projects wedge-like into the Sinaitic Peninsula. It is bounded on the north by the Mediterranean Sea and the mountains of Judah; on the west by the Isthmus of Suez; and on the east by the Arabah, that large valley or depression which runs between the Gulf of Akabah and the Dead Sea.[28]

Wilson had not had the time in 1868–9 to survey this barren region in the northeast of the Sinai Peninsula, which was so vital to communications between Egypt and Palestine. Instead, in the winter of 1869–70, he entrusted this task to two Cambridge men after briefly training them in survey and astronomical-fixing techniques: the Arabist Edward Palmer, who had been involved with the Sinai Survey, and Charles Tyrwhitt-Drake, a tall, asthmatic undergraduate with an interest in natural history who received a travel grant from Cambridge University's Worts Fund.

Following Wilson's instructions and mapping as they went, Palmer and Tyrwhitt-Drake returned to Mt. Sinai (Jebel Musa). They then proceeded to Erweis Ebeirig, which they claimed to be the first permanent halt of the Israelites at Kibrothe Hattarah on their way to attack the Canaanites. It was here that the starving multitude's desire to eat flesh was rewarded with a covey of quail and then was punished for its unbridled lust with the plague, which killed thousands. On the trail of the Israelites, Palmer and Drake then marched to 'Ain Hudherah, which they regarded as Hazeroth, the second permanent encampment, on the threshold of the wilderness of Paran (the Desert of Tih), the scene of the Wandering. Since Palmer and Tyrwhitt-Drake did not examine the country northeast of 'Ain Hudherah and southwest of the 'Azazimeh mountains, they could not identify the exact locations of the individual stations of the Israelites' march. But they were certain that their route led to Akabah (or Ezion Gaber, which was at the head of the Eleritic Gulf) and did not enter the plateau of the Tih by the southern passes. They found at 'Ain Kadis ('Holy Fountain') what they claimed to be Kadesh, the camp of the Israelites in the Wilderness of the Paran. This was on the threshold of the Promised

Land, where Moses struck the rock and brought forth a gush of water. It was from Kadesh that 'Moses, by the commandment of the Lord' sent a dozen men 'to spy out the Land of Canaan'. They went via the Negeb, or south country, and the Wilderness of Zin, as far as Hebron, bringing back the grapes of Eshtol. Their unfavourable report, leading to cowardice and the rebellion of the Israelites, resulted in their defeat by the Canaanites at Hormah and in forty years of wandering in the wilderness. This was followed by the Israelites' eventual reassembly, in the fortieth year of the Exodus, at Kadesh for the final advance upon Canaan. Their route took them south towards the head of the Gulf of Akabah. They went up Wadi Ithm to the mountains, a few hours north of Ezion Gaber (Akabah). From there the Israelites crossed the plain of Moab by the road running between Edom and the great eastern desert. (It was here that Palmer and Drake came away empty-handed when looking for another Moabite Stone near the Dead Sea.) Then followed the death of Moses on Mt. Pisgah, the crossing of the Jordan, the destruction of Jericho and the final entry into Palestine. Palmer and Tyrwhitt-Drake claimed to have identified all the key sites of the Exodus, thus completing the biblical survey of the Sinai:

> We cannot perhaps ever hope to identify all the stations and localities mentioned in the Bible account of the Exodus, but enough has been discovered to enable us to trace the most important lines of march, and to follow the Israelites in their several journeys from Egypt to Sinai, from Sinai to Kadesh, and from thence to the Promised Land.[29]

Palmer and his companions did all this on foot, trekking 600 miles from Suez to Jerusalem, with their few belongings on camel-back, as they were handed from tribe to tribe by their Bedouin guides. Palmer seems to have been a *wunderkind* when it came to languages, having an instinctive, almost musical, ear for intonation and vocabulary. During his 'energetic winter wanderings', he acquired a knowledge of all the local tribes and their Bedouin words.[30] There were the powerful and warlike Teyahah, who roamed the central part of the Desert of Tih and the south country, or Negeb, the semi-fertile areas at the southern end of Palestine. They were in some cases well-disposed to the Franks, or European Christians. They subsisted by providing camels for the haj caravans from Egypt to Akabah and thence to Mecca or for travellers taking the long desert route to Palestine from Nakhl to Gaza. The south country was in Turkish territory and was also inhabited by the Lewehat, the Amarin, the Azazimeh and part of the Teyahah. Palmer was incorrect in stating that the Azazimeh inhabited the mountain plateau to the northwest of Nakhl. They were to be found to the west of Wadi 'Arabah in Turkish territory. Of them, Palmer remarked:

> They are superstitious, violent and jealous of intrusion upon their domain, suspecting all strangers of sinister designs upon their lives and property, to examine the country and wrest from them the secrets of its topography and nomenclature, when the use of the prismatic compass exposes you to execration as a sorcerer and when to ask the simplest question is to proclaim yourself a spy, is as our own experience has taught us, neither an easy nor an agreeable task.[31]

Palmer might have added that this truculent tribe was always at war with its neighbours. Palmer was one of the very few travellers to have visited that tribe. Then there were the Terebin, a large and powerful series of tribes, who could put some 2,000 fighting men into the field. They lived mainly around Gaza, but there were detached minor tribes near the Suez Canal and an important one at Gizeh, near Cairo. This connection among the Bedouin tribes of the Sinai was hard for Europeans to grasp because it seemed contrary to their view of traditional Bedouin life. All the Sinai Bedouin had relations and allies among the Bedouin and *fellahin* (peasants) of Egypt and Palestine. Although the Egyptian Terebin had become mainly sedentary *fellahin*, they retained close connections with the Sinai or Syrian Terebin around Gaza. The latter had an unenviable reputation for being fanatically anti-Christian, untrustworthy and deceitful. Some of their sheikhs were kept hostage in prison by the Ottoman Turks to compel the good behaviour of the tribes, but this did not seem to alter their behaviour, and Turkish tax-collecting expeditions beyond Gaza were often driven out.

There was also the powerful Hawetat (or Haiwatat) series of tribes, to the east of the Gulf of Akabah and in the Wadi Arabah (where the tribes went by the name of Alawin). They had detachments between Akabah and Suez and were to be found in strength between Suez and Cairo and at Zagazig. The Towarah, divided into a number of minor tribes, inhabited the desert of the Sinaitic peninsula. They kept themselves apart from the other Bedouin. Palmer was sometimes mistaken as to where these tribes were to be found in the Sinai. This could be because he, like many others, did not realize that the tribal grounds or *dar* (sing. *diyar*) were interlaced. In many parts of the peninsula, sections of different tribes were to be found living in relative peace and sharing the same wells.

Palmer's knowledge of the tribes appeared to make him a natural choice for the later secret service mission to the Sinai in 1882. His biographer, who knew him well, remarked upon Palmer's 'extraordinary gift of sympathy [which] was connected with his mesmeric power; he was a thought-reader'. Apparently, it gave him great influence over people and during this and subsequent expeditions, 'he never doubted his ability to manage any number of Arabs, friendly or hostile'.[32] This is an odd remark to make given that Palmer by his own confession had no real sympathy for the Sinai Bedouin. He thought:

> The noble savage is a simple and unmitigated nuisance ... wherever he goes, he brings with him ruin, violence and neglect ... half the desert owes its existence to him ... If the governments of Egypt, Turkey and Arabia would but act in concert, and consult the real interests of their subjects, this terrible scourge might be removed, and the Fellahin relieved from the constant dread of rapine ... I do not advocate a war of extermination against the Bedawin ... but I would put an end to their existence qua Bedawin ... If the military authorities were to make systematic expeditions against these tribes, and take from them every camel and sheep which they possess, they would no longer be able to roam over the deserts, but would be compelled to settle down to agricultural pursuits or starve.[33]

Despite his lack of sympathy bordering on dislike of the Bedouin, Palmer was convinced that he was able to persuade them, especially the Teyahah, to assist him and provide accurate information:

The reason is simple enough; an Arab is a bad actor, and with but a very little practice you may infallibly detect him in a lie; when directly accused of it, he is astonished at your, to him, incomprehensible sagacity, and at once gives up the game. By keeping this fact constantly in view, and at the same time endeavouring to win their confidence and respect, I have every reason to believe that the Teyahah Bedawin gave us throughout a correct account of their country and its nomenclature.[34]

Palmer's belief in his power of persuasion was in evidence in his haggling with Misleh, the paramount sheikh of the Teyahah, and his brother Suleiman, over the contract for the supply of five camels for the journey from Nakhl to Beersheba. Palmer characterized Misleh as 'an ill-looking surly ruffian, his features rendered more hideous than their wont by a scowl of mingled cunning and distrust ... his brother Suleiman, who was to accompany us in our wanderings, a tall, thin man, with a handsome countenance and a restless, eagle eye.' Palmer found Suleiman 'exceedingly hard to deal with' but by providing medicine and reciting Arab poetry he believed that he had 'moulded him to our will'.[35] Palmer's conviction of his power in his guise as Sheikh Abdullah (since the Bedouin could not pronounce his real name) over the Teyahah sheikhs was to prove fatal in 1882.

After travelling through the 'great and terrible' desert and taking in Jerusalem and Petra on the way, Palmer and Tyrwhitt-Drake fetched up in mid-July 1870 at Bloudan in the Anti-Lebanon Mountains. This was the summer quarters of the British consul in Damascus, Sir Richard Burton, the famous explorer of Africa and Asia who was accompanied by his formidable wife Isabel.[36] The four became firm friends and ventured to Ba'albek together, looked for the sources of the Litani River and explored the cedars and crests of the northern Lebanon. Palmer then journeyed into northern Syria, where he spent time among the secret Nusairiyeh sect and later gave an account of them to his fellow Freemasons. He returned to London via Constantinople and Vienna, where he met the 'Dervish of Windsor', the Hungarian Orientalist and British secret service agent, Arminius Vambery. Palmer was quick to defend Burton when the latter came under a concerted attack from the scion of British Jewry, Sir Moses Montefiore (whom his detractors referred to as 'the King of the Jews'), the chief rabbi and the Rothschilds. They accused Burton of not looking after the interests of British-protected persons, namely, Jewish moneylenders, in Damascus. Coupled with a protest from the Greek Bishop of Nazareth that Burton and Tyrwhitt-Drake had brawled with some of his congregation during Easter Week in 1871, these complaints led the Foreign Office to demote Burton from Damascus to Trieste. Embittered, Burton sought solace in looking for what proved to be fool's gold in the Land of Midian on the Arabian shore of the Gulf of 'Akabah. He preferred this as the site of the Mountain of the Giving of the Law since Moses's wife was a Midianite. Ever anxious to return to the desert, the ungovernable Burton was to force the Foreign Office to send him to Egypt and Palestine in an attempt to rescue Palmer in 1882.[37]

Burton later thought that Palmer's details on the Bedouin of the 'Pharian Peninsula' as he preferred to call the Sinai, 'require copious revision'.[38] Even Palmer's biographer, or rather hagiographer, lamented the fact that Palmer alighted so early on 'Ain Gadis as the Kadesh of the Exodus. If Palmer and his companions had explored the neighbourhood, they would have found a more likely location at 'Ain el-Quedeirat ('Fountain of God's Power'), the largest spring in the Sinai.[39] There is no denying that Palmer's crossing of the Sinai on foot was an impressive physical feat, but it is difficult to avoid the conclusion that he was determined to return to England having discovered the path of the Exodus. This stemmed, in part, from a natural desire to have something to show for his tremendous efforts; still, one can't help thinking that it was also due to the showman in him. He wanted people to believe that he had solved one of the great biblical mysteries and to give Wilson and Holland of the PEF, and later Burton, the results they sought in order to gain their approbation. Palmer craved the esteem of his peers and society, not only as a way of validating his belief in his ability to win friends and influence people, but also to benefit materially from these connections. His lack of a secure and regular income was to drive him to consider any and all moneymaking schemes and to take increasingly greater risks.

Deathwish in the desert

The defeat of France by Prussia in the war of 1870 temporarily removed the French as a threat to British interests in Egypt, in particular to the Suez Canal, Britain's route to her eastern empire. The French had also withdrawn their military surveyors from Palestine, which they had intended to map with the aim of extending their 1860 survey of the Lebanon. They had managed to survey 2,000 square miles of Galilee by the time they withdrew. The threat to Britain's influence in the region now came from the far north. Russia's repudiation of the Black Sea neutralization clauses of the 1856 Treaty of Paris challenged the post-Crimean War balance of power in the Near East and allowed Russia to remilitarize the Black Sea region and once again cast covetous eyes on the Ottoman territories in the Balkans, Constantinople and further afield. Wilson and the PEF feared that if the Holy Land fell to the Russians, then British scientific and strategic mapping activity would cease. The British consul in Jerusalem, Noel Temple Moore, noted that the defeat of France, 'the first Roman Catholic Power', and the decline of the papacy with the unification of Italy in 1870 had led the Russians to purchase more property in and around Jerusalem and thus 'to extend their foothold and increase the influence of Russia in the country'.[40] As one of Wilson's intelligence officers later pointed out:

> If Russia occupies Turkish Armenia, she will have the valleys of the Euphrates and the Tigris at her disposal and she will completely dominate the Gulf of Seuderum if indeed she does not occupy it. Syria especially the Valley of the Jordan will become of great importance as offering the easiest road for an advance on the Suez Canal—under such circumstances it is of the utmost importance that we should have good maps of the country.[41]

While time allowed, the PEF pressed ahead in 1871 with Wilson's long-desired comprehensive survey of Palestine. This was to be a survey of the western part, since the American Palestine Exploration Society had agreed to survey Palestine to the east of the Jordan River. As it turned out, the Americans failed to carry this out, and that survey, too, had to be done by the PEF. Over a period of seven years, interrupted only by illness, injury and the death from malaria of Tyrwhitt-Drake, a dedicated party of Sappers led by Captains Stewart, Conder, and Kitchener carried out the great survey of the Holy Land which plotted every feature, road, ruin and watercourse in Palestine. This was not only a great scientific and strategic achievement, but it was later to form the basis upon which the frontiers of British Palestine and later Israel were drawn. However, in 1875 further plans to carry out a survey of sites connected with the life of Jesus around the Sea of Galilee had to be put on hold due to the deteriorating security situation and the threat to the lives of British surveyors from the Arabs. This was as a result of the revival of 'the Eastern Question', namely, the question of how to handle the dismantlement of the crumbling Ottoman Empire without sparking a war between the great powers of Europe.

While Turkish auxiliaries, *bashi-bazouks*, were massacring Orthodox Christians in Bosnia-Herzegovina and Bulgaria, leading Pan-Slavs in Moscow called for Russia to intervene and carry out its duty to protect fellow Christian Slavs. In a further development, the Russian ambassador to Constantinople, Count Nicolay Ignat'yev, sought to activate a secret agreement of 1870 with Ismail, the Khedive of Egypt, for the purpose of their joint support, with arms and agents, of a coordinated revolt by the southern Slavs and the Arabs to shatter the Ottoman Empire. These elaborate plans were undone by Ismail's disastrous Abyssinian campaign and his slide into bankruptcy, which had been encouraged by French bankers as they sought to reassert French control over the country and the Suez Canal. The British Conservative government of Benjamin Disraeli sought to check the renewed Russian and French threats by purchasing in 1875 the Khedive's 44 per cent shareholding in the Suez Canal Company and in the following year participating in the increasing Anglo-French control of Egyptian state finances.

Wilson stressed the need for more up-to-date information in case the British military needed to intervene in Egypt in defence of British interests against Russia and a recalcitrant Khedive. The head of Wilson's new Intelligence Department in the War Office, Major General Sir Patrick MacDougall, was despatched to Egypt ostensibly 'for his health' but in reality to carry out a military reconnaissance of the Suez Canal. He informed the British cabinet that if a British army corps held Port Said, at the northern end of the canal, then it should be able to repulse any Russian amphibious attack in the eastern Mediterranean or an overland invasion from Palestine.[42] As the Russians began to step up their political and military pressure on Turkey in 1876, a bevy of British Sapper officers was also sent to Constantinople and the Straits to draw up plans for British defence and to monitor Russian military activity. It soon became clear to Disraeli that Britain did not have the troops to defend Constantinople from the Russians and that Turkey's only salvation lay in removing the *casus belli* by agreeing to have the rights of Christians within the Ottoman Empire safeguarded by the great powers. The Sublime Porte's refusal to concede this led to war with Russia in April 1877.

The see-saw nature of this war, fought mainly in the mountains and plains of Bulgaria, put a premium on accurate and current intelligence being relayed by British intelligence officers from the front lines back to London to ensure that the British government could make well-informed decisions. The War Office Intelligence Department also sent officers to other Ottoman provinces in the Balkans, the Levant and North Africa to gather military information. As the Russians approached the gates of Constantinople in March 1878, the Turks capitulated and conceded territory under the Treaty of San Stefano to an independent and enlarged Bulgaria under Russian control.

In order to prevent Russia from gaining a stranglehold over Turkey and the Straits, Britain countered by sending its Mediterranean Fleet to Constantinople and also sent Indian troops to Malta and assumed a protectorate over Cyprus. This was to give Britain a *pied- à-terre* in the eastern Mediterranean to protect the northern end of the Suez Canal and, if necessary, to project force to Alexandretta (İskenderun) on the Syrian coast. British intelligence officers were sent to the Dardanelles, Syria and Cyprus to carry out survey work and to monitor Russian activity. Forced by Britain and other European powers to the negotiating table in Berlin in June/July 1878, Russia conceded some of its gains in the Balkans. Sapper officers were sent by the Intelligence Department to the Balkans to counter Russian chicanery on the commissions demarcating the boundaries of the new states. They were also deployed to eastern Turkey to act as an intelligence screen of military consuls under the ubiquitous Wilson and to monitor Russian activity in Armenia, Syria and Mesopotamia. Both Lord Salisbury, the British Foreign Secretary, and Wilson feared that the next threat to the British routes to India would be played out in the Fertile Crescent and wanted to deploy more military consuls to Syria and Arabia to counter Russian activity. The advent of the Liberal government under the 'grand old man' of British politics, William Ewart Gladstone, in the spring of 1880 put paid to all such schemes for the defence of British interests in the Near and Middle East. Gladstone had no desire to defend the 'terrible Turk' against the Russians and did not believe the Suez Canal needed to be defended from the Russians, the French or the Egyptians. Gladstone preferred to trust to the Concert of Europe to arbitrate any disputes in a peaceful manner, and meanwhile he concentrated on domestic politics and on solving the intractable 'Irish problem'.

Unfortunately for Gladstone, the 'Egyptian problem' would not go away. The growing Europeanization of Egypt, symbolized in the reinstitution of the Anglo-French dual control after the deposition of Khedive Ismail in 1879, had the effect of separating the regime of his son Tewfik from his subjects, thus provoking the latter into an Islamo-nationalist revolt. In February 1881 this unrest led to a military coup by the fellah colonels; the coup was orchestrated by Ahmed Arabi Bey and ended Turco-Circassian domination of the Egyptian Army. Further unrest was caused in North Africa from the Algerian Sahara to the Sudan by the French expedition to Tunis in May 1881, which compensated France for Britain's seizure of Cyprus. A second military revolt in Egypt in September 1881 led to Arabi becoming the real power in the land. In January 1882 a joint Anglo-French declaration of support for Tewfik only further weakened his position.

The internal situation in Egypt and the Sudan continued to deteriorate, threatening to destabilize the Sinai and the Negeb. Wilson and Major General Archibald Alison, the new head of the War Office Intelligence Department, stressed the need for accurate and up-to-date intelligence on Egypt and the southern Levant. This was because they suspected the French, with a naval squadron based at Bizerta in France's new protectorate of Tunis, of stirring up discontent in the Egyptian army and in Syria in order to have an excuse to intervene militarily in Egypt. Ignoring the objections of the Foreign Office, Alison and Wilson sent two Sapper officers on secret missions to

North Africa in the winter of 1881–2. Major Alexander Tulloch went to Egypt for a spot of snipe-shooting in the delta. In reality he spent his time laying the ground for a possible British military intervention. He made notes on the coastal defences at Alexandria and Damietta. He collected facts and figures about the state of the Egyptian army and recruited agents among the European rail and telegraph communities for future sabotage missions. Tulloch was bold enough to inspect Arabi's troops at the Abdin Palace in Cairo and to persuade the Egyptian ministry of war to divulge its plans to meet any invading force from the canal at Tel el Kebir. This was to be the site of the future battle to decide the fate of Egypt. Tulloch also came up with plans to counter any attempt by the Egyptian army and the Bedouin of the Sinai to block the Suez Canal and interrupt British imperial trade.[43] Meanwhile, Captain Gill was despatched to Tripoli to monitor the French conquest of Tunis and to discover whether the French had any designs on the Ottoman provinces of Tripolitania and Cyrenaica on the western frontiers of Egypt.

William Gill was the very model of a British intelligence officer. He was a consummate professional down to the very tip of his luxuriant moustache. He was intrepid, devoting his life to exploration and adventure in the service of his country. His maxim could have been: 'England's necessity is my opportunity.'[44] Moreover, unlike most Sapper officers, he was self-financed because he had come into a substantial inheritance when he was young.[45] This enabled him to seek adventure where he could find it. He served his apprenticeship with Colonel Valentine Baker exploring the border country between Persia and Trans-Caspian Russia and monitoring Russian activity. But he earned recognition as an explorer (and gold medals from the British and French geographical societies) after his journey in 1877 through Szechuan, eastern Tibet and Yunnan in China to the Irrawaddy in Burma.[46] In the spring of 1879 he was sent by the Intelligence Department to Constantinople to assist the commission set up under the Treaty of Berlin to delimit the Asiatic boundaries of the Ottoman Empire. Owing to disagreements between its British and Russian members, the commission never carried out its work. In the summer of 1880, following the British defeat at Maiwand, Gill rushed to Afghanistan, where he joined Sir Charles MacGregor as a survey officer for the expedition against the Maris. After that Gill returned to Persia to discover whether the Russians were moving on the Turkoman oasis of Merv. He was recalled before he could accomplish this task as a result of the diplomatic protest by the Russian foreign minister, Nicholas de Giers, about British officers 'haunting the frontier'.[47] In October 1881, Gill was drawn to Libya, travelling through the Tripolitanian desert while the French conducted military operations against the Tunisian tribes. Gill was pessimistic in his outlook, confiding to his travel diary (later shown to the War Office) that

> the French would be compelled to cross the Tripolitanian frontier, that Tripoli would follow the fate of Tunis and Benghazi would probably be seized by the French. Benghazi ominously near to Egypt where thanks to our miserable government we have lost the last semblance of influence of any kind. There is only one chance left to us now, and that not worth much. That is to get hold of Syria, make a railway and thus do without the canal.[48]

As for the Turks, Gill thought they wanted 'to stir up all Islam against Christendom, and I believe myself that the troubles in Egypt are all part of the scheme—the Turkish officers now have orders never to be on friendly terms with Europeans'.[49] Gill was constantly frustrated by Turkish officialdom in his travels in Libya. But he was a painstaking military surveyor, and his detailed report on Tripoli and Benghazi and on the intelligence activities of French and Italian military officers was commended by both the commander-in-chief of the British army, the Duke of Cambridge, and his rival General Wolseley. However, Gill's relentless adventures hid a dark and fatal impulse. He had a morbid horror of growing old. He told a close friend: 'Life is worthless without activity. I do not wish to live long.' His wish was to come true within a year in the sands of the Sinai.

4

On secret service in the Sinai

Just as events in Pharaonic Egypt drove the Israelites to embark on the Exodus, it was the deteriorating internal situation in Ottoman Egypt in 1882 which drew Gill, Palmer and eventually Warren to Sinai. The final breach between Khedive Tewfik and his nationalist ministers came in April 1882 with the arrest and intended show trial of forty Turco-Circassian officers. They were accused of conspiring to murder the newly promoted Ahmed Arabi Pasha, the minister of war. Anticipating an Islamo-nationalist backlash and growing anarchy, Europeans began to leave Cairo. The British considered an Anglo-French intervention in Egypt on behalf of the European powers. This was to demonstrate support for the Khedive and the protection of European interests. Some officials in London equated Egyptian nationalism with Irish nationalism following the murder of the Chief Secretary for Ireland, Lord Frederick Cavendish (the younger brother of the Secretary of State for India, Lord Hartington) on 6 May in Phoenix Park, Dublin, by former Fenians. A 'cabal' of ministers in the British cabinet decided on 12 May that Tewfik should be pressured to dismiss Arabi and the nationalist government. The 'cabal' ordered that two ironclads from the Mediterranean Fleet under Sir Frederick Beauchamp Paget Seymour should be sent to Alexandria. Success in Egypt was intended to make up for failure in Ireland. The arrival of British and French ironclads at Alexandria from 17 to 27 May only strengthened Egyptian popular support for Arabi, and Tewfik was forced to restore him to the ministry of war. This worsened relations with European residents, many of whom fled to the canal towns and then left Egypt. The Egyptian army began to throw up earthworks between the old masonry forts in Alexandria's eastern and western harbours opposite the ironclads. The Egyptians also assembled forces on the banks of the Suez Canal, but these were withdrawn on 7 June. The anti-Christian riots in Alexandria on 11 June, which led to the deaths of some fifty or sixty Europeans, turned public opinion in England against Arabi, who was blamed for the massacre.[1]

It was an Egyptian rather than a canal crisis.[2] The growing disorder in the delta threatened not only European residents, the dual control and its European officials but also the financial and economic interests of the foreign bondholders, the Levantine cotton merchants and the Khedive. There was no immediate and direct threat to the canal. The crisis was played up by Liberal ministers in the name of the protection of world communications and free trade and to rally Liberals, advocates of free trade and Radicals behind the Conservatives in support of military intervention in Egypt. Gladstone refused to believe that the canal was in any danger. But he was depressed by the failure of his policy in Ireland as well as by the murder of Cavendish, his former private secretary and nephew by marriage. Gladstone failed to keep the service departments in check, and after the Secretary of State for

War, Hugh Childers, received on 16 June a report on the vulnerability of the canal and the necessity to occupy Port Said and Suez, he met with the Duke of Cambridge and General Wolseley to discuss the preparation of an expedition to Egypt. Hartington presented plans for the protection of the canal to the Secretary of State for Foreign Affairs, Lord Granville, and gave advance warning to the Viceroy of India, Lord Ripon, of the possible need to send a force from India to Suez. The First Lord of the Admiralty, Lord Northbrook, prepared on 17 June to send a naval task force to seize the canal so that it could be used by Wolseley to attack Arabi from the rear via Ismailia in order to avoid damaging the cotton crop and becoming bogged down in the delta. Northbrook ordered the commander-in-chief of the East Indies Station, Admiral Sir William Hewett, to go to Suez on 23 June. Intelligence had been received that day from Major Tulloch, who had returned to Egypt and reestablished contact with members of the European rail and telegraph communities, that the 'Egyptians have three small vessels filled for explosion in the canal between Port Said and Ismailia. They have been in position one week. They also intend operations in the canal from Damietta.'[3] The builder of the canal, Ferdinand de Lesseps, did not believe that the canal was in any danger other than from foreign intervention. Nevertheless, on 24 June he asked the Egyptian prime minister for a guarantee of the safety of the canal, and the minister promptly placed a cordon of armed Bedouin along the banks of the canal. But Northbrook was worried about the possible threat the Bedouin, whether under the Khedive or Arabi or in search of plunder because of the disorder in Egypt, posed to the operation of the canal. The Bedouin had to be won over or neutralized. Accordingly, Northbrook instructed Admiral Seymour that 'in the event of your having to protect the Canal, it will be of the greatest importance to send some men who knew the Bedouins and their language, and will have influence with them'.[4] At this point the War Office and the Admiralty sought out Palmer for advice on the Bedouin of the Sinai.

While this crisis unfolded, Gill arrived back in London from Tripoli to resume his job at the Intelligence Department of the War Office under the supervision of Wilson. He was immediately asked by Northbrook (probably at the suggestion of a mutual acquaintance, Lt. Col. Bradford of the Indian Army, also the governor general's agent for Rajputana) to collect information about the Bedouin tribes of the Sinai. It seems to have taken Gill eight days to discover the existence of Palmer and to track him down to his house in Mecklenburgh Square, London. Here Palmer was living with his second wife and two daughters, supporting them on the proceeds of jobbing journalism to supplement his inadequate academic stipend from Cambridge.

When he visited Palmer on the evening of 24 June, Gill voiced the concern of the War Office and the Admiralty that Arabi was in contact with the sheikhs of the main tribes in the Sinai through the pro-Arabi governors of Nakhl and El Arish. It was feared that they would join Arabi to attack ships transiting the canal and stir up a holy war, or jihad, in Syria. In this and subsequent meetings with Gill, Bradford, Northbrook and Granville, Palmer answered their questions about the Bedouin tribes of the Sinai. He expostulated on how their sheikhs could be persuaded not to join Arabi and perhaps even to act against him if someone they trusted talked to them. Palmer spoke of how easy it would be to do so and impressed upon his listeners that the Teyahah of the Tih desert and the Towarah at the southern apex of the peninsula were the most important tribes in the Sinai. 'It may be said that, with the co-operation of these two, the Canal would be perfectly safe on the east, and that those tribes might be relied on to completely keep in check any others on this side … [namely] the Terabin, Hawetat, Azazimeh, Alawin, Ammarin, Beni Sikhur, Beni Ali (part of the Towarah), and Halebhi.'[5]

Palmer knew the paramount sheikh of the Teyahah and of the Sagairat branch, the 'suspicious and brutal' Misleh, but thought he could be 'managed through his brother, Suleiman Ibn Hamd, who is a very superior person'.[6] Palmer was under the mistaken impression that the Egyptian government preferred to deal with Moussa Nassier, sheikh of the Sowalihi branch of the Towarah, based in the Feiran valley, recognizing him as 'the Chief Sheikh of all the Arabs in this region'.[7] The Egyptian government had certainly dealt with Moussa Nassier in the past, by throwing him into prison in 1870 when he refused to supply a Towarah tribal guard for the Suez Canal. Although he was highly esteemed by the other sheikhs for his commonsense, he had no power over the Terebin, the Hawetat and the Teyahah when it came to war. The Egyptian government listened instead to Sheikh ibn Shedide who exerted a form of control over the Egyptian Bedouin thanks to his wealth and influence. The Teyahah could muster some 7,000–8,000 fighting men and 14,000–16,000 camels. Although superior in fighting capability to the Egyptian army, the Teyahah lacked discipline and were armed only with matchlocks. The Towarah numbered some 4,000 fighting men and 8,000 camels under the command of Hasan ibn Ahmar, sheikh of the Walad Said branch, and Eid, sheikh of the Jabaliyi branch, who controlled the route from Jebel Musa towards the canal. The Towarah lacked the fighting ability of the Teyahah, and Palmer seems to have suggested that they provide labour for any work required to repair any damage to the canal. The Towarah were less prejudiced against Europeans and were thus regarded with suspicion by other Bedouin. However, contrary to what Palmer seemed to think, this did not mean that the Towarah would side with the British in time of war if it was uncertain whether the British would win. Palmer said that because the Bedouin were 'desperately poor and very fond of money', he would advise that 'in dealing with these people, their self-interest and cupidity should be appealed to'. With regard to the Greek monks at St. Katherine's monastery at Jebel Musa, who were friendly with the Egyptian government, Palmer had this to say: 'Should any agent be sent amongst the tribes, these monks must be carefully watched, as they would probably send information to Cairo. Any monk leaving the monastery should be followed, and means might be found, without injuring him, to prevent the completion of his journey.'[8] In fact, any approach by a British agent to the tribes had to be kept secret from the Egyptian government, which meant departing from Gaza rather than Port Said or Suez.

Palmer drafted letters of introduction from him to the two principal sheikhs of the Teyahah and the Towarah and to any Arab. These were sent on by Northbrook to Seymour to be used by him in the event of the latter sending a force into the canal. It must have been clear to Gill, Bradford, Northbrook and Granville that Palmer was the best man to liaise with the Sinai Bedouin. Thus, Palmer had effectively talked himself into the job. After the event, however, his biographer, Walter Besant, thought that Captain Sir Richard Burton, who as a soldier was used to 'the peril of death', should have gone instead of Palmer. The latter, despite his expeditions across the Sinai, was, after all, a civilian.[9] Besant stated that Palmer never asked for remuneration for himself or for compensation for his wife if he did not return alive, but Northbrook seems to have made some general promise to this effect. In fact, Northbrook arranged for Palmer to receive £500 of secret service money and £400 from Northbrook's own account.[10] As a friend, Besant played down Palmer's pressing need for money to support his family. In contrast, Wilfrid Scawen Blunt, a vocal critic of British intervention in Egypt, emphasized that Palmer was 'an impecunious man, making a poor living from journalism and weighted in his struggle for life by a recent marriage'. Blunt argued that the money advanced to 'poor Palmer' and 'promises of large pecuniary reward in case of success' drove him to accept with alacrity the mission offered him by the Admiralty.[11] As evidence of this, Blunt quotes from Palmer's journal, written during his desert mission: 'Lord Northbrook told me that I was to have the £500 for this first trip, and that as soon as I began negotiations with the Arabs they would enter on a fresh arrangement with me. I shall save at least £280 out of this, which is not a bad month's work! ... I don't think they can give me less than £2,000 or £3,000 for the whole job.'[12] Besant also saw and used Palmer's journal, but he cut out this passage from his biography.

On the eve of his departure from London, Palmer talked with Besant of the dangers of the mission. He anticipated that this would not come from the Arabs but from the Turks and the Egyptians, who might have him murdered, at the beginning or end of his journey across the Sinai. Besant later related that Palmer had received no written but only verbal instructions for his mission.

He was to proceed to the Desert and Peninsula of Sinai: he was to get there the best way he could, and at his own peril: he was to travel about among the people, to pass from tribe to tribe, and this was the first thing—to ascertain the extent of excitement aroused among the people, and how far they were inclined to join Arabi. Next, he undertook to attempt the detachment of the whole of the tribes, if he could, from the Egyptian cause, and in order to effect this he was to make arrangements with the sheikhs: he was to find out on what terms each would consent to make his people sit down in peace, or, if necessary, join and fight with British forces, or act in any other way for our interests which might seem best. He was, if possible, to agree to those terms, and his promise would be regarded as binding. Thirdly, as to the Canal ... he was to take whatever steps he thought best for an effective guard of the banks of the Canal on the Eastern side, or for the repair of the Canal, in case Arabi should attempt its destruction.[13]

Before he left England on 30 June, Palmer had submitted to Whitehall estimates of the probable cost of preventing the destruction of the canal (through Bedouin patrols) or of repairing it if damage could not be prevented. As Besant pointed out, 'the safety of the Canal seemed at that time the most important point of all.'[14] Palmer may have also received instructions on arrival in Alexandria as to whether 'camels in sufficient numbers could be purchased, and at what price.'[15] As a 'cover' for his journey, it was put out that Palmer was going out as a war correspondent for his paper, *The Standard*. He represented himself as such to Blunt, according to the latter, before he left London, asking for introductions to Blunt's 'Nationalist friends there [in Egypt] for whom he felt, he said, a strong sympathy and would favour in his writings'.[16] There is no evidence from Palmer's writings that he was so inclined. Blunt gave him some introductions, though not to Arabi Pasha, but Palmer does not seem to have used them. For the sake of secrecy, Palmer's reports and telegrams were to be addressed to his wife, who would then pass them on to the Admiralty. Palmer also kept a short journal of his journey, intended for his wife's eyes only, which was later sent back to London. This journal and his few letters from Egypt constitute the only records of his 'adventurous journey' across the Sinai.

Palmer's return to Sinai

Palmer had a tiring and dusty three-day rail journey from London to Brindisi, but he had a comfortable crossing of the Mediterranean on board the SS *Tanjore* and arrived in Alexandria early on the morning of 6 July. He wrote to his wife that, 'I am sure this trip will do me an immense amount of good, for I wanted a change of air and complete rest from writing, and now I have got both. Of course, the position is not without its anxieties, but I have no fear ... It is quite a chance!'[17] He received a telegram from his wife passing on instructions from the Admiralty for him to report to Admiral Seymour. The latter had reported to Northbrook on 1 July that the Khedive believed that 'by the exercise of some diplomacy' the majority of the Bedouin could be brought over to his side and that of the British. Seymour thought that it would 'require a clever man, and one who is a good Arabic scholar, to conduct the negotiations successfully.'[18] He had been informed that

Palmer was to join him, and as 'the Pundit' spoke Arabic and knew the Bedouin, Seymour was to 'keep him at his disposal'.[19] On board the admiral's yacht—'the Swell of the Ocean', as Seymour was satirically known, gave Palmer a rifle, revolver and plenty of cartridges and told him 'to go at once to the Desert and begin work'.[20] As Palmer was rowed across Alexandria harbour from ship to shore, he marvelled at the sight of 'thirty-four huge men-of-war' facing the Egyptian shore batteries, waiting for the outbreak of hostilities. Many European residents of Alexandria had fled to the relative safety of the ships from Britain, France, Spain, Germany, the United States, Russia, Greece, Austria and the Netherlands. Palmer was excited at the prospect ahead of him. 'Though I shall be a long way off, I shall be able to do something towards winning for our side.' Seymour reported to Northbrook that Palmer 'seems to be very sanguine of success'.[21] According to Blunt, Palmer reported to his wife that Seymour 'congratulated the country on finding so able a man to undertake such a difficult task'.[22] The next day, after breakfasting with the admiral, Palmer boarded an Austrian Lloyd steamer for the three-day passage to Jaffa and put in at Port Said. The first leg of the journey was over a rough sea, and Palmer felt 'ill and miserable'. To add to his discomfort, the ship was crammed to the gunwales with refugees. 'The first class was crowded with Greeks, Armenians, Italians, Germans and all sorts of people … [in steerage] Jews and Syrians packed like herrings, fighting, being sick, howling, poor babes and little children screaming … [and] some Turkish ladies, the wives and mother of a great Pasha, and with them two eunuchs in fashionable Paris costumes.'[23]

The old town of Jaffa is built on a rock facing the sea, and it was 'crowded with noisy picturesque people' when Palmer arrived on the morning of 9 July. Despite a thorough inspection of his baggage by some surly Ottoman customs officials, he managed to get his guns and cartridges ashore. According to Blunt, Palmer lodged 'with the British consul, the Jew Shapira [sic]'.[24] Blunt was referring to the Reverend Schapira, a Christian convert who acted for the Church Missionary Society. Palmer bought provisions and 'Arab costumes' and arranged by a letter that was carried by Schapira's son to meet Sheikh Suleiman at Gaza. 'The heat here is just like a Turkish bath, and the perspiration runs down my face. In the Desert it will be hotter still, but better to bear because dry, and this is so damp. I am already as brown as a gipsy. I have had to cut my hair quite close, and I already begin to look a savage.'[25] Palmer was quite sure of the success of his mission and not afraid, for the Arabs were 'always good friends to me'.[26]

Armed with a *laissez-passer* from the Khedive, on 12 July Palmer left Jaffa for Gaza with his Jewish cook Bakhar Hassan, who was posing as a Muslim. Palmer endured an excruciatingly painful eighteen-hour journey in a jolting carriage, in the course of which he 'disappeared' and became Sheikh Abdullah, the old friend of the Teyahah. On 13 July he joined a company of the latter in Gaza though Suleiman was absent. As Palmer told Seymour in a letter written two days later, he gained 'most important information' from the large number of Bedouin there.[27] He proposed to take the short route of about 100 miles from Gaza to Suez as he had been asked to get there as soon as possible. He planned to halt at a place unmarked on the map and about four days distant from Gaza. Palmer would then send a Bedouin courier to the P&O agent at Suez, asking for instructions as to the best way to come into Suez because he was aware that the approach to the town might still be in the hands of the Arabists, and he wanted to avoid being captured and perhaps killed by them as he had notes on his contacts with the Bedouin with him. He proposed heading for Ayun Musa and to be taken off by boat. Palmer was leaving at once for the interior because he had heard of the bombardment of Alexandria by Seymour's ironclads on 11 July (the French had decided not to take part and had withdrawn their squadron beforehand). There was a distinct danger that when the denizens of Gaza found out, they would turn on the Christians and massacre them. Anti-Christian feeling was very strong in Palestine, and several murders of Christians took place in Gaza while Palmer was there. The bombardment of Alexandria on 11 July succeeded in neutralizing the Egyptian shore batteries and the threat to Seymour's ships. The Arabs wrought their revenge by burning down the commercial district of Alexandria. But the bombardment led to the rallying of Egyptian Islamo-nationalist opinion around Arabi. Arabists cut the telegraph line between England and India, rendering the Red Sea cables useless and forcing the resumption of use of the Indo-European line through Persia. Concern for the security of the canal led to the despatch of Admiral Anthony Hoskins to Port Said and his use of gunboats from 14 July to escort British vessels through the waterway. That same day the Secretary of State for War, Hugh Childers, instructed the Woolwich Arsenal to prepare to send an expeditionary force of 21,000 men to Egypt.[28]

Palmer left Gaza on 15 July with Bakhar Hassan, a headman and five or six Teyahah. He posed as a senior Syrian officer as he travelled through the lands of the Terebin. At his first camp, which was 'quite picturesque and romantic', he slept with a loaded gun at his side.[29] On 16 July he rode his camel 'through the most scorching heat, wind, and dust that I ever felt. We stopped for two hours at noon and slept, but the heat was so great it did not refresh me at all.'[30] He believed that he had elicited more information from the Terebin than they had learnt from him. 'I now know where to find and how to get at every sheikh in the desert, and I have already got the Teyahah, the most warlike and strongest of them all, ready to do anything for me. When I come back I shall be able to raise 40,000 men.'[31] He did not expand on how he had managed to accomplish this feat.

On 17 July, he wrote in his journal that during an eleven-hour stretch over 'white, glaring sand' and in 'burning heat', he had seen nothing important except two Turkish soldiers near Nimieh. Fortunately, they kept their distance; otherwise they would have risked being killed by Palmer's men. The two soldiers were actually travelling from Nakhl to Gaza. 'I am getting on capitally with my mission, and am longing to get instructions from Suez and know if our troops have landed [this was not to happen for another four weeks]. I did not expect to find out as much as I have done this first trip.'[32] According to Blunt, Palmer commented, presumably to his wife: 'I think our fortune will be made.'[33]

On 18 July Palmer boasted that he had won over to his views 'the great sheikh of the Arabs hereabouts' even though Sheikh Misleh of the Teyahah had told him that 'Ahmed Arabi is with the Muslims— you belong to our enemies'. The Teyahah had made a spectacular entrance into Palmer's camp at El Bawaty, riding in 'at full gallop with a host of retainers all riding splendid camels as hard as they could run; when they pulled up all the camels dropped on their knees and the men jumped off and came up to me.'[34] He also met one Meter Abu Sofieh, apparently of the powerful Hawetat tribes (alternatively spelt by Palmer and others as Haiwatt or Haiwatat), who was to accompany

Palmer to Suez and beyond. Meter was about seventy, of commanding stature, haughty, with a peremptory manner and wealthy by Bedouin standards. He was introduced by Sheikh Misleh as being the sheikh of the Hawetat, occupying all the country northeast of Suez. Palmer did not realize that Misleh had misled him. Meter was of the far less powerful Lewehat; he had broken away from his tribe and taken up residence with two or three families of the poor M'Said Bedouin, a branch of the Lewehat near Suez. They called themselves the Sofieh tribe, but they had no power or influence among the tribes. Palmer pressed Meter into service and had him carry messages to the P&O agent at Suez about their imminent arrival. Later, in the course of his investigation, Warren said that Meter was 'a most undesirable person to act as escort to travellers at such a critical time'. Warren concluded that this 'unfortunate deception' was to have fateful consequences.[35] One wonders whether the torrid heat of the desert in midsummer was affecting Palmer's judgement. He was certainly revelling in his role as 'Abdullah Effendi –which is what they [the Bedouin] call me – ... a very grand personage indeed.'[36] On 19 July, he noted of the Teyahah:

> It is wonderful though, how I get on with them. I have got hold of some of the very men whom Arabi Pasha has been trying to get over to his side, and when they are wanted I can have every Bedawin at my call from Suez to Gaza. I have also found out the right men to go to in every tribe, and where they are camped, and what men they have got with them.[37]

Palmer proceeded with Sheikh Misleh, who had been promised £500 for his cooperation, to his brother Suleiman's camp at Jebel

Moghara, three days from Suez (Suleiman was away in Cairo). It was Misleh

who engages all the Arabs not to attack the caravan of pilgrims which goes to Mecca every year from Egypt, so that he is the *very man* I wanted. He has sworn by the most solemn Arab oath that if I want him to, he will guarantee the safety of the Canal even against Arabi Pasha, and he says if I can get three sheikhs out of prison, which I hope to do through Constantinople and our ambassador, all the Arabs will rise and join me like one man. In fact, I have already done the most difficult part of my task and as soon as I get *precise instructions or see Colonel Bradford the thing is done, and a thing which Arabi Pasha failed to do, and on which the safety of the road to India depends.*

I hear from the Bedouin who has just come on from Egypt that Arabi Pasha has got 2,000 horsemen from the Nile Bedouins and brought them to the Canal – but when I get to Suez they will soon go back, for my men know them, and if fair means won't do I shall send them ten thousand of the Teyahah and Terabin fighting men and drive them back.[38]

According to Blunt, Palmer boasted in his journal to his wife:

I have been so successful that I shall write for more money, saying I have been obliged to spend all mine on presents a few hundred pounds is a great deal to us and nothing to the Government, who would, I know, have given thousands for what I have already done – of course I shall make the most of the difficulties and they have been really great. I will send you a hundred or so as soon as

I get the chance from Suez …I have had to give away a great deal, but have still nearly £300 left after paying my journey to Suez! That is better than newspaper work, £300 in a month![39]

On 27 July Palmer and Meter left with their six-man Teyahah escort for the coast via Arif, Wadi Hadirer, Jidi, and Wadi El Haj. On 28 July Palmer wrote that 'I have just got the great Sheikh of the Haiwatt Arabs with me now, and get on capitally with him. In fact I have been most wonderfully successful throughout. I have been sitting out in the moonlight, reciting Arabic poetry to the old man until I have quite won his heart.'[40] Palmer seems to have been under the impression that this moonlight sojourn was due to Meter Abu Sofieh being of the Hawetat tribe. This was to prove a fatally wrong assumption: Meter Abu Sofieh was in fact a renegade Lewehat. Palmer arrived at Ayun Musa on the night of 31 July. The oasis was inhabited by a few Christian families who were protected from Hawetat raiders by two sheikhs of the Aligat, Ode Ismaili and Umduckhl. It was the latter who supplied three camels to Palmer to take his baggage down to the beach since the Teyahah refused to do so. While the Teyahah returned to their tribe, Meter Abu Sofieh made for his camp at Tusset Sudr, a location of sinister future significance for Palmer. A dhow took 'Abdullah Effendi' to the P&O steamer offshore. 'It cost me a lot of money, nearly £10, but I escaped the Egyptian sentries.'[41] Palmer was relieved to have arrived safely. 'The last thing I saw in the Desert was the bones of a camel and the head of its rider! I am quite well, a little thinner and dried up perhaps, but quite strong.'[42]

Palmer's revelation

The Egyptian crisis had moved towards its climax while Palmer had been among the Bedouin. Arabi had reacted to the revelation in the 19 July issue of *The Times* of Wolseley's intention to attack via the canal by designating an army corps for its defence. But the rumours that he had diverted salt water from Lake Timsah into the Sweetwater canal proved unfounded. For his part, Gladstone was forced by his cabinet on 20 July to send an army corps to Egypt. His attempts to secure French and even Italian military collaboration came to nought when the idea was rejected by the Italian and French parliaments in late July. This ensured that the government of India would have to send troops to Suez. On 31 July the Khedive authorized the British occupation of the canal to expel the nationalists from the main towns. Northbrook commented that this was 'the key to the whole situation. It is no question of war, and does not involve the neutrality of the Canal. We are acting at the request of the Khedive to put down the rebels. The Khedive is the ruler of the country and of the territory through which the Canal passes. We are engaged in supporting his authority there.'[43] Arabi responded by moving his troops by train to Tel el Kebir, which was intended to be 'the Egyptian Plevna'.[44] Northbrook duly instructed Admiral Hewett to occupy Suez, now abandoned by its European and Egyptian population, which he did on 2 August. Hewett hoped that this would have a catalytic effect upon the Bedouin: 'These will flock to us as soon as they see us in possession here, and bring us any number of camels we may want.'[45] The Egyptian council of war responded by despatching troops to occupy the railway between Suez and Ismailia, Nefiche and Salihiyeh as well as sending 2,000 Nile Bedouin to occupy the canal along its banks and then to block it at Ras el Esh, Kantara, Guisr and Chalouf. Arabi withdrew his garrison and administration from Ismailia and entrusted the defence of the canal to Lesseps, who had protested against what he saw as the British violation of the neutrality of his creation. Since the British were intercepting and reading Arabi's telegrams, they knew that he continued to receive intelligence on British military movements (troop transports arrived at Alexandria and Suez on 10 August, at Port Said and Ismailia on 20 August) from de Lesseps and the telegraph to Syria. This made it imperative for the British to cut off these sources of information, a job with which Gill was to be tasked. While Admiral Hoskins at Port Said declared de Lesseps to be 'an enemy of England' and threatened to hang his son Victor from the yardarm, Lesseps announced that he would personally kill the first Englishman to land at Ismailia.[46] Hoskins was reading de Lesseps's 'affectionate' telegrams to Arabi, in which the former promised that no act of war would occur in the canal and the latter in return promised to leave the canal alone and not cut off the freshwater to the canal ports. His later attempt to revoke this promise was prevented by the British. Northbrook felt sympathy for Hoskins:

> It must have been abominably provoking to be worried by a fidgety vain Frenchman, who is, moreover, exceedingly voluble ... [b]ut, after all, he has been playing our game by keeping the Canal open ... [w]hen the moment arrives to act in the Canal, and we are strong enough, we must shove M. de Lesseps out of the way, and act on the authority of the Khedive. It is a pack of nonsense to parade

the neutrality of the Canal against the Ruler of the country and in favour of the rebels; and now that the Sultan has denounced Arabi the case is stronger, for we are acting also for the Sovereign. All this tall talk will evaporate when the moment arrives; and I don't believe M. de Lesseps will commit himself so far as to block up his own Canal out of spite against us, though I dare say he has plenty of it, and must be tearing his hair at the way France has effaced herself by the conduct of her Chamber.[47]

This was the context for Palmer's short stay at Suez and his preparations for his return to the desert. Palmer had reported to Admiral Hewett that during 'his preliminary journey through the Desert of Tih' he had:

found the Bedawin in a very unsettled state, at war with each other, turbulent and distrustful of strangers. Agents of Arabi Pasha have been amongst them for some time, as well as other secret Turkish emissaries, endeavouring to stir them up against the Christians and to induce them to join in a jehad. Arabi Pasha has also frequently summoned the great sheikhs to Cairo at different times; some have obeyed the summons, but no engagements have been entered into by them. I learn, however, that the Pasha has succeeded in obtaining 2000 men from the tribes under the protection of Ibn Shedide ... [these were the five clans of the 'Nile Arabs': the Shedide, the Suwalineh, Ma'azeh, Ubili, and 'Ayaidi]. Ibn Shedide had died within the last three days and I think it better to leave these last for the present; there is a feud between them and the Terabin, and the latter will only be too glad of a chance to drive them back should they show themselves near their territory ...

Arabi Pasha's emissaries have set the Bedawin thinking. They have, for instance, to a great extent kept the fast of Ramadan, which is the first indication I have ever seen of their paying any attention to religious duties.

At present the Bedawin hesitate with which party to side, because they do not know whom to trust. I believe that if they saw a determined occupation once begun, it would be possible to engage at least 50,000 men to protect the Canal, furnish camels etc; but they would require to be provided with ropes and shebekat, or camel-nets, for holding loads. In case of any arrangement being entered into with these Bedawin, it would be of great assistance if a gunboat were stationed at Gaza to protect the Christians and give the necessary confidence to the Bedawin.

If provided with funds, and furnished with precise instructions as to what services are required from the Bedawin, I feel confident of being able to bring them over.

A glance at the map will show that the only Arabs who can exercise an important influence on the Canal are those of the Tih and the Sinai, these I can control . . .

The task was a delicate one, and I have had to give exorbitant sums in backshish, payment for escorts, etc. I think from £20,000 to £25,000 would secure the whole of the tribes hereafter mentioned [the Teyahah, Terabin, Azazineh, Hanajirah, the Sowriker, the Hawetat and the Lewehat].[48] I can call a meeting of sheikhs within a fortnight, and lay the case before them. In case this should be thought necessary, I should like for the sake of effect to take a large company, say of 200 or 400 Bedawin of the Haiwatt, Teyahah and Terabin with me to the rendezvous.

I can trust the Arabs to keep quiet until they hear from me, no matter what Arabi may say.[49]

But there was another factor in the equation because Palmer had also reported that he had seen 'some Turkish troops at Gaza who had apparently been sent from Jaffa and were trying to prevent the Bedouins from joining us and were preaching the Jehad'.[50]

Palmer's report was forwarded by a 'delighted' Hewett to Hoskins, Seymour and Northbrook.[51] The latter was also 'delighted' that Palmer had 'arrived safely at Suez, and that the Bedouins are right. Their disposition has always seemed to me to be of the utmost consequence'.[52] Yet Northbrook and the others do not seem to have acted on one of Palmer's key points for winning over the Bedouin. 'There are seven sheikhs imprisoned at Jerusalem [they were Jubr ibn 'Atiyah, Hasan Abu Shennar, Zani el-H'zazil, Salem Abu Hejjaz of the Teyahah, Hama des Sofi, 'Auda ez Zara, and Hejjaz of the Terabin]: if their release could be obtained by direct or indirect means from Constantinople, the tribes would rise like one man and follow us.' Perhaps to cover up this failure to act on Palmer's advice, the Admiralty and the Foreign Office omitted this passage from the published version of Palmer's report, but it is contained in the correspondence submitted to Parliament.[53]

Both Seymour and Hoskins sent £10,000 each by the hand of Gill to Hewett for Palmer's use with the Arabs. This was later disputed by Lord Northbrook, who argued that the money was a carried by a naval officer, Lt. Grove, who travelled on the same ship as Gill. Northbrook maintained that this large sum was handed over to the paymaster of Hewett's flagship, the *Euralyus*, and was intended for use in support of the operations of the East Indies Squadron in Egyptian waters.[54] The Admiralty ordered Hewett to instruct Palmer to keep the Bedouin available to patrol or provide camel transport along the canal. 'A reasonable amount may be spent, but larger engagements are not to be entered into until General [Wolseley] arrives and has been consulted.'[55]

After the British occupation of Suez on 2 August, Palmer acted as chief interpreter to Admiral Hewett, assisting in reassuring the inhabitants. According to Blunt, Palmer boasted to his wife that he had 'a staff of about Forty men working under me. The Admiral told me the other night that I was sure of the Egyptian medal and the Star of India.'[56] He was also trying to hire camels. The Admiralty had asked Seymour, Hoskins and Hewett to hire all available camel transport near the Suez Canal in time for the arrival of British and Indian troops. Accordingly, Palmer gave the camel contractor at Suez, Sheikh Salamen, £40 and sent him forth to buy camels. Unfortunately, Salamen made straight for Chalouf and the rebel forces under Raschid Pasha and told them about Palmer's plans to suborn the Bedouin. Salamen was incarcerated for his pains and deprived of his money; he was not released until after the occupation of Cairo.[57] Unaware of this, Palmer was falsely confident that in four days he would have 500 camels and that within ten to fifteen days he would have 5,000 more. He should have taken heed of the fact that he was having trouble just hiring enough camels to convey his own small party to Nakhl, where he was due to meet Sheikh Misleh. Hewett asked Consul Moore in Jerusalem (this message had to go by ship to Jaffa since the consul did not have the relevant FO cipher, 'N') to send a 'trusty horseman' to Gaza to deliver a message to Sheikh Misleh, who was in the neighbourhood, to meet Palmer—Kawadja

Abdullah—at Nakhl on 12 August. In fact, it was to be Sheikh Suleiman who showed up.[58]

On 2 August Palmer recorded: 'I am off to the desert for a short trip in about two days. I have been asked to go to the coast and cut the telegraph wires and burn the poles on the Desert line, so as to cut off Arabi's communications with Turkey.'[59] He made several trips to Ayun Musa in order to buy camels. He tried to obtain the assistance of Ode Ismaili, sheikh of the Aligat, But the sheikh was not inclined to assist because of the threat of the Egyptian Bedouin crossing the canal and attacking him. He stated (later) that he had warned Palmer that this was not the time to enter the desert and advised Umduckhl, a minor sheikh, not to become involved. The Bedouin thought Ode Ismaili partly responsible for Palmer's ultimate fate, presumably because the former failed to dissuade Palmer from going into the desert. Palmer then asked the Christian Mr Zahr to buy camels, and the latter paid £181 10/ to the Jebeliyeh Bedouin for ten camels. Palmer also sent a messenger and a written message to Meter Abu Sofieh asking him to come to Ayun Musa with twenty armed men and one hundred camels to escort Palmer to Nakhl. Meter received the message on 6 August, but he could not read it because he was illiterate, and so instead he started for Suez. That same day the Hawetats sent a message to Cairo to inform Sualem Abu Farag that there were plenty of Christians at Ayun Musa to plunder and a party of English with money just about to start into the desert. Farag duly went to Marbrook and sent a Hawetat, Mosellam Suleiman, to spy on Palmer (he was to visit Palmer on 9 August). On 7 or 8 August, according to later evidence, a Hawetat named Nafil took a message from the Shedides at Chalouf to the Bedouin at Marbrook ordering them to stop the Christians from going into the desert 'at the risk of their throats'.[60] But the messenger arrived too late for the grisly deed had already been performed by others.

Meanwhile Gill had been sent out to Egypt to help Seymour and Admiral Hoskins at Port Said to deal 'with the Bedouins if we go into the Canal'.[61] He was 'a good traveller, with some knowledge of them', according to Northbrook,

> and was employed by me to get up all the information you have about the Bedouins. He knows all about Professor Palmer and his whereabouts. I think you will find him useful. If necessary, do not hesitate to spend money to a reasonable extent to secure the Bedouins, and you can quite trust to Professor Palmer when you get hold of him to advise you as to this.[62]

The Admiralty and Admiral Hoskins ordered Gill to Ismailia on HMS *Orion*, where he conferred with Pickard, the district telegraph engineer, as to the best means of cutting the telegraph line from Egypt to Syria and to Constantinople by which Arabi received information and support from the Porte, the Ottoman government (the cutting of the line had been requested by the Khedive). This line was to be cut at a point between Kantara, where the cable crossed the canal, and El Arish on the Mediterranean coast of Sinai. As Gill pointed out in one of the last pages of his journal (sent back to his mother), this was more difficult than it appeared. It had 'to be done without breaking the neutrality of the Suez Canal, so we cannot simply pick up the cable where it crosses the canal, and take it away, nor can we land at Kantara. To land at or near El-Arish would be very risky, unless we were in communication with the Bedouins near'.[63] There is no indication that

Pickard warned Gill about another problem with the telegraph line between Kantara and El Arish. This problem was due to the telegraph poles in or near the hollows between the sand dunes being covered up as the dunes moved with the wind. Alternately, the poles towards the crest of the dunes could be left suspended in the air. The dunes were like waves with each grain of sand blown up the gentle windward slope, then falling by its own weight down the steep leeward slope. The particles of sand vibrated as they fell down the steep slope striking an odd musical note. The dunes increased in size as they moved inland from the coast, reaching heights of 300–400 feet. After consulting Pickard, Gill thought it best to go on to Suez to see Palmer.

Gill arrived at Suez at 4.00 am on 6 August and after an interview with Hewet the discussed with Palmer the arrangements for entering the desert. After 'mature deliberations' with Palmer, Gill decided to cross the desert from Suez and cut the telegraph himself (according to Blunt he did not trust Pickard to do it), while Palmer attended his meeting with Sheikh Misleh at Nakhl.[64] Gill wanted to judge for himself 'how far Palmer's hopeful opinions are true'.[65] Gill bought Arab clothing, cooking pots and food at Suez. From Lt. Brand, the gunnery instructor, he received guncotton, the Bickford mining fuse, detonators, axes and so forth to cut the telegraph line, 'one of the greatest works of civilization ... war is always melancholy to me'.[66] Palmer noted in his journal (intended for his wife to read) on 6 August that he intended to start for the desert in a few days to buy more camels. Gill and Harold Charrington, flag lieutenant to Admiral Hewett (thus giving the mission the authority of HMG), were to accompany him, and 'we shall all be jolly'. According to Blunt, Palmer went on to write:

my position seems like a dream. The Admiral said as I preferred leaving the Government to settle my pay, that in the meantime I might draw to any amount for private expenses – so I will send you another £500 as soon as I come back. I could do it now, but do not want to look hard up. I have £260 left, after paying all expenses of my journey, etc., in hard money in my despatch box, and today twenty thousand pounds in gold [about £923,000 today] were brought by ship and paid into my account here! I have *carte blanche* to do everything. I give passes to the sentries. If I see a dozen horses I buy them off-hand. Yesterday I found thirty camels and gave a man £360 for them by just writing on a slip of paper.[67]

He also noted: 'Of course it is wartime, but as I am on the staff of the Commander-in-Chief I am not likely to go to risky places.'[68]

On 7 August Meter Abu Sofieh arrived at Ayun Musa where Mr Zahr read him the message from Palmer. Since Meter could not read, he had not brought the twenty armed men and one hundred camels requested by Palmer. Zahr's son, Farag, escorted Meter to Suez by sea where he met Palmer, Hewett and West, the British consul, in the drawing room of the Suez Hotel. Hewett presented Meter with a naval officer's sword as a souvenir. Zahr's son later said that Meter gave it to him for safekeeping because he expected Palmer's party, which he was guarding, to be attacked by Bedouin and feared for his own life if he was found with a sword. But Meter later denied this, saying he had the sword with him in the desert and that it was captured by the Bedouin. Palmer asked Meter to escort him to Nakhl and suggested that on the way they should go to Meter's camp at Tusset Sadr, via the Wadi Sadr, to pick up Meter's camels and send back those he had bought or hired for use by the troops. Meter said he believed that the country was quiet or so he believed, and he repeated this after the events.

By 8 August all necessary preparations had been made for Palmer's expedition. However, there existed no formal agreement with Meter Abu Sofieh for escorting Palmer's party into the desert; such an agreement should have been drawn up and witnessed by Consul West. Gill informed Hoskins on 8 August that he was to leave Suez that day and hoped to cut the wire on the Thursday or the Friday, after which he would rejoin Hoskins at Port Said. Gill thought he could make arrangements with the Bedouin to prevent repair of the wire. Gill was accompanied by his dragoman, Khalil Atik, a Syrian Christian who had been with him in Tripoli, and they joined Palmer, who was travelling with his cook Bakhar, and Charrington, Meter and his nephew Salameh ibn Ayed aboard Hewett's flagship, HMS *Euralyus*. They then sailed from Suez down to a point offshore near Ayun Musa, where they took a ship's boat to the beach and camped the night in one of Mr Zahr's tents. Palmer took with him a bag about 18 inches long, containing three bags of £1,000 each in English gold sovereigns, and this had been generally known at Suez. The next day the group disappeared into the interior.

5

Manhunt in the desert

A week after Palmer, Gill and their companions had set off into the Desert of the Exodus, there had been no communication from them as to how they were faring with their mission. This silence began to disconcert the admirals. On 14 and 17 August 1882 Hoskins expressed his worry to Seymour (relayed to the Admiralty) about the whereabouts of Gill, who should have cut the telegraph wires between Kantara and El Arish by then and should have reported to Port Said. But the telegraph was still operating. Therefore, Hoskins decided to send Colonel Tulloch's agent, Pickard, the engineer who worked for the Egyptian telegraph service, to Gaza in HMS *Beacon* to cut the wires and to try to obtain news of Gill's fate. Pickard later reported to Hoskins that he had hired one Abu Root, a linesman, to cut the wire between Mazar and Beir-al-Abd (i.e., between Kantara and El Arish). He had also bribed the Ottoman telegraph operator at Gaza to prevent any communications from El Arish from reaching Constantinople. Pickard had also examined the telegraph registers and discovered that there had been no telegrams between Cairo and Constantinople for the last twenty days prior to his arrival on 17 August, and no messages had been passed through El Arish up to the time of his departure on

11 September. This may have been because the governor of El Arish, Said Bey Muhammad, was fanatically in favour of Arabi and was trying to prevent the Porte from communicating with the Khedive about the rebellious Arabists. Pickard also reported that Gill had been at a Terebin camp before returning to Suez and should have arrived there by 25 August. But this was difficult to reconcile with disturbing news from some Terebin and Tehayah Bedouin that two white men and four Bedouin had been murdered at a place two days east of Suez. What was the truth?[1]

On 16 August Palmer's old paper, *The Standard*, contained a short, stark news item:

> It is reported that Mr. Palmer, the chief interpreter, and Lieutenant Charrington have been robbed by Bedouins, but they have not been harmed. There is probably some foundation for the tale, which is, however, regarded as an exaggeration.[2]

Three days later *The Standard* elaborated further:

> No news has been received of Chief Interpreter Palmer and Lieutenants Charrington and Gill. The story of their having been robbed was brought in by some Bedouins of their escort, who left, however, without seeing the General, and their improbable story has not, therefore, been sifted. They say that the Sheik in command of the escort, hearing that an attack was imminent, persuaded the officers to go off with him to a place of safety, leaving their luggage, which, after their departure, was looted. We hope to receive the true version of the story shortly from the lips of the missing men.[3]

British newspapers, with their stringers in the major Egyptian ports, were faster with the news on this and other stories during the Egyptian crisis than Britain's official representatives in the country. The Admiralty officers saw this newspaper report, for on 22 August they asked Seymour for news of Palmer and Gill. Hoskins had no news from Port Said, but Hewett at Suez reported that although there were all sorts of rumours circulating about the missing men's fate, which he knew had reached the British public, he could not substantiate them. In order to find out what happened, he sent Captain Foote of HMS *Ruby* and the Greek consul at Suez, Mr Mitzakis, in the Indian government's steamer *Amberwitch* to Tor, the small port on the western side of the Sinai Peninsula. There they were to talk to the Greek archbishop, who was known to the Bedouin. Four days later Hewett informed Northbrook that Saad, one of Palmer's Bedouin escort, had returned to Ayun Musa and informed the Zahr family that Palmer's party had broken camp in a hurry and left their baggage behind to escape an imminent Bedouin raid. They had been led off on fast riding camels by Sheikh Meter Abu Sofieh. The camp had been looted but nothing had been heard of Palmer's party since. Hewett then informed the acting Egyptian governor of Suez, Raschid Bey, of this, and the latter sent two officials to Ayun Musa to bring back Saad for questioning. But the Bedouin would not let him be taken away. Fearing Bedouin reprisals, the Zahrs and the other Christian residents of Ayun Musa shortly afterwards fled to Suez, after which their properties were looted.

Despite 'the disquieting rumours', Hewett thought it 'undesirable' to show his anxiety 'as the Desert is so difficult to communicate with, that I hoped, after all, news might soon arrive which would be re-assuring.'[4] He had telegraphed to Consul Moore in Jerusalem, asking him to send a messenger to Nakhl to enquire as to whether Palmer's party had arrived there. Sheikh Misleh went himself, but Palmer did not appear. Northbrook was 'very anxious' about Gill and Palmer and hoped that the latter had not carried a large sum in gold on him.[5] Hoskins informed Northbrook on 27 August that Gill was safe and would arrive at Port Said the next day.[6] This optimism was reflected in the report by Palmer's old paper, *The Standard*, on 29 August (also in *The Globe* of the same date):

> It is now known that Professor Palmer and Flag Lieutenant Charrington were waylaid by the garrison of El Arish with a party, by Arabi's orders, but no more than this is authentically known. It appears that Captain Gill had left them before they were seized, and he travelled to El Arish, where he executed his mission, and was heard of near Gaza. He has probably arrived at Suez by this time.[7]

But by 1 September Hewett at Suez was beginning to feel anxious about the safety of Palmer's party since they had been away so long. Foote had returned from Tor and reported that Palmer's party had been attacked shortly after leaving Ayun Musa, that the son of a local unnamed sheikh had been wounded and that Meter Abu Sofieh had gone with Palmer to Syria. There was no report of Gill and Charrington, but Hewett thought they were probably prisoners and that the £3,000 of gold that they were carrying had been seized. Hewett expected more information in a week's time from Tor. For the first time this information was conveyed to the mothers of Gill and Charrington and to the wife of Palmer as well as to Queen Victoria.[8]

It was at this point that Lt.-Colonel Charles Warren arrived at Suez accompanied by his fellow Sappers, Lieutenants Haynes and Burton and Quartermaster Sergeant Kennedy. Warren had instructions from Northbrook and Seymour 'to ascertain the fate of Professor Palmer and his party. They were told that no expense would be spared for this object.'[9] Although Warren had volunteered on 24 July for active service in Egypt, he had not been involved with that country or Palestine for a decade. Since 1871 he had served with distinction in a number of postings at Royal Engineer establishments in England. Following the diamond strike at Kimberley in South Africa, he had acted as the British commissioner who settled the disputed boundary between Griqualand West and the Boer-run Orange Free State. He had commanded the Diamond Fields Horse during the Transkei War of 1877–8. He had been badly wounded fighting the Griquas the following year, which was mentioned in despatches. However, Warren believed that he was still 'well acquainted with the Arabs, and particularly the Bedouin' as a result of the three and a half years he had spent in Syria.[10] When the call came on 24 August from the Admiralty for Warren to prepare to leave his post as Instructor in Surveying at the Royal Engineer barracks at Chatham and to proceed to Egypt, he had already submitted to the War Office a memorandum and a longer report on how to neutralize any Bedouin threat to the canal. The report contained the following pertinent warning passage about guarding against treachery and assassination:

The Bedoui, though courteous and hospitable, is strangely wanting in faithfulness where white people and Christians are concerned; but, although he will not scruple to rob and murder those whom he finds in his power, yet he is very chary of doing either if his victims are capable of active, though maybe on the whole ineffectual resistance. Thus, to be well-armed, and to be alert and to be able to use one's efforts with effect, goes far to render one secure from ill-treatment by the Bedouin.[11]

With this in mind, Warren proposed to go into the desert without a Bedouin escort, relying instead on his Sapper companions to guard against any sudden 'surprise or treachery' by the Bedouin.[12]

Warren and his party arrived at Suez at a time of almost 'indescribable tension', as Haynes later related:

The Arab population almost to a man sided with Arabi Pasha against the English; but they feared the Bedouin … and the air was filled with the shadows of panics relative to the town being attacked and sacked by hordes of Bedouin—all perfectly absurd in the face of ample precautions taken by Sir William Hewett. The Europeans were expecting every day to hear of the great battle which was to wipe out the Egyptian Army [at Tel el-Kebir]; while the Moslems were expecting to hear of the British being swept into Lake Timsah … a great alarm of impending water-famine was paralysing the people at Suez [as a result of Arabi cutting the Canal at Nifichi, afterwards repaired by Wolseley]. In former days the town had been dependent for its water upon the springs at Ayun Musa; but that supply was now insufficient for the wants of the modern town, and it was also in the hands of the Bedouin.[13]

Amid this panic, Warren reported for duty to Hewett, who introduced him to Osman Bey Rafat, a Syrian from Hebron who was an aide-de-camp (ADC) to the Khedive. He had been especially sent to Suez to assist in the search for Palmer's party by liaising with the Bedouin. Warren was informed that he and Osman Bey were to act as colleagues together. They were to proceed to Tor in HMS *Cockatrice* with wheat and other foods for the starving monks of the Greek Orthodox convent at Jebel Musa. The monks were 'in want' because their mother convent at Alexandria had been destroyed during the anti-European riots. Warren's mission was also intended to persuade the Greek monks to exert influence on the Bedouin who protected the convent and to find out what had happened to Palmer's party. All that Warren knew was that

> the baggage had been plundered; that Palmer had escaped with Metter Abu Sofia; and that Gill had probably left the party to cut the telegraph wires, and had returned in safety. Robberies have so often taken place in the desert, and murder of Europeans so seldom, that there was no reason for supposing that any foul play had occurred, and all the Arab stories went to show that the party had escaped unhurt.[14]

Before leaving Suez, Warren visited the Greek families who had fled from Ayun Musa, but he obtained little information from them except that Moussa Nassier of the Towarah was implicated in the attack on Palmer's party. A Persian merchant named Ossad told Warren that Moussa Nassier had left the vicinity of Tor after receiving a letter from the governor of Suez about the disappearance of Palmer. Moussa Nassier had feared being taken prisoner and punished. Hewett thought this 'very suspicious, and I believe our party are held as captives. Professor Palmer was so well-known and respected by all the Arab Chiefs in the neighbourhood that I cannot think that any harm has befallen them, except that they are detained in hopes of a ransom being offered.'[15] Hewett was pessimistic about the chances of parleying with the Bedouin because they were so 'hostile'. Both Hewett and Ossad commented that the Bedouin had been incited by the Arabists to kill Christians, quite independently of the attack on Palmer. Warren also visited two Bedouin in prison (captured at the action at Shalufi) who would not take letters to the tribes in the desert because they said they would be killed by the Bedouin there. This showed 'a very curious and unusual state of affairs in the Desert'.[16]

On the southern crossing

Like Alexander the Great and Napoleon Bonaparte, Warren, Wilson and Palmer believed that the Israelites had begun their Exodus with a southern crossing of Red Sea in the vicinity of Suez. As Warren and his party (consisting of the British consul at Suez, Mr West, the Greek consul, Mr Mitzakis, the Khedive's ADC, Osman Bey, the Sappers Haynes and Kennedy, the interpreter, Del Burgo, and the lazy cook, Hassan) steamed south from Suez in Captain Grenfell's small paddle wheeler gunboat HMS *Cockatrice*, they gazed upon 'the red, castellated mountains of the peninsula, cut and crannied by innumerable fissures [which] stood out boldly in the clear azure sky'.[17] As they nimbly navigated their way through the coral reef protecting the small settlement of Tor whose few whitewashed stone houses stood out against the dun-coloured plain and the verdant green palm groves, they witnessed a sudden flurry of activity onshore as the Towarah Bedouin present fled with their donkeys and camels. Apparently, they feared that the arrival of HMS *Cockatrice* presaged an imminent attack. Previously, after Foote's arrival, the Bedouin had blocked two passes in the mountains because they mistakenly believed that they were about to be attacked by five hundred British troops. Prevented by fear of the British from wandering into Suez to trade, the starving Bedouin had ridden into Tor to extort food from its Greek Orthodox inhabitants and the monks, who kept a depot at this 'miserable' little place for provisioning the convent at Jebel Musa. Welcomed by the frightened inhabitants, Warren's party was put up by the monks at the depot, which they proceeded to fortify against a possible Bedouin night raid.

The archbishop and his monks had little news to impart. The general view was that Palmer's party had been attacked, had been taken prisoner and were still alive. This news was soon conveyed by Warren to Hewett and the Admiralty, who in turn relayed it to the British public.[18] Two Greek Christian merchants informed the Greek consul, Mitzakis, that on the evening of 11 August Palmer's party were attacked by twelve Hawetat Bedouin, of whom one was wounded by a pistol shot in the ensuing skirmish. Palmer and his men then surrendered, were stripped of their clothes, leaving them no protection against the sun, and were carried off captive into Syria. The Hawetat threatened to hand them over to Arabi if they did not receive a ransom for the release of their prisoners. Apparently, Meter Abu Sofieh, who had escaped with Palmer's money, had offered too little (first £10 for each hostage, then £30) and had then broken off negotiations because of his doubts about the 'good faith of the captors'.[19] Warren wanted to verify this story from Bedouin sources, but the Bedouin refused to talk to Europeans. A reluctant Bedouin by the name of Sala was found to take a letter, for a small consideration, to the paramount sheikh of the Towarah, Moussa Nassier. But Sala disappeared with the money and did not deliver the message, which asked for Warren to be escorted to Nakhl. Warren then proposed 'to make arrangements with "Misleh", Chief of the "Tiyahah", for the ransom of the party if they are yet alive, or for a full punishment of the offending Bedouin if any evil has befallen Professor Palmer's party'.[20]

Meanwhile the British consul, George West, was pursuing his own line of enquiry. He had found what he thought was Palmer's old servant Eid Raschedi from a decade before, and the latter spun him a story about Palmer being at Wadi Sidri, near Tor. The faithful old retainer had allegedly tried to rescue Palmer but had turned back when he learned that either Palmer was dead or it was not Palmer who had been taken prisoner after all. Raschedi's friend Farrak Abu Haiz was convinced that Palmer was alive and took a letter from Warren to Palmer, dated 9 September, asking his 'old friend' for the best way to rescue him. 'If you cannot send a written reply send a token that you are well, one for each [person], a piece of cloth or string with three knots in it (one for each [person]), or some hair from your head or beard with three knots in it; otherwise we cannot tell that the messenger has seen you and we may lose time.'[21] With the letter was sent pencil, paper and a bottle of zinc ointment to treat wounds and sores. Farrak and Raschedi departed for Wadi Sidri and returned a week later. It then transpired that Raschedi had played a cruel trick on West and Warren, motivated by an intent to deceive and/or plain material gain (he was given £10 for his trouble). He had never been Palmer's servant and had never even known him. In fact, he had been Wilfrid Scawen Blunt's servant. Warren overlooked this, paid Raschedi once more and despatched him a second time into the desert with the letter for Palmer. But this letter was destined never to arrive as Raschedi had no clue as to the whereabouts of Palmer. Moreover, he had falsely led Warren to believe that the attack had occurred in the Wadi Sidri, not far from Tor, in Moussa Nassier's territory, and for that reason Warren surmised that Palmer's party was likely to be alive for the Towarah were not openly at war with the British.[22] Further confusion ensued a few days later when the archimandrite, or treasurer, of the convent at Jebel Musa arrived in Tor and proclaimed that vultures had been seen hovering over the Wadi Sidri, which led him to conclude that Palmer and his party had been killed there. He also related that Moussa Nassier had received a letter from Arabi ordering him to kill all Christians, but the sheikh had responded by burying the letter in the sand as an indication of his desire to maintain his neutrality.

By each pursuing his own lines of enquiry, Consul Mitzakis, Consul West and Warren were in danger of entangling their initiatives and thwarting their main purpose of rescuing Palmer's party. Accordingly, it was decided that Mitzakis, West and Osman Bey, who believed that Palmer was not in the desert at all but in Cairo, should return to Suez in HMS *Cockatrice*. Warren and his Sappers, Haynes, Burton and Kennedy, along with Del Burgo, the interpreter, prepared to move inland under the aegis of Moussa Nassier. Warren proposed going overland from Tor to Wadi Ghurundel on the Sinai shore, which he thought 'to be only three or four days from Professor Palmer's locality', and to await there the reply from Palmer carried by Raschedi. This plan would also allow Warren to open up communications with

Captain Grenfell on HMS *Cockatrice* because there was an anchorage in the vicinity, and it was only about four hours steaming from Suez.[23] Warren seemed to be glad to see the back of the civilians and Osman Bey, who demanded to be consulted on everything, for Warren believed that only the Sappers were fit to march to Nakhl to find out what had happened to Palmer.

While Warren and his Sappers waited in vain to hear from Moussa Nassier through Sala, they spent a nervous watch in the fortified food depot at Tor, prepared to defend it against any Bedouin raids. They learned that

[the] Bedouin firmly believed Arabi to be the prophet Isa (Jesus) foretold in the Koran, and who is to come and raise the Moslems to their proper place as the dominant power of the world. Arabi was credited with the power of working miracles, and was supposed to possess two familiar spirits, or angels, resting one on each shoulder; one told him of what was going on in the present, and the other foretold the future. He was supposed to have already vanquished the British in every contest, and was only staying his hand before entirely destroying them.[24]

Conflicting accounts of what had happened to Palmer's party continued to arrive from the Greek monks at Jebel Musa. The rumour that the governor of Nakhl had killed them with his own hands was discounted by Warren as an attempt by Moussa Nassier to clear his tribe of blame and deflect it elsewhere. That rumour was also contradicted by other news from Jebel Musa and Suez that indicated that Palmer and his party were still alive. The news from Suez that Wolseley had defeated Arabi's forces at Tel el-Kebir and was advancing on Cairo prompted Warren to pass on this key information to Moussa Nassier in a letter conveyed to him by the governor of Tor, Ali Effendi. The latter promised to persuade the sheikh to send twelve camels to convey Warren to Nakhl 'without delay'.[25] Warren had previously sought to destroy any mystique Arabi might have among the Bedouin:

What is Arabi to you Bedouin? If he is a prophet, how is it that he counsels you to act contrary to your faith, and if he is not a prophet he must indeed be an evil man, for he is a declared rebel by the Sultan, Commander of the Faithful, and he will be dealt with as a rebel according to the law of Islam! Judge for yourself! Do not be misled by him! He wants you to compromise yourself with your master so as to place you at his mercy so that you must do what he likes! Do not be blind! ... [the Sultan] has sent 6,000 Turkish troops with English officers to support the sultan's Khedive; to act with the English and reduce Arabi to submission. Your old friend Karvadje [Sir Charles] Wilson is with the Turkish troops who have landed at Port Said. The Governors of El Arish and Nakhl will soon be prisoners ... you cannot do wrong in keeping peace in the Peninsula until your Sultan, with the assistance of the English, has removed this false Arabi and the rebels against your faith ... I hear from the convent at Sinai that you imagine that the English are displeased with you on account of the abduction of Hadj Abdullah [Palmer]. Dismiss this from your mind. We know who are the guilty parties, and to them we shall look for satisfaction. As for you we have only friendship, but we expect you to show your friendship in return.[26]

Warren proclaimed Arabi's defeat to the disbelieving townsfolk of Tor. He sent a letter to this effect to the governor of Nakhl, ordering the latter to send his submission to the governor of Suez and to look after Palmer and his party until Warren arrived in Nakhl. In addition, Warren and West thought the pro-Arabi governor of El Arish, Said Bey Muhammad, should be dismissed from his post because he had been responsible for stirring up the desert tribes.

As Warren did not have enough camels to convey his party with their boxes of supplies to Moussa Nassier in the Wadi Feiran, he decided to wait for the latter at a camp in some mosquito-infested gardens that were 4 miles distant from Tor and offered a grand view of Mount Serbal. Warren hoped that by doing so he could demonstrate his peaceful intentions and persuade the sheikh to parley. Warren's party was

> without any escort or guide, thus placing ourselves unreservedly in the hands of the Bedouin, in order to show them that there was no distrust, this being the only method I could devise of inducing them to believe that the English did not intend to injure them indiscriminately for the abduction of Professor Palmer's party, whether guilty or not.
>
> It is scarcely necessary for me to say that though it was my knowledge of the native character which enabled me to attempt this with success, yet I could not have done so had I not been able to rely upon my subordinates to carry out the necessary arrangements for our safety.[27]

This was just as well, for Moussa Nassier had his tribesmen watch the camp where Warren mounted a guard in case he and his men

PLATE 1 *Portrait of William Gill*

PLATE 2 *Lt. Charles William Wilson*

PLATE 3 *Charles Warren's party in Jerusalem, 1867*

GENERAL VIEW OF THE CITY, FROM THE MOUNT OF OLIVES.

PLATE 4 *Panoramic view of Jerusalem from the Mount of Olives*

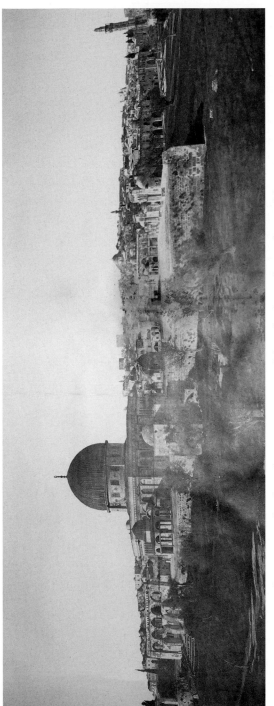

PLATE 5 *Interior of Haram-ash-Sharif. Eastern view of the platform from the Golden Gate*

SOUTH ENTRANCE TO KUBBAT-AS-SAKHRA.

PLATE 6 *South entrance to the Kubbat-as-Sakhra*

INTERIOR OF THE HARAM-ASH-SHÁRIF.

INTERIOR OF KUBBAT—AS—SAKHRA

PLATE 7 *Interior of the Kubbat-as-Sakhra*

EASTERN WALL NEAR SOUTH EAST ANGLE

EASTERN FACE OF SOUTH EAST ANGLE

PLATE 8 *Eastern face of the south-east angle of Temple Mount*

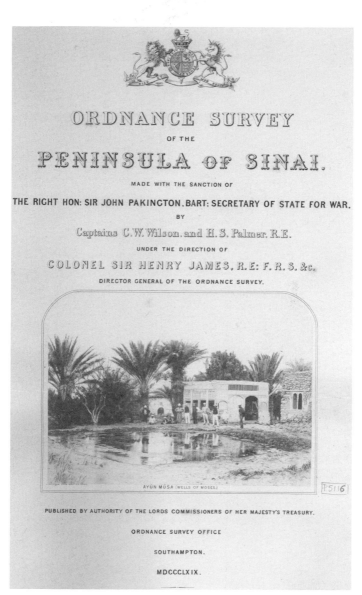

PLATE 9 *Frontispiece of the* Ordnance Survey of the Peninsula of Sinai

MEMBERS OF THE SINAI SURVEY.

1	CAP. H.S. PALMER R.E.	5	CAP. C.W. WILSON R.E.
2	SALVO, COOK.	6	C. WYATT ESQ.ᵉ
3	REVᵈ F.W. HOLLAND	7	EISA, SERVANT
4	E.H. PALMER ESQ.ᵉ		

PLATE 10 *Members of the Sinai Survey*

NON COMMISSIONED OFFICERS OF THE ROYAL ENGINEERS ON THE SINAI SURVEY.

1   LANCE CORP! J.MALINGS, R.E.   4   COLOR SERG! J.M°DONALD R.E.
2   CORPORAL J.H.BRIGLY, R.E.   5   CORPORAL W.GOODWIN R.E.
3   JEMMA, ARAB GUIDE

PLATE 11 *Non-commissioned officers of the Royal Engineers on the Sinai Survey*

CAMP IN WADY ED DEIR, AT FOOT OF JEBEL MUSA FROM AARONS HILL.

PLATE 12 *Camp in Wady ed Deir at foot of Jebel Musa from Aaron's Hill*

PLATE 13 *Convent of St. Katherine and steps leading up to Jebel Musa*

PLATE 14 *Interior of convent of St. Katherine, west wall*

PLATE 15 *Jebel Katherine from summit of Jebel Musa*

PLATE 16 *Plain of Er Rahah from cleft of Ras Sufsafeh*

PLATE 17 *Rock inscriptions in Wady Mukatteb*

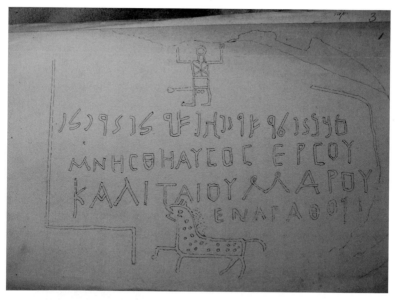

PLATE 18 *Palmer sketch of inscription in Sinai*

GROUP OF BEDAWIN.

PLATE 19 *Group of Bedouin*

ENTERING THE DESERT BY AYÚN MÚSA (WELLS OF MOSES)

PLATE 20 *Entering the desert by Ayun Musa*

would be rushed. The Sappers were plagued by mosquitoes, hyenas who knocked over their cooking pots and made off with their dinner, and a strange, unidentified beast, which seemed like a large ant or spider (but may have been a jerboa), which ran around them in circles at night, eluding capture or destruction.

Ali Effendi reported back on 19 September from the Wadi Feiran that Moussa Nassier wanted to await confirmation from Suez as to the defeat of Arabi and the surrender of Cairo before going over to the British and coming to Tor with Ali to see Warren. The latter wanted to travel to the Wadi Feiran to see Moussa Nassier but was dissuaded from doing so on security grounds by West, Captain Grenfell and the archimandrite. Warren gave up waiting for Moussa Nassier on 24 September, broke camp and returned to 'the miserable town of Tor' and embarked on HMS *Cockatrice* for Suez.[28] Warren found it:

difficult to comprehend the meaning of Moussa Nassier's conduct; he had ample opportunity for ascertaining the truth with reference to the surrender of Arabi, and it appears to be possible either that he is himself implicated in the capture of Professor Palmer and party, or else that the Bedouins east of the Canal have agreed to ignore the authority of the Khedive; further news at Suez may explain this ... [f]rom the conduct of Moussa Nassier I am beginning to be doubtful whether they are still alive, although we have every reason to suppose they were alive a few days ago.[29]

Warren arranged with the monks at the depot at Tor for messengers to be sent overland to Suez with any news of Palmer. Two days after Warren left Tor, Moussa Nassier arrived at Warren's previous camp with camels for the journey to Nakhl but found that Warren's party had gone. At the time Warren and Haynes believed their expedition to Tor had been unsuccessful because they had not been able to open up a channel of communication with Moussa Nassier and the Bedouin. Haynes, echoing West, attributed this to an unnamed Bedouin intermediary who, acting secretly for Arabi, had successfully dissuaded Moussa Nassier from meeting with Warren. On reflection, however, they regarded the Tor episode as important and having 'so strong an effect on the Towara, that they became pacified and changed their views regarding the English', and establishing 'the basis of a firm friendship' with Moussa Nassier.[30] Perhaps its greatest value, as will be seen, was that it prevented Warren from entering the desert from Tor in a fruitless pursuit of Palmer's captors into Syria.

Sojourn in Egypt

Although the war in Egypt had ended and the Arabi revolt quelled, the Bedouin in the Sinai and between Suez and Cairo were still in a disturbed state, which made it unsafe for Warren to enter the desert in search of Palmer and his party. Warren's first thought was to suggest to the new governor of Suez, Raoulf Pasha, that he should send a new governor with thirty *zaptiehs* (soldiers) to replace the hostile, pro-Arabi governor of Nakhl and his garrison. Raoulf Pasha thought this a splendid idea except that he did not know of thirty Egyptian soldiers who could be trusted because force would have to be used. Warren then offered the services of his Sapper party with thirty Indian soldiers or the unit of one hundred troopers of the Aden Horse that was then based at Suez to accomplish the task. But Raoulf Pasha again demurred with the excuse that it would be unsafe on account of the Bedouin and that the governor of Nakhl only took his orders from the pro-Arabi governor of El Arish.[31] It was eventually worked out that since there was only one well between Suez and Nakhl–the one at Marbook–this meant that one hundred and fifty camels would be needed to carry the water for the horses, and the latter would be rendered ineffective by having to move at the same pace as the plodding camels. As Haynes later put it: 'The Egyptian authorities, who took no interest in the rescue of Palmer's party, gave us no assistance.'[32] However, they were prepared to turn a blind eye to Warren's organizing an intelligence service with agents who reported on the comings and goings of Bedouin between Ayun Musa and Suez (including the son of Meter Abu Sofieh) to spy on the English. Warren's arrest of certain Bedouin elicited some significant information, namely, that Meter Abu Sofieh had left his tribe, the Lewehat, and was 'a man of no great influence' and that the Hawetat were the most important tribe around Suez (contrary to Palmer's belief). Moreover, as Haynes elaborated:

> We found out that amongst the various Bedoui tribes each one in the desert was connected by marriage with one in Egypt; pressure might thus be brought to bear on the tribes in the Arabian desert through the tribes in Egypt. Indeed, we discovered that this was the secret of the power of the great Bedoui sheikh (the Shedid) at Cairo; and that he, in turn, was kept by force at Cairo, that thus the ruler in Egypt might have control over the Bedouin of the desert. This was an important discovery, and gave us the key which was to open the desert to us.[33]

Warren realized that the only way he could bring pressure to bear on Moussa Nassier and the Towarah (whom he still thought responsible for capturing Palmer) was to arrest members of a connected tribe, the Nofiat, who dwelt near Zagazig. Hewett had also asked Osman Bey Rafat to request from the Khedive 'the assistance of a very influential Bedouin there [Cairo], the eldest son of the late Sheikh Ibrahim Shedide, who is the most powerful Sheikh [of the Hawetat] in the country where the attack on the party was made, and who has it in his power to at any rate find out the truth.'[34]

While Hewett summoned Warren to Cairo to see Wolseley, Lt. Burton kept watch on Ayun Musa. As Warren and Haynes journeyed by freight train from Suez to Ismailia and Zagazig, they would have been aware that they were passing through the biblical Land of Goshen where the Israelites had spent their 'sojourn' or bondage in Egypt. As they approached Cairo on 29 September, they could see the main railway station burning and with the telegraph cut, they thought they might be looking at another Arab revolt. They had to walk into Cairo in the heat, dehydrated and famished, carrying their baggage. In a meeting with Wolseley, it was decided that Warren should continue his 'search mission' for Palmer's party. He was to report to the Admiralty (through the new senior naval officer at Suez, Captain Stephenson on HMS *Carysfort* since Hewett was returning with the East Indies Squadron to Bombay) and the Foreign Office. As far as possible, Warren was to work through the Egyptian government, and he could draw upon £5,000 of secret service money made available to him by Admiral Seymour.[35]

Accompanied by Sir Charles Wilson, the new intelligence chief in Egypt, Warren convinced the British consul-general, Sir Edward

Malet, that it was necessary to replace the pro-Arabi governors of Akabah, El Arish and Nakhl. The two men asked that Salami Shedide, the paramount sheikh of the Hawetat Bedouin, should cooperate with Warren. The latter then saw Riaz Pasha, the interior minister, who agreed to issue orders to the mudir of Zagazig 'to deliver up the bedouin we required' from the Nofiat tribe and to order Selami Shedide to put his brother 'at our disposal'.[36] The Shedide proved evasive at a subsequent meeting,

bringing with him an Arab who he introduced as his brother, and to whom he gave instructions to obey Colonel Warren's directions. The brother seemed to have a touch of the Fellah [peasant] about him, so Colonel Warren at once taxed Shedid with duplicity, stating his belief that the man was not his brother. After many lies Salami admitted that the man was not his brother, but merely a sheikh of cameleers who had just been released from prison [it was Selami, whom Palmer had sent off to buy camels]. He was not in the least abashed, but highly amused, at being found out in a lie; however, he promised faithfully to bring his real brother over in the afternoon, a promise he did not keep, for we saw nothing more of him, and Colonel Warren had to draw the attention of Sir C. Wilson to the fact that Shedid showed no inclination or desire to assist us.[37]

But Warren left word with Wilson that the Shedide's brother, Saad, should be sent to Suez.

Before leaving Cairo, Warren watched the British Army of Occupation march through the city, thereby witnessing the beginning of the seventy-four-year British 'bondage' in Egypt. At Zagazig, a town of some 'forty thousand inhabitants, mostly fanatical Moslems', Warren, who by then was suffering from the heat and a plague of sandflies, arranged on 1 October with the local mudir for the arrest of three sheikhs and four Bedouin of the Nofiat tribe, men he intended to use as messengers from Suez to Palmer's party.[38] Warren and Haynes also interviewed Pickard, the telegraph engineer, about his cutting of the telegraph wire across the Sinai. Haynes said they did not find Pickard much help because he was not familiar with Bedouin manners and customs and did not know what had happened to Palmer's party. Yet, Warren asked Pickard to go back to Gaza to arrest the Bedouin who had boasted that he had assisted in killing 'the accursed Feringhees [Franks or Christians] near Suez'.[39] Pritchard also stated that 'he had evidence that the Governor of El Arish had sent out a party of Souwaki Bedouin to get Palmer, dead or alive, when on his journey from Gaza to Suez'.[40] The Souwaki were a powerful tribe living in the vicinity of El Arish and were in a blood feud with the Terebin.

Warren left Zagazig on 2 October, filling an entire train truck with the Zagazig (Nofiat) Bedouin and their guards, and Selami, the cameleer, and his family. As the party was passing the battlefield at Tel el Kebir, Warren learned that the Bedouin were busy exhuming the Egyptian and British dead and stripping them of their uniforms. Haynes exclaimed that a 'Bedouin will strip his own dead father if he has a chance'.[41] Reaching Suez on 3 October, Warren learned that Lieutenant Burton, Colonel Griffiths (CO Troops Suez) and West had contemplated sending a small force to Ayun Musa to seize four Bedouin of the tribes who had captured Palmer's party and who were spying on the English. However, that plan seemed to have been thwarted by the Egyptian governor of Suez, Raoulf Pasha. Warren also learned that Moussa Nassier had submitted to the Khedive, and letters were sent to him requesting he bring twelve camels and come to Suez with all the Towarah who had accompanied Palmer's party or who were implicated in the attack.

Saad, the 'morose, incapable' brother of Salami Shedide, arrived at Suez from Cairo on 4 October accompanied by, and with precedence over, his more able and authoritative uncle, Hadji Muhammad. Warren demanded that the Hawetat and Nofiat sheikhs 'show their mettle at once' and sent them to Ayun Musa to seize the four Bedouin spies, including Ali Shwair, who had boasted of having 'killed an Englishman'.[42] The Shedide's kin allowed the latter and two Hawetat to escape, but they brought back Isma Selami of the Sabaha tribe, one of Palmer's camel men. Warren received from the latter the first informative account of what had happened to Palmer's party. The Englishmen had ridden off without their baggage on the second day out from Suez, leaving the cameleers to escort the baggage to the next camp. The following day a large Bedouin band had attacked the cameleers and looted the baggage. Isma Selami identified two of the looters as being Sheikh Salem and Salem ibn Subheh of the Hawetat. The other marauders were from the Dubur and Terebin tribes. This happened in the Wadi Sadr on the way to Nakhl, not in the Wadi Sidri, as Warren had been led to believe. But Isma Selami knew nothing of the fate of Palmer's party. This emphasized to Warren the importance of renewing his efforts to establish contact with the desert tribes.

Warren's plan of action was to visit Akabah first to secure the agreement of the Egyptian governor to block any attempt by Palmer's captors to spirit him and the others off into Arabia. On his return from

Akabah, Warren proposed to enter the desert from Suez to retrace the steps of Palmer's party and 'to thoroughly pacificate the desert'.[43] Since the desert was 'closed' and it was necessary to avoid another 'incident' there, Warren decided that a parallel, powerful Bedouin force should also go into the desert to find out what had happened to Palmer's party.[44] Warren was concerned that the Bedouin sheikhs might instruct their tribal cousins to destroy the evidence of Palmer's murder before Warren could arrive on the scene. At a meeting with the Cairo and Zagazig sheikhs or their representatives, Warren and West told them that they must help find the tribesmen who had retained Palmer's party and that they would be held responsible for anything that happened to their prisoners. The sheikhs remonstrated that they would need some of their own tribesmen if they were to go into the desert. Accordingly, the governor of Suez sent a telegram to Riaz Pasha, the interior minister, asking him to send 20 men from each of certain tribes in the Kalyub and Dukola districts, that is, a total of 160 men, to Suez within nine days.[45] In the meantime, Warren embarked on HMS *Eclipse* for Akabah.

Sailing to Midian

A motley crew sailed from Suez on 8 October bound for Akabah, saluting as they passed the white hulled ships of the East Indies Squadron on their way out of the harbour. On the deck of HMS *Eclipse*, underneath an awning 'tween the guns, camped various Bedouin, including five Cairo and Zagazig sheikhs and the newly appointed governor of Nakhl, Hassan Effendi, a captain in the Egyptian artillery. They catered for themselves, supping off 'quantities of vegetables and watermelons, Bedoui bread, pots of rancid butter, etc., with a variety of queer pots and pans for cooking'.[46]Together with Warren and Haynes, they were welcomed aboard by Captain Garforth and his sailors, who were amused by the antics of the more 'lively' Bedouin. Passing Tor, they navigated their way around the sunken reefs and rocks at the toe of the Sinai Peninsula and very cautiously made their way into the Gulf of Akabah, taking soundings as they went. No ship of the Royal Navy had ventured up the Gulf for forty years, and as we have seen, the Admiralty had lost the records of that survey. Anchoring at Dhahab, a small fishing village on the Sinai shore, the travellers sent one of the Zagazig Bedouin, Marbruk Abu Atwa, ashore to question the locals about the fate of Palmer's party. Marbruk returned to say that he had learnt that Moussa Nassier and the Towarah had fled with Palmer to Syria. Warren and Haynes were not fooled by this. 'In fact, it was a genuine case of thought-reading; Marbruk told us exactly what he thought we knew, or wanted to know, and no more.'[47]

Proceeding up to the head of the gulf, the palm groves of Akabah on the eastern shore were sighted around noon:

A happy relief to the eye after the continuous red mountains, and blue sky and sea. We could see the green flag of Arabi waving above the castle-walls; but as we approached nearer and passed the fort it was quietly hauled down, and no flag was to be seen. The officials were evidently not anxious to be too defiant, at the same time they did not hoist the Egyptian (Turkish) flag. We could see through our glasses that a general exodus of all the flocks was taking place, and many people were hurrying away up the mountain side, while armed men were coming in and assembling near the castle.[48]

The castle was a fortified caravanserai, built by Suleiman the Magnificent in the sixteenth century to provide safe accommodation for pilgrims at the third stop on the haj route from Egypt across the Sinai. The place was a journey of three days or a hundred miles from Nakhl, which was itself a hundred miles from Suez, this being the farthest a loaded camel can go without water. Akabah castle was commanded by an Egyptian or Turkish governor with a garrison of 'sturdy' North African irregular troops, who had no fear of the Bedouin. The latter were banned from entering the castle. As HMS *Eclipse* approached Akabah, which had been a bone of contention between warring tribes and empires since the Midianites, 'numerous parties of armed men were to be seen running along the shore and gardens following us, and stopping opposite to us when the *Eclipse* anchored, about three-quarters of a mile above the fort.'[49] The townsfolk of Akabah had not heard about Arabi's defeat, and being 'Arabists to a man', they were preparing to repulse an expected attack from the *Eclipse* and capture the crew. As Haynes later remarked: 'we were somewhat curiously situated; for *we* were at peace with them, and had a strong additional incentive to risk much rather than engage in an encounter, for Professor Palmer and his party might be in their hands—might even be prisoners in the castle.'[50]

Warren, Haynes, their Persian Armenian interpreter Ossad and the new governor of Nakhl, escorted by Lt. Henderson RN and twelve armed blue-jackets, tried to land from a cutter while another cutter containing twenty armed marines waited offshore. But they had to stand off after encountering 'hundreds of muskets levelled at us over the walls'. Waving a white flag, Warren's Bedouin and the new governor of Nakhl encouraged the governor of Akabah to come alongside.

At first there was a cry that we were taking the Governor prisoner, and more excitement; but this calmed down, as he was to be seen from the shore hugging and kissing the Moslems in our boat. He was meanwhile taking in the news, and when he realised the truth he expressed his great delight at Arabi's capture, suddenly become a staunch Khedivist, and shouted to the people that we must be allowed to land.[51]

Warren, Haynes and Henderson were then borne ashore on the shoulders of their 'swarthy antagonists' and found themselves among a throng of townsfolk on the beach:

The excitement of the people now reached its zenith; some wanted to shoot us on the spot, while others shouted to make prisoners of us and carry us off to the castle. The only man who seemed to have any authority or to possess any common-sense was a Bedoui sheikh who suddenly appeared on the scene. He stated that he was Mohamed Gad of the Alawin [a branch of the Hawetat], and at once took a prominent part in the proceedings, allaying the excitement by drawing his sword and belabouring all he met with the flat of it. We exerted ourselves to spread the news of the peace; but the majority of the people would not believe it, and kept behind the walls with their muskets levelled on us. The Governor and his officials exercised their ingenuity in devising reasons why we should go up to the fort; but we were quite as loth to be made prisoners as they, at this stage, were anxious to get us into their power, and Colonel Warren politely and flatly declined the invitation. Matters were at a deadlock, when Colonel Warren told the Governor to send for coffee at once, being anxious that the ceremony of drinking coffee and eating salt might be performed as soon as practicable, as that would tend to subdue the feeling against us.[52]

After coffee on the beach, when Warren tried to win over his interlocutors by buying some 'miserable' sheep and offering free passage to Suez to any who wanted to avail themselves of it, 'the women began to wail and lament, declaring that if we were allowed to remain on shore they would all be murdered, and they rushed about exciting their spouses to attack us.'[53] Sensing danger as dusk descended, Warren decided to re-embark with his party in the cutter and make for *Eclipse*, leaving behind some Bedouin to discover any information on the fate of Palmer.

Warren's Bedouin drew a blank on Palmer. But Hassan Effendi, who was to be the new governor of Nakhl, learnt that the governor of Akabah was in possession of a letter from the Arabist incumbent governor of Nakhl. This contained incriminating evidence about the governor with regard to Palmer. The governor of Nakhl also called on the governor of Akabah to arrest and imprison Warren and his party. Warren and seven Europeans landed again the next day on the beach at Akabah and were escorted to the fort by Muhammad Gad and the governor who did

their best to keep the crowd at a safe distance from us; but the people soon hemmed us in on all sides and tried to hustle us, until, when we got within the great archway of the fort, the massive iron-cased gates were closed and bolted, and the excited Arabs left outside to beat at the gates and shout themselves hoarse. It was not an agreeable position to be in, locked up in a fort among a hostile soldiery, with an excited swarm of barbarians without; but we made the best of things, and settled ourselves on the cushions which had been spread in the gateway, waiting until coffee should be served. But speech was impossible, for the disturbances outside increased, and the Governor, Mohamed Gad and the *zaptiehs* were continually running outside beating the people off with their sticks … at last Colonel Warren considered it time to do a little shouting himself. So he commenced to harangue the Governor in a loud voice, pointing out that if we met with any evil not one stone would be left upon another in the castle or houses; that though the people might not suffer, the Governor and his *zaptiehs* could not possibly ever be employed again; that they would be outcasts among the Bedouin, who hated them; that Mohamed Gad would cease to be sheikh over his tribe, and that his tribe would lose the care and lucrative custody of the Hadj pilgrims. These threats were direct home-thrusts to all those in the castle; and they made a final dash outside, beat the excited crowd indiscriminately all round, locked the gates of the fort, and begged us to come into an inner room in the court out of the noise, where we could talk.[54]

After a meal of *talaf* (rice boiled in *gieh*) and meat:

Colonel Warren turned on our host and demanded the reason why he had refused to give him any information about Professor Palmer's party; insisting that it was quite certain that they knew all about them, and telling him that he would suffer severely if he did not assist us. Colonel Warren had a theory that the best time for brow-beating an Arab host is just after he has fed you; when he thinks you ought to be satisfied with what you have eaten, and when he is himself a little gorged and unable to resist your importunities. On this occasion the onslaught was successful; our host was taken aback by the sudden attack upon him, and began to assert his readiness to assist in anything in accordance with the orders of the Governor of Suez. He was at last induced to admit that he had received a letter from Nackl, whereupon Colonel Warren insisted that this was only a further proof that he was an accessory to the imprisonment of Professor Palmer [Warren even wondered whether the latter was languishing in the castle dungeons]: eventually, to prove his innocence, he produced, with much mystery, the letter written to him by the Governor of Nackl—a letter which proved to be of the greatest importance, though, alas! it completely destroyed our hopes that we should ever see our missing countrymen alive.[55]

The letter revealed that the son of Abu Murshed, one of the sheikhs of the tribes living in the Wadi Sadr, had killed 'three Christians'. Moreover, the news of this crime had been sent to the Shedides in Cairo in early September. The latter had then sent instructions to the tribes not to kill Christians but to take them prisoner. This sobering news clearly shocked Warren and his party. At first they wondered whether the letter was a forgery, but the governor's seal and reference number on the letter seemed to discount this possibility. They were also aware that it contradicted the governor of Nakhl's previous claim to have killed the Christians himself. Then Warren hoped the governor might be mistaken and misinformed. He resolved that as long as one of Palmer's party might be alive, he would continue the search for possible survivors.

Muhammad Gad blamed Meter Abu Sofieh for the murders, for the Bedouin considered the man who betrayed the party more guilty than those who had actually carried out the slayings. Mohamed Gad pledged to find out more about the murders and send the information overland to Warren. He promised to seize the Arabist governor of Nakhl if he came near Akabah. 'It was now getting late in the evening, and the Akabese again began, under cover of the approaching darkness, to get disagreeable—wanting to know what we were waiting for, and crowding roughly round our party.'[56] Warren's party beat a retreat to the cutter, and the next morning the *Eclipse* weighed anchor without any extra Bedouin passengers; it arrived back in Suez on 16 October. Warren then had to report back to London, where the Admiralty and the Foreign Office were anxious for some news. Amid a flurry of brief telegrams that flew back and forth between Suez, Alexandria and London between Warren, West, Seymour, the Admiralty and the Foreign Office, it was the senior naval officer at Suez, Captain Stephenson, who best summed up the situation as of 17 October:

Information most conflicting on account of extreme reticence of Bedouins, who are in a very disturbed state and none come into Suez. By general concurrence of testimony two Englishmen were living some days after being taken prisoners, and general impression they were killed by order of Governor of Nakhl; important letter obtained by Warren at Akabah inculpates Governor of Nakhl. Sheikh Moussa Nassier promises to come here with some of the missing camel drivers and other witnesses demanded by Warren. On arrival valuable information may be expected, and course of action decided on. If party is alive great caution will be necessary, but if otherwise Warren proposes to start for Wady Sadur to procure evidence and particulars.[57]

6

Warren and the Bedouin

Warren was soon confronted with the difficult task of organizing the one hundred and fifty Nile Bedouin, under fifteen different sheikhs, who had arrived with their camels at Suez to help in the hunt for the suspected killers of Palmer and his party. They had to be fed and watered but also had to be prevented from clashing with one another. They looked to Saad Shedide for leadership, but the latter pleaded that he was too young to give orders to the grey-haired sheikhs. Warren decided to divide them into three groups, according to their district of origin, each under a responsible sheikh. The Hawetat, Ayeidi, Bili ibn Ali and the Maasi, from the Kalyub district around Cairo under Hadji Muhammad Shedide formed one group; the Tumeilat and Nofiat under the latter's Shaikh Muhammad Hassan from the Shurkia district about Zagary formed another group. The Terebin under Shaikh Abu Sarhan from Gizeh were kept apart from the others because they were engaged in a long-running blood feud with the Ayeidi, Bili ben Ali and Maasi, having driven the latter out of the desert east of the canal. The hostility of the sheikhs towards each other was palpable when they first met with Warren in council. It was clear that he was going to have to keep a tight rein on them if he was to succeed in his quest for Palmer's killers.

Warren's first test came with the 'lithe', 'active' but 'sullen' Sualem Abu Farag, the Shedide's 'right hand in the desert', with authority over the Hawetat both east and west of the canal.[1] With his Bedouin, Sualem had tried to block the advance of the Indian troops from Suez to Cairo, but had ended up being captured by them as he tried to cross the canal and escape into the desert. He had tried to stir up the Bedouin against the Christian invaders, thwarting Warren's attempts to contact the tribes. More than that, as Haynes later explained, 'he was a man of authority over, if not actual sheikh of, the very Haiwatat who had attacked Palmer's party; and here he was, sent to join our expedition for the solution of the mystery which enshrouded Palmer's disappearance, and to exact penalties of the guilty parties!'[2]

Warren suspected that either Sualem or the 'over-zealous' Arabist governors of Nakhl and El Arish had ordered the killing of Palmer and his party, but he believed the Shedides under Arabi had instigated the attack.[3] It became clear to Warren that the Shedides were 'playing a very double game' through Sualem. The latter had revealed that the Shedides were putting obstacles in Warren's way and were holding Sualem's son hostage in Cairo to guarantee that he would carry out their instructions to thwart Warren. Sualem suspected that they might use him as a scapegoat if and when it proved necessary to avoid any culpability themselves. For that reason he was prepared to cooperate with Warren to hunt down the guilty Bedouin. Certainly, the Shedides had provided no information to Warren on the whereabouts of the offenders, for which he reprimanded them and confronted them with the governor of Nakhl's letter implicating them in stirring up the Bedouin against Christians. He also threatened to report them to Cairo if they did not cooperate.

The Shedides had also tried to throw the blame for the attack on Palmer on the Towarah and especially on the subsidiary Aligat tribe. They were aided in this by the seeming reluctance of Moussa Nassier to meet Warren either at Tor or at Suez, which seemed to indicate his guilt. On Moussa Nassier's eventual arrival at Suez on 19 October, this tall, stately 'fine specimen of a Bedoui' who 'was not unworthy of the name of the great Law-giver [Moses], who led Israel through the desert', explained that his delay had been due to the need to prevent his tribesmen, stirred up by Hawetat emissaries, from sacking Tor and killing its Christian inhabitants.[4] Warren also suspected that he feared being thrown into prison by the Egyptian authorities as a result of 'the machinations of the Shedides', who exerted a powerful influence not only over the Bedouin tribes but over Egyptian officials.[5] Moussa Nassier moved quickly to dispel Warren's suspicions of him and the Towarah by persuading the sheikh of the Aligat, Ode Ismaili, and his camel drivers to tell what they knew of the fate of Palmer's party. It seems that the Englishmen were attacked by a mixed band of Hawetat and Terebin around midnight on 10 August (it was later revealed that the attackers numbered some two hundred and fifty men). The Bedouin surrounded the party and Captain Gill's dromedary camel was shot from under him. The party then dismounted, taking up firing positions across the humps of the kneeling camels. Meanwhile Meter Abu Sofieh fled on foot while his nephew rode off on Professor Palmer's camel, which carried the saddlebags filled with £3,000 in gold sovereigns. The Bedouin waited until first light before resuming their attack on the three Europeans and their two Arab attendants.

They overran the party with ease, seized their rifles, revolvers and clothing and then carried them to their camp at the top of Wadi Sadr. A highly strung Ode Ismaili then gave a dramatic account of the last moments of the party, later reported in the London newspapers as a result of an indiscreet remark by the Duke of Connaught:

> Palmer and his companions were taken to a very steep place in the mountains, hard-by to some water, and there their captors gave them the choice of being thrown over the precipice, or shot. Palmer [Sheikh Abdullah, as the Bedouin called him], seeing that they were surely to die, stretched his arms towards heaven, and, calling down the vengeance of the almighty on their cruel captors, jumped over the cliff.[6]

Gill followed suit, while Charrington, the dragoman and the cook were shot. Sheikh Hassan ibn Murshid of the Terebin, assisted by Abdel Rahman Guma Bissuni, a soldier from Nakhl, were supposed to have given the actual order to kill. Although based on hearsay since Ode had not accompanied Palmer's party, this accorded with the earlier account given by Salami, one of Palmer's camel drivers. Warren had to substantiate the story by venturing to Wadi Sadr where the bloody deed was said to have occurred and whose actual location was confirmed by Moussa Nassier. Sualem Abu Farag and the Shedides had feigned ignorance of the place in an attempt to keep Warren away from it.

Moussa Nassier drew up a contract with Warren, witnessed by the governor of Suez, to provide him with camels for his desert mission. This made Moussa Nassier responsible for protecting Warren and his party, a move Palmer had failed to make. Warren's plan was to go straight to Nakhl with his 150-strong Bedouin escort. There he would install the new governor, Hassan Effendi, and send the old Arabist one, Ali Effendi, back to Suez under guard. The Bedouin force would then be divided into two parts. Seventy men under Sualem Abu Farag would track down the Hawetat and Terebin suspects. Meanwhile, Moussa Nassier and eighty men would seek Meter Abu Sofieh and his nephew of the Lewehat tribe. Letters were also despatched to Sheikh Misleh (the amir of the Tiyahah) requesting his help in finding Meter Abu Sofieh. After the sheikhs had been summoned by the governor of Suez to hear Warren's plan, they voiced their objections to it on the grounds that it would lead to tribal feuds. Some sheikhs would only agree to provide an escort for the new governor of Nakhl. Others wanted to return home arguing that only the tribes with suspected offenders should provide men for the manhunt. Consul West had no time for such protests and called upon the sheikhs to do their duty. 'Justice had to be satisfied, and the stain on Bedoui hospitality wiped away by the delivering-up of the perpetrators of the crime to suffer the just penalties of the law.'[7] West's harangue seems to have had the intended effect because the sheikhs then departed with their men for Ayun Musa to await Warren's arrival. A few of the older sheikhs stayed at Suez to act as guarantors against the safe return of Warren and his party. Unlike Palmer, Warren had secured protection against attack by having an escort of Nile Bedouin, who had blood ties with the key tribes east of the canal. In addition, according to Haynes, Warren had achieved 'a personal ascendancy' over the Bedouin due to his 'rigid straightforwardness' as opposed to Palmer's 'happy way of treating them'. Warren was also in a position of strength, basking in the prestige of Britain's defeat of Arabi and having the support of the newly restored Khedival government.

While his Bedouin escort rode to Ayun Musa, 'marking with a black line the glaring desert in the distance', Warren and his Sapper officers, Haynes and Burton, went by sea in a *felucca* and then landed on the beach near the oasis. They speculated

> on the course of events before us. In our quest for information about the business we had in hand, we had heard much of the country we were now going to enter for the first time, but the testimony of our informants was obscured by contradiction. Was it an arid desert, which the fringe bordering on the Canal had often shown to us—a desert with waters small and far between, and therefore supporting a sparse population; or was it a fat land, with a company of fifty thousand fighting men? If the latter (and Palmer, than whom there was no better authority, had said so), where would we be with our party of one hundred and fifty Bedouin, impressed into our service by the orders of the newly-established Government, and possessing neither cohesion, discipline, nor love for their leaders?[8]

It was a sobering thought as Warren's party made its way across the sands towards Ayun Musa for their rendezvous with their Bedouin escort, now numbering some three hundred and seventy men and two hundred camels. The Bedouin had assumed that they would escort the Europeans to Nakhl by the *haj* route. But Warren was intent on making the journeying via the Wadi Sadr in order to find the remains of Palmer's party before the rains would wash away all the evidence. The Bedouin sheikhs immediately objected, exclaiming that: 'Wadi Sadr was a wild place, where they might all perish for want of water; the road was rough and little known, and it would be impossible to take the convoy of grain [for the Nakhl garrison] that way.'[9] Warren warned the sheikhs that if they did not follow his orders he would report them to Cairo. He had the camels loaded and then made a start with Moussa Nassier for Wadi Sadr. Sualem Abu Farag and the Bedouin then followed 'docilely' in Warren's footsteps.[10]

Warren in the wilderness

While Warren and his Bedouin made for the Wadi Sadr, the lack of news from Egypt was causing anxiety among the families of Gill, Palmer and Charrington. They attributed it to a lack of urgency and initiative on the part of the British authorities at Suez. They enlisted the help of prominent Eastern travellers, such as Colonel Henry Yule (also a Sapper officer) and Wilfrid Scawen Blunt, to make their case to the Gladstone government in letters to *The Times*. Yule's letter, of 16 October, elicited a short statement from the Admiralty to the effect that 'up to date nothing authentic had been ascertained respecting them [Palmer and his party]; but the reports obtained from the Arabs were very unsatisfactory'.[11] *The Times* took up the case of the families of the missing men, publishing a series of news reports, editorials and letters that assessed the available news and asked some searching questions of the government. It is clear from the very accurate editorial of 18 October that *The Times* had been briefed by the Admiralty regarding the latest information contained in the telegrams from Seymour at Alexandria and from the naval officers at Suez.

The same day Blunt offered his services to the families to search for Palmer's party. It was a good thing that the government refused to

sanction his plan given that Blunt mistakenly believed that neither the
Hawetat nor the Tiyahah were implicated in the murders. Charrington's
family wanted to accept Blunt's offer and saw the government's refusal
as solely due to Blunt's opposition to the Gladstone government's
Egyptian policy. After all, Spencer Charrington had been granted
permission to go to Suez to join the search for his brother and his
companions.

Gill's brother, Robert, suggested to Lord Northbrook that the
advice and assistance of the explorer Captain Sir Richard Burton
(then British consul at Trieste) be sought. Burton's fame and
familiarity with the Sinai, which he had crossed on his 'haj' to
Mecca, had led Besant of the PEF to recommend him to Robert
Gill because Burton 'knows every inch of the Desert', a pardonable
exaggeration in the highly charged circumstances.[12] Warren's fellow
Sapper, Captain Charles Watson (who later became the biographer
of Sir Charles Wilson) advised Robert Gill that a search should be
made for his brother from El Arish or Gaza because Captain Gill had
been instructed to destroy the telegraph wire between Kantara and
El Arish. Pickard had reported that Captain Gill had been seen in
Simkin's encampment near Gaza and had then left for Suez. Robert
Gill thought that his brother may have separated from Palmer and
Charrington, who were going east to Nakhl, and that Captain Gill
might have gone north towards Kantara and El Arish. Robert Gill
held out the hope that since there were reports of only two white men
being murdered, Captain Gill might still be held in captivity. Robert
wanted this drawn to Warren's attention although by this stage it was
clear to the latter that Captain Gill had perished with Palmer and the
others at Wadi Sadr.

Consul Moore at Gaza was equally in ignorance of the fate of Palmer's party. He believed that Captain Burton's services would be of great use in finding the missing men. Moore had requested that a local Muslim notable, Hussein Effendi, who possessed great influence with the Bedouin, go into the desert to search for the party, provided Constantinople agreed. He would be accompanied by a 'native agent' who would go anyway.[13] At the suggestion of Walter Besant of the PEF, this was to be Moses Shapira, the well-known antiquities dealer in Jerusalem 'who will do anything for money'. His name was kept out of the Parliamentary Blue Book because he had been used as an agent by the British. Shapira later disgraced himself by faking Moabite pottery and selling it to the gullible curators at the museum in Berlin. Moore was authorized to fund Shapira's search, but this was to cause difficulty later on.

While Consul Moore prepared to launch a small search party into the desert from Gaza, Warren, Haynes and Lt. Burton followed in Palmer's footsteps towards Wadi Sadr. By Haynes's own admission, they made

a rather incongruous appearance, made up of corduroy-trousers, gaiters, flannel shirts, any sort of coat, mushroom pith-hats, swords, revolvers, and very red faces. We had not yet learnt to discard our hats for the Bedoui head-dress, and cover ourselves during daytime with the goat-hair *abba*, which forms an excellent protection from the burning rays of the sun: these improvements came later with the teachings of experience.[14]

Warren and his men were accompanied by their Beiruti interpreters, Selim Mosalli and Josef Raad, a Persian merchant, Ossad, who knew the Bedouin well from trading in turquoise with them, and their culinarily challenged cook, Adam. After they entered Wadi Sadr, as it broke the outline of Jebel Rahah (the Bedouin name for the mountains east of Suez, on the edge of the Tih, or 'the Desert of the Wandering'), the Bedouin wanted to make their customary halt at the Ain Abu Jerad for water. But Warren pushed them on, in extended order:

> sweeping up the wadi in search of any traces of the baggage, which we knew had been plundered close to this spring. Our search was quickly rewarded. First a piece of tin was found, then some broken wood and pieces of paper; and a mile from the spring we reached the spot where the baggage had been looted, and found the remains of a portmanteau, a sponge, an iron camp-fireplace, and several smaller articles. Here we also found a quantity of note-paper with envelopes of the flag-ship Euryalus, letters to Lieutenant Charrington, and a mutilated copy of 'Don Juan' with following on the cover, 'John Charrington, 1823'. Following up the valley we found more paper, parts of maps, a Bradshaw's Guide, old news-papers, the peak of a forage cap, two cakes of moist water-colour, and a bottle of essence of camphor. There was nothing, however, among all these articles that could be surely identified as belonging to either Gill or Palmer.[15]

But the evidence of the looted baggage did confirm the Aligat cameleers' story. Warren despatched four Bedouin from different tribes so they would not be attacked to deliver a note on his finds to Captain Stephenson at Suez; the latter immediately telegraphed the news to the Admiralty in London.

After camping the night among rocks with their backs against a precipice in case their Bedouin turned against them, Warren and his men continued up the Wadi Sadr looking for 'any vestiges of Palmer's party'.[16] As they approached the water at Abu Rigem, they espied a number of men trying to escape towards the hills and gave chase. The Bedouin camel men, led by Sualem Abu Farag on his horse, soon outpaced Warren, Haynes and Burton, who were 'tryos at the art of galloping our camels'. The Britons dropped out at Abu Rigem and searched for any Bedouin who might be hiding in the scrub around the waterhole. They soon discovered the wife of Sheikh Hassan ibn Murshid. She was in possession of a silver pencil case, which she had used to ornament her hair. It must have come from Palmer's baggage train. Ibn Murshid had been surprised by Warren's party and had made good his escape. This was probably with the connivance of Sualem Abu Farag and his Bedouin, which was a cause for concern to Warren. They also captured an old man, one Salami, an Aligat tribesman, who had a tobacco pouch inscribed with the name 'H. Charrington'. He said it had been given to him by Ibn Murshid. At the urging of Moussa Nassier, Salami revealed that Palmer and his party had been murdered by Ibn Murshid and his Bedouin near Abu Rigem and that he knew where the bodies of the Britons lay. Four had been eaten by hyenas and vultures, but one was intact having 'fallen into water at the bottom of a gully'.[17] On 24 October Warren lost no time in setting off with about sixty men for the murder site before the Shedide's Bedouin could remove the bodies or the rain came and swept them away down the gully. In order to reduce the danger of being attacked, Warren sent Sualem Abu Farag and seventy camel men to attack a Bedouin camp half a day's ride to the east and to seize some prisoners while he kept Mohammed Shedide and four men as a scouting party. The latter soon disappeared. Since it was clear that none of the Bedouin could be trusted out of sight, Warren kept the remainder of the party close together as they marched up the right bank of the Wadi Sadr from Abu Rigem. They followed a tortuous path as

> the valley began to narrow, with ledges shelving in on either side. The sides got steeper and steeper, until there was merely a camel-track along the ledge, with precipices above and below us—on our right to the cliffs above, on our left to the gully below. The gully was about twenty feet broad and fifty deep, with pools of water in places at the bottom; and the edges at the top so rounded off that it was with difficulty we could see down to the bottom. On we went till we reached a post about six miles below Abu Rigem, where the ledge broadened out, making a cave in a re-entering angle; in the middle of which, in a cistern formed out of limestone rock by the dripping of the water from the roof above, was a pellucid pool of water. Salami tells us that the bodies were beneath us in the gully; but we could see nothing of them from above … …we retired to the cave to lunch before commencing what we inferred would be a lugubrious and sickening task.[18]

While they were lunching, Muhammad Shedide arrived with his scouts from the gully below, a suspicious occurrence given that they had no guide and had said that they knew nothing of the country or the murders. It was important to act quickly as there was a Hawetat camp in the vicinity. Haynes later described what happened next:

Leaving Burton ... with the Bedouin to look after the ropes at the
top, Colonel Warren and I were next lowered to the bottom of the
gully, which was here forty-seven feet deep, and from ten to twenty
feet wide, with precipitous sides. Below we found the remains of
our unfortunate countrymen—a skull, jaw-bone, numerous ribs
and broken bones, much knawed [sic] by wild beasts; a truss of
a very small man, supposed to be Professor Palmer; two socks
marked W.G. (W. Gill), with the feet still in them; and parts of
socks and drawers marked H.C. and H. Charrington: also a pair
of duck trousers, with buttons marked with the name of a Bombay
tailor; these latter were in such a condition that we burnt them. The
bones were much scattered over the bed of the gully, where were
pools of water and clumps of reeds; and on the ledge, and on the
side of the gully, there were traces of blood, showing that one or
more of the party must have been killed or wounded above. Never
could a better place have been chosen for the concealment of the
tragedy: after the first rain all trace of it would have been washed
away from the gully beneath, and even on the sides, and above on
the ledge, where the marks of blood were, the rocks would have
been washed clean, for there was here the flood of a little torrent
that, after rain, courses down the side of the ravine and traverses
the ledge from the above-mentioned cave to the gully.[19]

Warren and Haynes gathered up the human remains and placed
them in a case, which was to be conveyed back to England. After
sketching the wadi, they were hauled up the cliff and set off back
to camp, where they had left the new Egyptian governor of Nakhl,
Hassan Effendi, and a party of Bedouin. Warren scribbled a note on

his grisly discovery from this 'wild romantic spot' for Stephenson and Consul West at Suez. He asked for his Bedouin, who bore this message, to be sent to rendezvous with him in Nakhl and to bring with them some 'lunar caustic … as we have touched the stuff on the bodies and have cuts on our hands'. They were also to bring five rifles, either Remingtons or Martini-Henry carbines, with ammunition. 'We are at a disadvantage when attacked with only revolvers; five of us can keep off 30 or 40 Bedouins with rifles, but with revolvers we are only useful for a minute or so at close quarters.'[20] Warren thought that 'the guilty ones are going to fight if we do not succeed in capturing them by strategy, but I think I can manage it without very much bloodshed. There are likely to be a few killed, as they fire when pursued, and may attack us.'[21] Stephenson and West flashed this news to the Admiralty and the Foreign Office in London on 26 October, and the telegrams were duly printed in *The Times* the next day. The news was also read out to the House of Commons by Secretary to the Admiralty Sir Henry Campbell-Bannerman in answer to an enquiry about the fate of the Palmer party by Joseph Cowan, the Radical MP for Newcastle.

In answer to another enquiry by Cowan on 27 October as to the fate of Palmer's party, the purpose of his mission, and Blunt's offer to assist in the search, Campbell-Bannerman (or C-B, as he was known) stonewalled and said he had no further information to impart. This did not impress the *Saturday Review*, which the next day called the government and the naval authorities at Suez to account for being dilatory in their search for the missing party. The great Orientalist Arminius Vambery, a sceptic of Gladstone's Eastern policy, was critical of the very premise of the Palmer mission. As reported by *The Times*, Vambery thought it:

a most foolish and unhappy idea ... for Mr. Gladstone's Government to think of purchasing camels and sympathy with English gold among tribes which could not, in the circumstances, but be animated with the deepest fanatical hatred towards England.

Were, then, Mr. Gladstone and Sir Charles Dilke really so simple as to persuade themselves that the Bedouin Sheikh of Nakhl or Akaba would identify himself with English interests as to please the Liberal politicians on the Thames by siding with the Khedive and disavowing Arabi, who had emerged from among the people, and was surrounded with the prestige of Moslem zeal? That is truly ridiculous. And yet such hopes were cherished in London. Is it not irony to see English statesmen, knowing so little about Asia, seeking to exercise influence on the destinies of the Asiatic world?[22]

On 30 October the Irish nationalist MPs Ritchie and O'Donnell sought to discomfort the government further over the Palmer expedition. They asked about its covert purpose (spying and bribery) and whether it had received adequate protection, given that if caught its members faced the death penalty. Campbell-Bannerman answered by issuing a statement to the House of Commons giving the bald facts about the Palmer mission. He made a point of saying that Palmer and Hewett had not anticipated any threat to Palmer's party from the Bedouin. He said more detailed government documents would be laid before the House by way of information (i.e., the Blue Books, which were published in 1883). Lord Northbrook found the news of the murders 'most distressing' and vowed 'to consider how the guilty persons shall be punished'.[23] Seymour concurred but thought 'it will be difficult to get at the tribe[s] which committed these atrocities, and if it is to be done by England, as I presume it will, native cavalry from India must (in my opinion) be brought into the affair'.[24] Clearly, Seymour was unaware that light cavalry could not operate in the Sinai because it would be tied to the pace of its camel water-train, a fact that makes Warren's one-man effort all the more impressive.

Since Palmer's body had not been found and it was believed that he might be still alive, being held by the Bedouin, the Foreign Office instructed Sir Richard Burton in Trieste to proceed to Gaza to assist Moore in the search. Moore had not wanted to wait for Burton, preferring to proceed into the desert with Hussein Effendi, who had received permission from the Porte in Constantinople to accompany Moore. The latter had learnt from a Teyahah sheikh that Palmer might have survived. He came into possession of Palmer's rifle, given him by Admiral Seymour, which had been seized by the Turkish commander at Khan Younis from a passing Bedouin, and Moore wanted to follow up this clue.

However, the local Ottoman authorities thwarted Moore's quest by pressuring Hussein Effendi to withdraw at the last minute from the search party. The authorities denied Moore his own escort on the spurious grounds that his life would be in danger. Moore managed to persuade the *kaymakam* (governor) of Gaza, Youssef Effendi, to call a meeting of the sheikhs of the Terebin and Hawetat and some other tribes near Gaza. This was 'at the encampment of the great Chief Sheikh Hamoud El-Waheidi, when the most competent of them would be selected to be employed in the search'.[25] Just before the meeting, Moore learnt from Warren that it was unlikely that any of Palmer's party had survived. Still, Moore offered the sheikhs a reward of one hundred pounds sterling for information leading to the discovery of any survivors. He had originally wanted to take some of the Terebin sheikhs as hostages to effect this result, but the Porte had objected. With the arrival of Sheikh Abu Sirhan, of the Egyptian Terebin, Moore concerted with him, the other sheikhs and Youssef Effendi, measures to hunt for two of the murderers who had fled towards Syria.

With the receipt of Warren's despatch from Suez dated 20 October, it became clear to the Foreign Office by 31 October that it was very unlikely that Palmer had survived. The Foreign Office tried to stop Burton from taking ship to Egypt and then Gaza, but he had already booked his passage, and so the Foreign Office acceded to his request to dash to Alexandria, Cairo and Gaza to make sure of the fate of Palmer.

Warren and his fellow Sappers had not expected 'to arrive at so rapid a solution of the mystery of Palmer's disappearance'. However, bent on vengeance, they made their way, with their mutinous Bedouin escort, up and out of the Wadi Sadr onto the central plain of the desert of Tih; this was

> covered with sun-blackened stones, stretched before us as far as the eye could see, and rising therefrom into the dazzling sky were the dim outlines of the mountain-peaks of Jebels Yeleg, Ihkrim, and Bodia. North of us were the mountains of Rahah, through which the Hadj route from Suez to Nackl passes; and to meet this route, where it debouches onto the plain, we now bent our course to the northward.[26]

On the morning of 27 October they came, in sight of the square-built fort at Nakhl, 'lying in the centre of a wide depression, the Wadi el Arish, the Torrens Egyptii, and Biblical "brook of Egypt"';

there they were joined by Sualem Abu Farag and his Bedouin. Warren was sceptical about Sualem's alleged reasons for his delay, namely, that he had been ambushed by hostile Bedouin. But this had at least diverted attention from Warren's party and allowed them to proceed to Nakhl. Warren was unsure as to how much of a fight the Arabist governor of the fort, Ali Effendi, would put up. If the Effendi called for the support of the tribes who had murdered Palmer's party, Warren thought it likely that he and his fellow Sapper officers would be captured. Ali Effendi also controlled the only water source in the vicinity. But Warren's bargaining chip was the store of grain the garrison would need for the next year. Warren threatened to send this back to Suez or burn it if Ali Effendi did not send out an honour guard to greet the new governor, Hassan Effendi, and then receive the party in the fort. This seems to have done the trick because Warren was soon questioning Ali Effendi about his part in Palmer's demise. The old governor did not give much away and mostly repeated what he thought Warren already knew. But it was suspicious that he had visited Meter Abu Sofieh's camp at Tuset Sadr. Because Meter was absent with Palmer, Ali Effendi had moved on to Meter's brother's tents at Rahah on 10 August. It was from this place that the Bedouin had ridden down to ambush and capture Palmer's party in the Wadi Sudr, some five miles away. Ali Effendi denied any knowledge of this, saying that it was only when he reached Marbrook, a well on the way to Suez, that he learnt of Palmer's presence in the desert en route to Nakhl. He had then returned to Rahah 'in the hope of conducting the English gentlemen to their destination'.[27] It was there that he was told by Meter of Palmer's fate and was also told the names of the murderers, which he passed on to Warren. The governor returned to Nakhl with one of Meter's camels. Perhaps he was carrying his share of the £3,000 in gold sovereigns, which had last been seen on Palmer's dromedary as it was ridden away from Wadi Sadr by Meter's nephew, Salami ibn Aid. (Meter was to give up his £1,000 share, and it was suspected that Sheikh Misleh of the Teyahah and the Shedides also took their cut). Despite this, it was not possible to incriminate Ali Effendi 'directly in Palmer's capture and massacre. He must have bound the Bedouin over with the terrors of officialdom to absolute secrecy as to his part in the business.'[28] Warren sent Ali Effendi back to Suez, under escort, making sure that his baggage was searched en route in case he was carrying any of the Palmer party's property.

In order to avoid causing blood feuds, which the Shedides were trying to stir up to stymie the murder investigation, on 28 October Warren despatched Sualem Abu Farag and his Bedouin to visit their own tribe, the Hawetat, near Marbrook. There they were to arrest the headman Sheikh Salem who was implicated in Palmer's murder. They were to go via Jebel Maghara to see Palmer's 'friend' Sheikh Misleh and via Gatie, east of El Kantara, whence Meter Abu Sofieh had fled. Meanwhile Sheikh Sarhan would take his Bedouin to Gaza and ask the Turkish governor, whom Warren knew from his Jerusalem days, to help him seize Hassan ibn Murshid, the headman of the Terebin. This was always going to be difficult because this tribe dwelt partly in Syria. The next day Warren made for Gatie, some one hundred and fifty miles to the northwest of Nakhl, to ensure that Sualem Abu Farag carried out his instructions to arrest Meter Sofieh. Afterwards Warren intended to go to El Arish to secure the support of the new governor. Warren's party consisted of Moussa Nassier and about one hundred men from the Maasi, Ayeidi, Bili ibn Ali and Nofiat tribes with Muhammad Hassan, the sheikh of the latter tribe, leading them.

It was hard going, and the party suffered from excessive heat and shortage of water, which affected both men and camels. Both dropped out under the increasing strain at frequent intervals, with Haynes succumbing to heatstroke and congestion of the lungs near Mahada. Warren had to abandon his planned march and head to the canal and Ismailia, with the delirious Haynes being borne along on a stretcher by willing Bedouin. They showed more application to this task than to tracking Meter Abu Sofieh through the desert. They had baulked at the chance of seizing him when Warren espied four men on two camels (one of the men later proved to be Meter) among the dunes travelling south from Gatie to Suez. Accordingly, Warren sent the Nile Bedouin back to their homes and asked for new contingents of Hawetat and Terebin to be sent to Suez to continue the hunt for the murderers from their own tribes.

After nursing Haynes back to health in the Anglo-phobic environs of the Hotel des Bains in Ismailia, Warren and his men returned to Suez. There Meter Abu Sofieh had surrendered on 6 November, and the next day Sualem Abu Farag brought in Sheikh Salem. The latter proved resistant to Warren's questioning even when confronted with an animated Meter and Robert Gill. The latter had arrived at Suez and bore a remarkable likeness to his dead brother William. Warren's subsequent interrogation of the shifty Meter helped fill in the gaps in the account of the last days of Palmer, Gill and Charrington. Among other things, Warren found out that Ali Effendi had instructed the Bedouin at Rahah to capture the Christians and send them as prisoners to Arabi. There had been a spy watching the movements of Palmer's party. Warren forced Meter to take him to Wadi el Hadj, some forty miles from Suez, to recover his £1,000 share of Palmer's gold. This was buried in a crevice on a rock-strewn slope. Meter denied any knowledge of the whereabouts of the remaining £2,000, which had been in the charge of his nephew but was never found. As mentioned earlier, it is likely to have been shared out among Ali Effendi, the Shedides and perhaps even Arabi Pasha himself.

The inquisitor of Suez

The Shedide, the paramount sheikh of Hawetat, the most powerful of the desert tribes of Sinai, had proved obstructive to Warren's enquiry at every turn. The reasons for this lay in his resentment at British interference in his private desert domain and in his fear of being held responsible for the murder of Palmer and his companions. It was to take all of Warren's investigative skills and his steady cross-examination of suspects and witnesses at Suez to build up a comprehensive picture of what had happened to Palmer in the desert. Only then was Warren able to identify with some certainty the roles played by the Shedides and others in this tragedy. Gradually, the missing, and key, pieces of evidence began to fall into place. By about 24 July the Shedides had learnt from Sheikh Misleh's brother Suleiman of Palmer's presence in the desert. Fearing for their lives in Cairo if the desert tribes opposed Arabi, as Palmer wanted them to do, the Shedides sent instructions to Ali Effendi, the governor of Nakhl, that arrived about 2 August to apprehend Palmer when he re-entered the desert and imprison him, thus taking him out of harm's way. The Shedides may have calculated that by following these instructions, they would gain Arabi's approval and could also profit from this undertaking by capturing Palmer's gold.

Ali Effendi duly left for Wadi Sadr on 7 August, but the plan seems to have gone awry when the Bedouin possibly exceeded their instructions and murdered Palmer, Gill, Charrington and their cook. The Shedides reacted by sending explicit instructions to the Bedouin that Christians were not to be killed but sent as prisoners to Arabi (this was reflected in Ali Effendi's letter to the governor of Akabah, which the latter had shown to Warren). The Shedides tried to cover their tracks by falsely blaming the Aligat section of the Towarah for the murders. When that failed, they lined up their right-hand man, Sualem Abu Farag, as a possible fall guy. Warren had passed within 2 miles of the murder site in Wadr Sadr without the Shedides' representatives, Sualem and Hadji Muhammad, alerting him to it and taking him there. Those two men would have known of what had occurred there because their Bedouin were not in the habit of concealing their actions from their sheikhs. Nor did the two act in opposition to the instructions they had received from the Shedides, a failure that is an indictment in itself. Hadji Muhammad twice allowed key prisoners to escape so Warren could not question them. Moreover, he had coached one of the surrendered killers, Sheikh Salem, to stonewall Warren. The latter responded by having Saad Shedide thrown into prison by the governor at Suez and demanding that Salami, the paramount sheikh, be sent to Suez from Cairo. Hadji Muhammad allowed Sualem Abu Farag and his son to abscond and then threatened that the Hawetat would all leave Suez if Saad Shedide was not released from prison. Warren threatened to throw Hadji Muhammad into prison if Sualem did not return.

While Warren waited for Salami Shedide to arrive from Cairo, he interrogated all the witnesses available at Suez in order to piece together what happened in Palmer's last days. Haynes admired the tenacity with which Palmer pursued his mission in the face of the unwillingness of the Bedouin to accompany him because of the known dangers and the hostile attempts to delay him. As Warren established, from the moment Palmer left Ayun Musa, he was spied upon by Salem ibn Subheh of the Hawetat, who despatched messengers ahead to warn the Bedouin at Marbrook and Rahah of Palmer's approach. At some point, Salem tried to persuade Meter Abu Sofieh to betray Palmer and seize the gold. With Meter's connivance, Salem succeeded in stealing some of Palmer's camels, thus delaying the party and allowing the Bedouin time to arrange the attack. By separating Palmer from his baggage and servants and hustling the Europeans off on fast riding camels, Meter effectively divided the party and made the men easier targets for attack. When the attack occurred, Meter and his nephew rode off with the gold, abandoning Palmer and his companions to their fate. Meter deceived Palmer into believing he was a great sheikh of the Hawetat, when in fact Meter was a wealthy man living apart from his tribe. As Warren put it:

This party then were in charge of a Sheikh of no great local influence, who had no bedouins at his command, and no territory, and were about to pass through Wadi Sadr, occupied by Haiwatats and Debours [a section of the Haiwatat], who owe allegiance to Sheikh ibn Shedide of Cairo: the sheikh who Professor Palmer states in his report to have already furnished Arabi with 2,000 Nile Bedouins, and who he supposed was watching his movements.[29]

Haynes thought that Palmer had reposed too much faith in the Bedouin who ultimately outwitted him at every turn. Palmer seemed to have convinced himself that he was at one with them and able to think, speak and act like them. He believed that this gave him great influence over them, hence his overestimation of the number of Bedouin fighters that he could bring over to Britain's side. Possibly Palmer came to believe in his Bedouin guise as Sheikh Abdullah. He made a serious mistake in giving advance notice of his intention to meet the sheikhs at Nakhl under the beady eyes of its Arabist governor, Ali Effendi, and in proceeding there with no escort other than a few Towarah camel drivers. Far from being his friends, Sheikh Misleh and his brother Suleiman of the Tiyahah did nothing to avenge Palmer's death, let alone inform the authorities, perhaps because they feared arrest. Haynes surmised that Misleh may have been in league with Meter Abu Sofieh from the beginning to deceive Palmer and take his gold. Moreover, Suleiman later obstructed Warren's search for Salem Subheh, whom Salami Shedide had reported as being at a Tiyahah camp some 30 miles north of Nakhl.

When Salami Shedide finally arrived at Suez on 22 November, ten days after he had been summoned, he proved a most 'accomplished obstructionist'.[30] First he pretended that he knew nothing about the Palmer tragedy and even denied being the paramount sheikh of the Hawetat! Warren had to haul in his Hawetat prisoners to force Salami to acknowledge that he was, indeed, their sheikh. Warren refused to accede to Salami's request for details of the murders and the names of the prisoners because he wanted the sheikh to elicit the information from his own tribesmen. This was duly accomplished, and the uncommunicative Sheikh Salem was forced to tell what he knew and reveal the names of the five killers of Palmer, Gill, Charrington, Khalil Atik and Bakar the cook. These were respectively, Ali Schwair (a Terebin), Salem Abu Telhaideh (a Debour Hawetat), Abzar (a Terebin), Hamil Abu Telhaideh (a Debour) and Zeyed Ibn Hamid (an Ourdah Terebin). Ali Schwair had boasted throughout the desert of having killed Palmer. Informed of both the facts of the case and the names of sixty wanted men and witnesses, Salami proved reluctant to draw up and sign an agreement to bring in the culprits by a specified deadline. The following recorded conversation gives an idea of the often farcical lengths to which Salami was prepared to go to avoid cooperating:

Salami Shedide – Ah! Impossible. I shall be killed if I venture into the desert for such a purpose.

Colonel Warren – You must bring in all the persons I require in twenty-one days, or I shall report you as one of the persons implicated. There is plenty of proof against you.

Salami Shedide – I am undone. I am undone. It cannot be done in twenty-one days. Two months is the very least time.

Colonel Warren – You don't intend to do it. What have you done since you came here? Nothing!

Salami Shedide – I will die for the Government. But I must get some men from Cairo to take with me into the desert.

Colonel Warren – Do you mean deliberately to refuse to get these men?

Salami Shedide – By my father's beard, I am undone. I am undone.[31]

Eventually, after more hard bargaining, Salami Shedide agreed on 25 November to sign a contract committing him to bringing in all the offenders and witnesses within thirty-one days. He was to send them in by batches every ten days on condition that no other search parties operated in the desert. He was to be assisted by Abu Sarhan of the Terebin, who had failed in his previous mission to bring in the Terebin offenders. Moussa Nassier of the Towarah was persuaded to give up two cameleers who had initially been with Palmer's party. Sheikh Alayan of the Hawetat followed suit, giving up Meter's nephew, Salami ibn Aid, and several of his sons. Sheikh Misleh of the Teyahah sent two men. Muhammad Gad of the Alawin pledged to prevent any guilty parties from escaping into Arabia. By Christmas Day, nine offenders out of a total of twenty-one had been captured, and hostages had been obtained for five more. The remaining seven had either fled to Gaza or Akabah, and Warren was hopeful that they could be captured. All the principal men in the attack on Palmer's party had been captured except for Hassan ibn Murshid. As Warren pointed out:

> The recent unusually heavy rains have rendered the task of finding and securing these men more difficult and hazardous than it would otherwise have been, as the Bedouins are now able to live about all parts of the mountains without coming down to the waters which the Shedide has taken possession of, and in searching the mountains the culprits have resisted with their firearms and have wounded some of Shedide's men.[32]

Accompanied by Captain Stephenson and three naval officers from HMS *Carysfort*, Warren had arrived in Nakhl on 22 December to interrogate three of the men who had actually committed the murders. These were Salem and Salami Abu Telhaideh and Ali Schwair, as well as other Bedouin involved in the attack. The obstinacy of the accused is revealed in the following exchange:

Colonel Warren – Where do you live?

Telhaideh – Yonder on the Tih (with a wave of the hand all round the compass).

Colonel Warren – Whereabouts?

Telhaideh – Far away! Yonder!

Colonel Warren – What is your name?

Telhaideh – Don't know. The people call me Salem.

Colonel Warren – What was your father's name?

Telhaideh – Don't know.

Colonel Warren – Did you ever have a father?

Telhaideh – I once had three camels.

Colonel Warren – Where were your camels?

Telhaideh – Yonder in the hills, a long way off. I have tended them ever since I was born.

Colonel Warren – Do you meet any Bedouin in your country?

Telhaideh – No! I go wandering about and never see anything but camels.

Colonel Warren – When did you last see your brother Salami?

Telhaideh – What brother? I never had one.

Colonel Warren – Do you know this man (Pointing to his brother, who was here produced.)

Telhaideh – No! I never saw him before.

Confronted with evidence of their crimes by various witnesses, these men eventually broke down and admitted their guilt. More evidence was revealed which showed that it was Meter Abu Sofieh who had condemned Palmer and his party to death when he refused to give up their gold and that he had known of the Bedouin plot to seize them on orders from Cairo. Certainly, the Bedouin blamed him rather than the actual killers for the murders. He continued to thwart his pursuers when he died in hospital at Suez before Warren could return to interrogate him more.

Warren's hunt for the remaining killers at large was to be aided by Richard Burton from Gaza, who was supplied by Warren with the names of the culprits. Burton was also inclined to agree with the grieving relatives, Robert Gill and Charrington's brother and sister, who had travelled to Suez, that 'the five deaths of the Palmer party were "not proven"'.[33] There was a rumour that a European had been seen near Gaza. After conferring with Warren at Suez and with Moore in Cairo, Burton travelled by gunboat to Gaza to press the *kaimakam*, or governor, to discover and arrest the remaining fugitive Terebin murderers. He and the 'valuable and zealous' English consul at Jaffa, the missionary Rev. W. Schapira (not to be confused with Moses Shapira) came up with a plan for seizing the Terebin culprits through Gaza and for rescuing who they presumed to be Professor Palmer, who had been reported to be held at a Bedouin encampment near Petra.[34] At the same time, Moses Shapira tried with the help of his contacts at the British Museum in London to extract £200 or £300 from the British government to cover 'expenses' of his own search for Palmer. Robert Graves was covering in Jerusalem for Moore while the latter was on leave in Cairo and informed the British embassy in Constantinople that he had authorized payment to Shapira based on the latter's results. Sheikh Abdullah Reschid was to proceed to Petra with the objective of obtaining authentic information on the subject and, if possible, of obtaining Palmer's release. This proved to be a false lead, and it was later presumed by Warren that the story had originated from a report of a Syrian Christian 'wandering in a state of lunacy' near Petra; the man later turned up at Suez. Palmer was presumed to be a Syrian Christian by the Bedouin.[35] Warren had protested to Northbrook that he had found:

> Captain Richard Burton's presence in Egypt and Syria most embarrassing and likely to overthrow my arrangements … absolutely necessary for success of my operations that he should not enter desert from Gaza or take any actions for thirty days and Stephenson urges his withdrawal from the East for the present.[36]

Burton had sailed for Jaffa and proceeded to Gaza before the Admiralty could detain his gunboat, HMS *Condor*, at Alexandria. The Admiralty asked the Foreign Office to recall Burton to Trieste since Warren was taking care of matters. The Admiralty instructed the commander of the *Condor* to re-embark Burton at Gaza, convey him to Alexandria and put him on the first packet boat to Trieste, which he duly accomplished. Burton later wrote that he thought Palmer made a critical mistake in journeying across the Sinai when the tribes were in such a disturbed state. He regretted that he had not volunteered his services earlier since he knew tribes of Midian well and could have launched a rescue or reprisal mission from the East.

Warren on the Mount

While at Nakhl, Warren decided to postpone his journey to Wadi Sadr where he wanted to make a final re-examination of the tragic ground because Salami Shedide was in the area and wanted another ten days to pursue the remaining culprits. Instead, Warren made best use of the interval by journeying south to interview the monks at the Convent of St Katherine at Mount Sinai about the state of the desert during war. He also wanted to impress on the Towarah the need to cooperate with the government and to surrender any guilty persons for trial. Escorted by Moussa Nassier, Warren, Haynes and Burton encountered rain, mist and snow as they headed for Nutelghineh and the top of the Tih escarpment. Haynes provided a vivid description:

> The rugged masses of the Sinaitic mountains spreads out before our expectant gaze. The situation is of the grandest. The scarp, stretching out from our feet in a drop of some thirteen hundred feet, had at its base a broad valley of brilliant yellow sand, from which, as in an archipelago, rose abrupt masses of blue and dark maroon sandstone. Beyond was the rugged form of Serabit el Khadem; and, again, further in the distance, rose the peaks of the granite mountains of the peninsula, showing, by their elevated and jagged tops, the enduring character and tenacity of their component rocks, compared with blunt masses of the sandstone mountains at our feet.[37]

They were now in Towarah, or Tori, country and could afford to put away their arms in their saddlebags and contemplate the land of the Exodus and the sites discovered and surveyed by Wilson and Palmer. On arriving at the convent at Mount Sinai after their long manhunt in the desert, they could not help feeling that they were 'reaching the end of a pilgrimage and arriving at the long-looked-for shrine'.[38] They received a warm welcome from the monks, who remembered all Warren had done to sustain and help protect them from the

Bedouin during the recent war. However, the archbishop and the archimandrite were absent, having gone to Tor. The remaining monks could not provide Warren with any new information on the state of the desert during the war, the behaviour of Arabi's governors at Nakhl and El Arish, and the rumours stemming from Palmer's capture and murder.

After climbing Jebel Musa, Warren and his party left for Wadi Sadr via Moussa Nassier's encampment at Wadi Feiran. Warren and his companions learned from Moussa that when an Algerian had been murdered in the Wadi Sadr four years earlier, Salami Shedide's father, Ibrahim, had attempted to blame the Aligat section of the Towarah. Moussa and the sheikh of the Aligat, Ode Ismaili, had been thrown into prison and were only released after a suspect who was carrying the murdered man's purse was arrested in the Suez bazaar. This led to the seizing and execution of the culprit. Warren and Haynes could not but remark upon the similar behaviour of the Shedides in both cases. Having traversed the desert, Warren calculated that the Bedouin tribes could muster no more than 5,800 fighting men, not the 50,000 that Palmer estimated, and no more than half (or 2,800) could be engaged for war purposes. The Terebin were a very powerful tribe and were able to avoid Warren's manhunt. All but one of their men escaped justice.

Once Warren learnt from the Bedouin that Salami Shedide had left Wadi Sadr for Jebel Maghara in pursuit of the remaining culprits, Warren made for the killing ground in order to make a final re-examination. He and his companions commenced a compass survey of the wadi on 17 January and discovered many personal items belonging to the murdered men. They found Gill's journal (kept up to 8 August) and some of his official correspondence and a leaf and cover from one of Palmer's notebooks.[39] Haynes surmised that the Bedouin had 'taken umbrage at Palmer's Bedoui dress'. This would have wounded Palmer's pride because he had regarded himself as 'being a Bedoui amongst Bedouin'. The attackers stripped Palmer and his companions of their Bedouin clothes as being unseemly for infidels to wear.

When Spencer and Minnie Charrington, escorted by Lt. Burton from Suez, arrived, Warren read out the funeral service at the site of murder on 23 January. Haynes later described how:

> to the amazement of the Bedouin, we fired three volleys of ball-cartridge into the opposite cliff. Above the gully, on the north side, was a prominent flat-topped hill, and here Miss Charrington selected a site for a cairn of stones. The cairn was seventeen feet in diameter, with sides nearly perpendicular for four and a half feet, then sloping inwards to the apex, which was thirteen feet high. Into the centre was built an oaken cross, on which was cut the following inscription: – 'Prof. E. Palmer, Capt. Gill, R.E., Lieut. Harold Charrington, R.N., were killed by the Bedouin whilst on a special mission for the British Government.' On the back of the cross was carved the names of Harold Charrington, his brother Spencer, and his sister Minnie.[40]

A soda water bottle with the date was buried in the cairn and a consecration service held. In a nearby cave they found two naval swords that Palmer had carried into the desert, intended as gifts to the sheikhs at his planned meeting with them at Nakhl.

On Warren's return to Suez, he found that Salami Shedide had also returned, confident that he could capture the last fugitives, including Hassan ibn Murshid, when they returned to Wadi Sadr. But Salami Shedide had had no luck with the Terebin, who would not surrender any of their guilty men and had retired to Jebel Hillal. Warren also sent twenty witnesses out into the desert to search for and capture the remaining men. Warren had captured all the principal men involved in the attack on Palmer's party, with the exception of Hassan ibn Murshid (though his wife was still held hostage against his reappearance). Warren had been very effective in forcing the Hawetat sheikhs to cooperate. Seymour was pleased with the outcome and commended Warren to Northbrook for having 'acted with great judgement and *sang-froid* in his very difficult mission' and for having done 'his work exceedingly well'.[41] Arrangements now had to be made for the trial and punishment of the culprits. This entailed Warren's departure from Suez for the last time. He bid farewell to the estimable Moussa Nassier, before entraining for Cairo and Tanta where a native court was to try the prisoners.

7

The final judgement

Warren proceeded to Cairo to arrange for the trial of those Bedouin who had been arrested for the murder of Palmer and his party. The trial was to take place at Tanta, in the Delta between the Damietta and Rosetta branches of the Nile. A town of about 60,000 people, Tanta had been a storm-centre of the Arabi revolt, where some ninety-seven Christians had been chased through the streets and slaughtered by their Muslim neighbours. When General Sir Archibald Alison and three hundred Gordon Highlanders had arrived to take the surrender of the town on 17 September 1882, four days after the defeat of Arabi Pasha at Tel el-Kebir, he was confronted in the main square with a mixed Egyptian force of two thousand infantry, three squadrons of cavalry, four batteries of artillery, and an excitable mob in the side streets, who had not heard the latest news. Alison's coolheaded explanatory address to the assembled Egyptian soldiery and citizenry and the deployment of the Gordons around three sides of the square, succeeded in defusing the situation without bloodshed. Alison's departure and the renewal of khedival government left the townspeople in an ugly mood. When Warren arrived, he was greeted with the sight of five 'unfortunate wretches', victims of khedival justice for the massacre of the Christians, hanging from gibbets in the streets.[1] Since there were eighty prisoners awaiting trial for this atrocity, the president of the judicial commission informed Warren that he would have to wait until the backlog was cleared before the trial of the Bedouin could commence. 'This, however, would not do', as Haynes later put it.[2] Warren had no compunction in having the British consulate general pressure the Egyptian government into replacing the president and the two members of the commission. He then journeyed to Cairo to fetch the new president, Zekki Pasha, and returned with him to Tanta for the trial. Warren had not banked on the fact that he was ineligible to act as prosecutor because he had conducted the preliminary enquiry. Thus, Lt. Burton was appointed in his stead, and Warren acted as official observer for the British government. Moreover, he met Zekki Pasha's request that 'the whole history' of the Palmer expedition should be translated into Arabic for the commission's use.[3]

Under Egyptian law, which was based on the Napoleonic Code, the commission was responsible for taking evidence from the witnesses, but it fell to the mixed court-martial sitting at Alexandria to pronounce sentence. This division of responsibility was intended to safeguard 'the unfortunate Fellah from the too drastic methods of justice in vogue in the East'.[4] It was expected by all and sundry that the president of the commission would punctuate the proceedings with remarks about the prisoners, comments along the lines of 'vagrant, pig!' and 'biggest scoundrel'. In order to 'satisfy the more exacting ideas of law inherent in English minds', Warren suggested to the president that the prisoners' bare confessions be supplemented with the recording by the court of the evidence of the many witnesses whom Warren had brought to Tanta to testify. This was done in five days, with charges being brought against thirteen prisoners implicated in the murders of Palmer and his party as well as against twelve additional culprits who were still at large. The commission then retired to consider its report and make recommendations to the mixed court-martial at Alexandria. Warren, Haynes and Burton proceeded thence to hear the verdict on 18 February. General Harman, commanding the British troops in the city, and Captain Fitzroy, RN, the senior naval officer, were also present. One of the members of the commission, Chefik Bey, acted as prosecutor, outlining the case and the charges against each of the prisoners. The latter were arraigned, and after a short discussion, the court passed sentence. Five prisoners (Sheikh Salem, Salami Abu Telhaideh, Salem Abu Telhaideh, Ali Shwair and Merceh el Rashdeh) were condemned to death; seven (Salami ibn Aid, Muhammad Arthun, Murshed ibn Said, Aid ibn Salem M'Haisen, Salami Abu Owardeh, Aid Abu Rigal and Salim Sulman) were sentenced to various terms of imprisonment. Ali Effendi, the former governor of Nakhl, was discharged from service and sentenced to a year's imprisonment with hard labour. Meter Abu Sofieh's family property was confiscated by the Egyptian state as reparation for the £3,000 in gold sovereigns stolen from Palmer. However, Haynes did not know 'if any refund of money has been made to the national coffers thereby. If not, it is probable that the sentence of the Court has been utilized by the sheikhs to plunder Meter Sofia's family, and thus compensate themselves for their out-of-pocket expenses connected with the Inquiry'.[5]

Warren considered proposing that the murderers should be executed at Ayun Musa 'by their own countrymen living about Suez', but he was prepared to accept the court-martial's alternative recommendation.[6] This provided for the five condemned men to be taken to a place near Zagazig, among the Hawetats, and to be executed in front of a sheikh and two Bedouin from every tribe in Lower Egypt (thirty-three tribes in all). But Warren arranged with the Egyptian government that the sentence of execution should not be carried out until he had returned from El Arish. He intended to proceed to this town in northern Sinai in order to communicate with the Terebin sheikhs about the whereabouts of the wanted murderer, Hassan ibn Murshid. He would also enquire about the role of the Arabist ex-governor of El Arish, Said Effendi, who was imprisoned in Cairo, in the capture and deaths of Palmer and his party. Pickard, the engineer working for Egyptian Telegraphs, said he had conclusive proof of that person's involvement but was too ill to accompany Warren to El Arish. Intriguingly, Palmer's watch and chain, a pair of boots and a small bottle had been bought by an inhabitant of El Arish from a desert Bedouin (probably Salama Suleiman) and then sent on to Consul West at Suez. Warren thought it worthwhile to investigate this lead.

On the way to the land of the Philistines

Unlike Moses, Warren did venture to El Arish, the midway point along the Way of the Land of the Philistines between Egypt and biblical Canaan. Accompanied by Haynes and Burton, Warren had been conveyed by the gunboat HMS *Decoy* to El Arish. Landing in small boats through the surf, the men and their stores received a proper 'ducking'.[7] As they dried their clothes on the beach and emptied their weapons of shingle and seawater, they managed to overcome

the wariness of the local Arabs and negotiate their passage to El
Arish, several miles inland. The town, of some four thousand people
of Bosnian Muslim extraction brought there as frontier wards by
Muhammad Ali, was entirely dominated by a dilapidated fort, which
served as residence for the governor and a small garrison. The town
had lost its importance as a waystation and camel hub on the overland
route from Egypt to Palestine, and goods and passengers now went
by sea. The town's sole significance was its function as a transmitting
station on the telegraph line from Kantara to Gaza, hence Gill's failed
mission to cut the wire there. Its physical isolation had allowed the
new khedival governor, Mustapha Mamnoon, to behave as a petty
tyrant. He ruled with:

> The most barbarous severity, taking measures to make it almost
> impossible that his unlawful acts should become known to the
> administration. He administered the bastinado freely in the
> Queen's name, which so embittered and alarmed the people
> against the English, that on our arrival we were treated as enemies,
> and the women actually dug holes in their gardens and hid all their
> ornaments, so much alarmed were they at the arrival of the three
> British officers. It was impossible for us to avoid noticing that there
> was some peculiarity about the people of the place in their relation
> to us, but we could not tell what it signified; it only appeared as
> though there was a very intense feeling against us among all.[8]

The governor had gone to Cairo and had illegally appointed his son,
Hassan Effendi, to act in his place. The latter had invited Warren and
his fellow officers to reside in the fort, as de facto prisoners, pending

the return of his father. Warren baulked at this prospect, preferring to set up his tent in a howling gale, as the *khamsin* blew, outside the fort. While they were 'struggling with the tent-poles and guy-ropes', a young Syrian Christian telegraph clerk, Racheed Haddid, staggered into the tent with a story of having been badly beaten by Hassan Effendi's servant for not having informed the acting governor of the intended arrival of Warren's party even though Haddid had received no advance notice of this.[9] Warren reported the matter to the British consul-general, Sir Edward Malet, in Cairo, and as a result Hassan Effendi was forced to agree to investigate the matter. The investigation 'resulted in the culprit getting a severe flogging for the trouble he had occasioned his master'.[10] This incident encouraged the townsfolk to reveal to Warren that the new governor, Mustapha Mamnoon Bey, was far more brutal and oppressive than his predecessor, the fanatically pro-Arabist Said Effendi. Warren investigated a great number of allegations of bastinadoing and flogging despite the attempt of the new acting governor, Bekka Effendi (replacing Hassan), to thwart him. The imminent return to El Arish of Mustapha Mamnoon Bey and his telegraphic order to his son to detain Warren's party led to some quick-witted thinking by the Sapper officers. Calling a parade of the garrison in the fort at 10.00 am (two hours before the governor was expected), Warren demanded that Bekka Effendi assemble all the sheikhs and officials of the town. As Haynes later described it:

Taken somewhat by surprise, Bekka Effendi complied, although with some show of reluctance. But there was a further surprise in store. Colonel Warren, in a very loud voice, which could be heard in the village, addressing the officials and sheikhs with reference to the administration of the governor, assuring them that it was not in accordance with the wishes of the English Government. By this means he attracted the attention of the townspeople, of whose support he was pretty certain, and drew them near to the fort: the market square soon became crowded, the people thronging the gateway of the fort, and Colonel Warren ordered Bekka Effendi to admit all the principal men. Gradually they filtered in and came among the soldiers, crowding round them until there was not room for them to use their bayonets.

We did not understand what all this meant, but it appears that Colonel Warren intended, in case his proclamation did not take effect, to call upon the people to seize the soldiers, and at the same time we would seize upon Bekka Effendi and the chief officials, and he would take possession of the fort in his own name and in the name of the Khedive. But we were not driven to this. When all was considered ready, Colonel Warren produced a sheet of paper, from which he read:—That finding the governor, Mustapha Mamnoon, was endangering the peace of the country, and there could be no question but that his re-assumption of the government would lead to bloodshed, therefore, in the name of H.H. the Khedive, he (Colonel Warren) declared him temporarily suspended from his functions as governor, until the pleasure of His Highness might be made known; and at the same time he directed Bekka Effendi to continue to act as governor ... After speaking to the officials and sheikhs, Colonel Warren made a speech outside the fort to the townspeople of El Arish. He told them that all the restrictions that had been put upon them were removed; that they might visit each other in their houses, and speak to each other in the streets; and that when they were punished or imprisoned entries would be in the offence-book and sent to Dukolia [the central administration in Cairo], according to law. He also released the head-shaikh of the village, who, we now discovered, had been imprisoned in his own house for several months. Though somewhat doubtful at first, the people received all this with subdued joy, but as they still looked with terror upon the soldiers, Colonel Warren ordered these latter into the fort: then the general enthusiasm knew no bounds, and the air was filled with that peculiar, thrilling noise made by Arab women when they rejoice.[11]

Warren, Haynes and Burton then re-entered the fort and went through the official records to gather and certify evidence in support of the charges against the governor. One copy of the result was sent to the central administration in Cairo, one kept by Warren, and a consul-general *précis* was wired to the British consul general, Malet. The authorities in Cairo sent an order the next day that Bekka Effendi should continue to act as governor and that Mustapha Mamnoon should not be permitted to enter El Arish, but instead should be arrested and sent back to El Kantara under guard. Warren's *coup d'etat* had succeeded, and Mustapha Mamnoon was duly tried and found guilty on all charges at a court in Cairo and dismissed as governor of El Arish.

Mustapha Mamnoon had also prevented any combined action being taken with the Turkish governor of Gaza, Yusuf Effendi, against the Terebin at Jebel Hillal to compel this tribe to give up the convicted murderers of Palmer and his party. Moreover, it was unlikely that any expedition could be launched against the Terebin, given their blood feud with the Souwaki. Their 'sheikhs would shake their old heads and talk in a wild way, as only Bedouin can, of the steep mountains and rugged precipices in the Terebin country, of their enemies' enormous numbers, and how they gave the Souwaki such a thrashing a few years back, when five hundred of their young men were killed.'[12] Haynes noted that the Bedouin were prone to exaggeration when it came to numbers. In any case, the matter was resolved by the news from Cairo that the five men convicted by the Alexandria court-martial had been executed at Zagazig, despite Warren's plea for a delay while he conducted his enquiries at El Arish. As Haynes realized, this 'considerably militated against our chances of making any more captures in the desert'.[13] Warren's party had no choice but to return to Egypt. The manhunt was over.

The Promised Land?

As Warren, Burton and Haynes prepared to return to England, Parliament and the press gave consideration to the 'Professor Palmer expedition'. This was occasioned by the publication on 1 March 1883 of the official correspondence of the Admiralty and the Foreign Office pertaining to the murders.[14] *The Times* was quick to analyse these papers, probably with the assistance of Wilfrid Scawen Blunt, the great defender of Arabi Pasha. *The Times* was critical of Palmer for being misled by his 'sanguine temperament' into believing that 50,000 men could be raised as a fighting force from the Sinai tribes when 5,000 was a more accurate figure. 'The Thunderer' (as *The Times* was dubbed) also questioned Palmer's belief in the sincerity of those with whom he had been dealing. His intercourse with them was in reality slight, for, though admirably qualified for the work he had undertaken, he had neither sufficient time nor sufficient opportunity to test their character, his whole journey having occupied barely a fortnight, while the names of the chiefs mentioned do not appear to be those of the acknowledged sheikhs of the district.[15]

The fact that a similar remark had been made by Blunt (in a letter to *The Times* dated 18 October 1882) would seem to indicate that the editors were relying on his expertise, he having travelled in the Sinai in 1881 among the Terebin and the Teyahah. Blunt argued that neither 'Sheikh' Misleh nor 'Sheikh' Meter were the 'recognized' sheikhs of, respectively, the Teyahah or the Hawetat, as Palmer seemed to think. Blunt referred to twelve sheikhs of the Sinai Bedouin tribes who were imprisoned in Jerusalem by the Ottoman authorities. He later claimed that he had mentioned this at an unstated date (but probably before the British expedition to Egypt) to Lord Northbrook with the suggestion that the latter urge the Turks to release the sheikhs, 'since it might one day be found of importance to have these Bedouins friendly to England'.[16] Never one to underestimate his own importance, Blunt surmised that Northbrook had taken up this suggestion as a way, along with bribery by Palmer, of winning over the Sinai Bedouin. It would seem from the extant evidence that the Admiralty was aware of Blunt's suggestion, but the Foreign Office was not inclined to follow up on it. Thus, Blunt the Arabist may have been hoisted 'on his own petard', as he later put it, but not in the way he thought.[17] *The Times* also castigated the government for being as 'sanguine' as Palmer about the Bedouin and having apparently backed him with £20,000 to buy their allegiance.

While admitting 'the untiring zeal and ability' of Warren in discharging his duty of identifying and arresting the murderers of Palmer and his party, *The Times* felt the need to censor him for 'the stratagems and devices by which the "guilty ones", for so Colonel Warren throughout speaks of the accused persons, were entrapped and forced into giving evidence and confessions'.[18] As evidence of this, the editors cited the letter Warren had written to Moussa Nassier on 16 September 1882 in which he sought to entice Nassier away from Arabi Pasha on the grounds that the latter had allegedly already fallen from power, which was, however, not true, however. The editors were implying that Warren had played fast and loose with the truth. This criticism does not stand up to scrutiny given that Arabi's forces had been defeated at Tel el-Kebir on 13 September, which signalled the end for the pasha, and that Warren had been aware of this when he wrote to Moussa Nassier. Of greater interest was how the editors had managed to obtain a copy of this letter since it had not been included among the official correspondence. It was included in a draft of that correspondence and then excised before the printing of the final version. Someone in the Admiralty or at Eyre and Spottiswoode, who printed these Blue Books for Her Majesty's Stationery Office, must have leaked this letter or perhaps the entire draft to *The Times*.[19] The editors also criticized Warren for persuading 'a certain sheikh' (Salami ibn Shedide) to pressure Sheikh Salem, an eyewitness, to reveal the names of the murderers. The British consul at Suez, West, also came in for censure for his 'naïve' admission that the interpreters employed in the questioning of the Bedouin suspects did not always understand the import of the questions. For the editors, this cast doubt on the reliability of the evidence obtained.[20] In their view, this was exacerbated by a comparison of the various lists of 'guilty ones' obtained from the imprisoned witnesses, which varied considerably in the names they contained; this lessened the value of the confessions given by those who had been condemned to death. Lastly, *The Times* thundered that: 'though there can be no doubt that punishment has reached those who are immediately implicated in the murder of the three unfortunate Englishmen, yet in reading the papers on the subject, a painful impression remains that if the perpetrators of the crime have been brought to justice the instigators are still at large'. This was a reference to the ex-governor of Nakhl, Ali Effendi, the Shedides and their respective relationships with Arabi, regarding which there was not enough evidence for convictions.

When the official correspondence was laid before Parliament by the responsible minister, Secretary to the Admiralty Campbell-Bannerman, the opponents of the government's policy towards Egypt took up the criticisms levelled at Palmer, Warren and the Admiralty by *The Times*. Mr O'Donnell, the Irish nationalist MP for Dungarvan, cast doubt on 'the veracity' of the account of the Palmer expedition given by Warren and the government. O'Donnell accused them of 'concealing one of the most dubious and unpleasant transactions', namely, 'a mission of carefully-disguised spies for the purpose of cutting the telegraph wires communicating between Constantinople and Cairo, and seducing and bribing the Bedouin warriors who were prepared to assist us in the attempt upon Egypt ... this was not an expedition for the mere purpose of getting camels'. O'Donnell regarded such 'seducing' of the Bedouin from their allegiance to 'their liege Lord the Sultan' as 'double-dyed treason and trickery' by the British government. O'Donnell argued that 'the Mission was intercepted and found its death in consequence of that national resistance to invasion, and to spydom, bribery and treachery, and that the orders came from the Government in Cairo to intercept the English spies, just as the English government would give orders to intercept Arab spies'. As for Warren's conduct of the proceedings at Tanta, O'Donnell accused Warren and the government of conducting 'a bloody judicial trial' and characterized the Zagazig executions as 'a judicial murder of the most atrocious description'. Since Campbell-Bannerman had not been present in the House of Commons to hear O'Donnell's attack, another Irish nationalist MP, T. P. O'Connor, rose to demand answers of Campbell-Bannerman when he eventually arrived, to the three core questions:

> Was the Expedition one for the purpose of spying—he did not use the word in an offensive, but in a military sense? Were these men who were executed principals, or merely tools? Were they murderers acting for plunder, or soldiers acting under what they considered lawful authority? And, thirdly, was the evidence against the men obtained in accordance with the laws of justice and honour?[21]

In reply, Campbell-Bannerman (or C-B as he was called) stated 'very plainly and candidly' that the government had sought simply 'to utilize the Arabs for the protection of the Canal, and secure their goodwill'. In order to achieve this, Palmer had 'volunteered' to go into the desert 'to acquire certain knowledge as to the feelings of the Bedouins'. His journey had been made in disguise and from Gaza to

Suez, rather than in reverse, in order to facilitate his crossing of the desert and only in that sense was it 'secret'.

> He received no money on that journey to secure the allegiance of the Arabs. No sum whatever was given to him, and he was not encouraged to expect any money for that purpose. The object in view was to have him available at our disposal at Suez, if necessity should arise; and he had not authority to bribe the tribes.[22]

C-B truthfully denied that the Admiralty had seen Palmer's report of 1 August on his journey from Gaza (which Palmer had sent to Hewett and Seymour, and which had been printed in June 1883 in C.3761, pp.3–7), which had been mentioned in C.3494, page 2, and been picked up on by *The Times*. This referred to Palmer's belief that 'he could buy the allegiance of 50,000 [Bedouin] at a cost of from £20,000 to £30,000'.[23] It was this point that was contested by C-B and his opponents. C-B tried to shift the blame onto Palmer:

> He appeared to have taken a sanguine view of what he could do, and he described himself as able to secure the allegiance of 50,000 Bedouins for about £20,000 or £30,000. That proposal originated with himself alone. He had not been encouraged to conceive any such purpose at all, and he must say that the telegram which the Admiralty sent on receipt of that opinion was calculated to discourage him; and if it did not fully express that meaning ... it was intended to do so. It was not desirable, on the other hand, as it were, to snub him, or to imply any rebuke on account of over-zeal—nor did he now wish to attribute to him over-zeal—but he was instructed to keep the Bedouins available for control or

transport on the Canal, and for that purpose a reasonable amount might be spent ... He had no money given to him either at home or by the authorities on the Canal for any such purpose as the purchase of the allegiance of the Arabs.

The only money given him beyond his expenses was £3,000, which was handed to him at Suez by Sir William Hewitt [sic] to go into the Desert and secure camels for the use of the Indian Contingent. Sir William Hewitt [sic] said at first that the number of camels required was 1,500, but further information, after Professor Palmer had left, showed that 750 would be sufficient. That £3,000 represented only the cost of a fortnight's hire of 1,500 camels. Whether they would be ultimately required was doubtful; but they required to be collected near Suez, and the £3,000 was intended as a guarantee to their owners that, if the camels were not eventually needed, the loss of time would be paid for. That was the whole history of the transaction. There was no bribery, and no purchase of allegiance or goodwill. It was certainly part of [Palmer's] mission to conciliate the Bedouins, and to use his well-known influence to get them into a favourable state of mind towards us; but that was a very different thing from what was often suggested—that he was furnished with large sums of money for the purpose of bribing the Bedouins.[24]

As for the figure of £20,000, of which both *The Times* and the Irish nationalist MPs made so much:

That sum had nothing to do with the Palmer Expedition. It was an intimation that, under the authority given by the Admiralty,

Sir William Hewitt [sic], who was without money, had received £10,000 from Sir Beauchamp Seymour, and £10,000 from Admiral Hoskins, for the general purpose of the Indian Contingent. Professor Palmer had nothing whatever to do with that money. No part of it was given to him. It was required for the general purposes of the command at Suez, and therefore, all mention of it was omitted from these published Papers, which referred to the Palmer Expedition alone.[25]

If C-B is to be believed, there seems to have been a misunderstanding between the Admiralty, on the one hand, and Palmer and Gill, on the other, as to the intended use of the £20,000, which Gill believed he had conveyed from Admirals Seymour and Hoskins to Admiral Hewett at Suez. Palmer and Gill did think the money was intended to be used to buy the allegiance of the Bedouins or bribe them. As for the 'imaginative' allegations made by O'Donnell against Warren, C-B thought the published official correspondence 'showed with how much zeal, tact, courage and patience Colonel Warren had conducted the whole of the negotiations and search, first of all, for the unfortunate victims, and afterwards for those that committed the crime ... and [the latter] richly deserved the punishment they received ... [even if] those who incited them to crime could not be approached'.[26] This had been a bad-tempered exchange of views on the Palmer expedition in the House of Commons, with both C-B and O'Donnell walking out while the other was speaking (O'Donnell to have his dinner!). In his later account of the manhunt, Haynes expressed unease at C-B's failure to 'rebuff' with sufficient vigour the accusations of 'the irreconcilable party'.[27] If C-B had hoped to end the controversy about the expedition and its aftermath, he was to be soon disabused of that notion.

Blunt returned to the attack on 10 March 1883 in a letter to *The Times*. Mrs Palmer had shown him her husband's desert diary:

which records in detail his dealings with the Bedouins and not a little of his dealings with the Admiralty: and I affirm emphatically that the history disclosed stands, on every important point, in direct contradiction with the explanations officially made ... this diary proves conclusively:

1. That Mr. Palmer's mission, as intrusted to him by Lord Northbrook in June, was one of wide purport, wholly unconnected with the purchase of camels or the hiring of transport.

2. That it had for its ultimate, if not its immediate, object the bribing of certain Bedouin tribes.

3. That Mr. Palmer did in fact promise money with this object.

4. That he travelled, not as an Englishman, but disguised and under an assumed name.

5. That, on the 6th of August, he received from Captain Gill, at Suez, £20,000 in gold, distinctly for the Bedouins; and

6. That the purchase of camels was an afterthought, connected only with his last journey, and only accidentally with this mission.[28]

Blunt had also seen Gill's diary, which corroborated 'the true nature of Mr Palmer's mission just described' and mentioned 'the sum of £20,000 paid by him to Mr Palmer, and … it describes a report sent in by the Professor to Sir Beauchamp Seymour'. Blunt also believed that

> The vengeance taken upon the five Bedouins hanged last week at Tantah was the result rather of a supposed political necessity than of a true judgment of the facts. It is not necessary, in believing this, that we should regard the perpetrators of the deed as patriots, or even honest men; but murderers, in the common sense of the term, they hardly were.[29]

Blunt thought it suspicious that Palmer and his party were shot rather than despatched by 'sword or knife' as was the Bedouin custom of killing in the Sinai.

O'Donnell repeated Blunt's accusations in the House of Commons on 12 March, but C-B refuted them along the lines of his statement of 5 March. He admitted that

> Mr Palmer's mission certainly extended beyond the purchase of camels and hiring of transports, inasmuch as its object was that he should ascertain the disposition of the Bedouins, and use his well-known influence with them in order to conciliate them and obtain their support for the protection of the Canal should necessity arise. No money was given to him for the 'bribing of the tribes', nor was he authorised to promise it. I am not aware that anyone has ever asserted that Mr Palmer travelled as an Englishman; he wore the dress he had previously worn among the Bedouins, and went by

the name he was usually known by among them, so that there was no concealment in the matter.[30]

Although C-B denied that Palmer had received £20,000 in gold from Gill for the Bedouins, he provided more information on the means by which this sum was transported:

> The money was sent by the Canal in a picket boat under the charge of a Naval officer, who would deliver it to Sir William Hewett. It is possible that Captain Gill, on his journey from Ismailia to Suez, may have travelled as a passenger on this boat; but, if so—and this is pure conjecture—he had nothing whatever to do with the money or its destination. I cannot too strongly assert that the sending of the money in question had nothing whatever to do with Professor Palmer's mission, beyond the fact that £3,000 was subsequently given to him by Sir William Hewett for the hire of camels.[31]

Admiral Seymour (newly ennobled as Lord Alcester) and Sir Anthony Hoskins had confirmed this to C-B that very day. The latter had also spoken to Mrs Palmer, who had apparently not authorized Blunt to make public any part of the diary and had made this clear to him.

Undeterred, Blunt persuaded his brother-in-law, Lord Wentworth, to raise the matter of C-B's latest statement in the House of Lords on 16 March. Chairman of Committees Lord Redesdale had been reluctant to allow this 'since it was quite irregular to refer to the proceedings of the other House and comment upon them'.[32] But since C-B was a minister, Lord Salisbury thought this should be allowed. According to Blunt, he had sought Salisbury's help before the debate when the latter had admitted 'that in cases where secret service money was

concerned, it was conventionally permitted to Ministers to lie'.[33] As
a good opposition leader should, Lord Salisbury did not miss an
opportunity to hold the government to account. Accordingly, Lord
Wentworth asked Lord Northbrook, the First Lord of the Admiralty,
for 'some better and further explanation than Mr. Campbell-
Bannerman had been able to give'. In particular, Wentworth wanted
Northbrook to respond to the issues raised by the publication that
morning in *The Daily News* of further extracts from the desert diaries
of Palmer and Gill, which 'had appeared on the authority, apparently'
of their relatives.[34] Wentworth read out some of these extracts in the
House of Lords. First, quoting from Palmer:

> 'I have got £260 for paying all expenses for my journey; but £20,000
> in gold was brought by ship and paid to my account here.' The
> Daily News also quoted from Captain Gill's journal—'£20,000 will,
> according to Palmer, buy up 50,000 Arabs. I intend to urge that
> the money should be sent down to him at Suez.' In another extract
> from Captain Gill's journal, it was said that Professor Palmer had
> travelled much in the Sinai Peninsula, and knew all about the
> Arabs, and that he had just come from among them, and had said
> that 50,000 Arabs could be bought for £25,000. In another extract
> from Captain Gill's journal, it was stated that Professor Palmer
> had arranged for a great meeting of Sheikhs in a few days; and if
> he were to go North to cut the wire he would miss this meeting,
> which might do incalculable injury. He brought Palmer authority
> to spend £20,000 among the Bedouins. From this it was clear
> that Captain Gill and Professor Palmer considered they had the
> authority to spend £20,000.[35]

Wentworth asked the government to produce the journals of both Palmer and Gill for Parliament as well as Palmer's report to Hewett and Seymour of 1 August 1882.

Lord Northbrook was 'able most distinctly and categorically to affirm in every part and detail the accuracy of Mr. Campbell-Bannerman's statement'. Northbrook confirmed that he:

> gave [Palmer] no instructions whatever to bribe the Bedouins, or anyone else. My instructions to Professor Palmer were simply to obtain information as to the disposition of the Bedouins, and to hold himself in readiness at Suez to be deployed in case of necessity … On the arrival of Professor Palmer at Suez, he reported that he found the Bedouins loyal. I apprehend that he meant loyal to the Khedive, as we were informed from the first that the Bedouins of the Desert had a sincere attachment to the family of Mehemet Ali. That being so, we inferred that the Bedouins would be inclined to favour us rather than Arabi, who had rebelled against the Khedive. Professor Palmer also reported that we should have no difficulty about obtaining any number of camels, of which he was instructed to procure as many as possible for the use of the Indian troops who were shortly expected at Suez. In order that he might carry out his instructions to that effect, he was entrusted by Admiral Sir William Hewett with £3,000.[36]

Northbrook reiterated C-B's point that 'Professor Palmer and his party did not travel in disguise in the ordinary acceptation of the term', for despite the Arab costume, they were known to be Englishmen (actually the Bedouin thought Palmer to be a Syrian Christian). As for the question of the intended use of the £20,000:

It is settled beyond all possibility of dispute by the Naval accounts. It appears that £10,000 was drawn by the paymaster of the Penelope, the flagship of Admiral Hoskins, on the 26th of July, 1882, and another £10,000 on the 4th of August. This £20,000 was sent by Admiral Hoskins, from Port Said, to Sir William Hewett at Suez, in charge of Lieutenant Grove, R.N., and he went in the same picket boat which took Captain Gill from Ismailia to Suez. The money was not paid to Professor Palmer; it was taken on charge by the paymaster of the Euryalus, Sir William Hewett's flagship, and expended for the use of the East Indian Squadron in Egyptian waters, with the exception of £3,000 advanced to Professor Palmer. *It is clear that there must have been an impression upon Professor Palmer's mind that the £20,000 was intended for him.* The mistake must have arisen from the circumstance that the money came in the same boat with Captain Gill, and that Professor Palmer had shortly before reported to Sir Beauchamp Seymour that he could buy the allegiance of 50,000 Bedouins for from £20,000 to £30,000. This proposal was telegraphed by Sir Beauchamp Seymour to the Admiralty, on the 6th of August, *and as there did not seem any need at the time for such a proceeding,* we told Sir William Hewett, in reply, on the same day, to instruct Professor Palmer to keep the Bedouins available for patrol or transport on the Canal. We added—'*A reasonable amount may be spent; but larger arrangements are not to be entered into until the General [Wolseley] arrives, and has been consulted*'... Thus whatever may have been the impression on Professor Palmer's mind, it is clear that the sum in question was not paid to him. I should like to say that I attach very little importance to the controversy about this £20,000, whether Professor Palmer received it or not, excepting in so far as the accuracy of the statement of Mr. Campbell-Bannerman in 'another place' is concerned.[37]

It was clear that Northbrook intended to end the controversy over the intended use of the £20,000. But some of his remarks (in italics above) leave one with the distinct impression that if necessary, this sum would have been used to win over the tribes to the British, to patrol and provide camels for transport along the Canal, and that Palmer was prepared to undertake this task. In other words, the money was not just intended to cover the logistical expenses of the Indian contingent of troops. Northbrook confirmed this when he allowed himself a dig at Blunt,

> who was one of Arabi's allies during his rebellion … [who thought] it a most abominable thing for any money to have been paid to Bedouins by us for any services; but, as we desired to dispose of Arabi, I should not have hesitated for a moment to authorise expenditure for the purpose of doing anything I considered desirable to protect the Suez Canal, and dispose of Arabi and his rabble.[38]

Northbrook reiterated C-B's support for the way Warren had conducted the search for Palmer and his party 'with gallantry, determination, good judgement, and a perfectly judicial mind. He has taken the greatest care to ascertain who were the really guilty parties; and I must protest against the inference of the noble Lord that in prosecuting these murderers … there has been anything whatever done of which an Englishman can for a moment be ashamed.'[39]

Northbrook refused to produce the diaries of Palmer and Gill as they were private, and both Mrs Palmer and Robert Gill had protested against Blunt's use of the diaries by allowing extracts to be published in *The Times* and *The Daily News*. According to what Northbrook wrote in a private letter to Hewett, Blunt had also tried to convince Mrs Palmer to issue a public statement forgiving the murderers of her husband and his party, an attempt that failed. Although Wentworth continued to dispute Northbrook's account of the intended use of the £20,000 and of Mrs Palmer's behaviour, he was prevented from quoting further extracts from Palmer's journal by the Liberal peers, Earl Stanhope and Earl Granville, the foreign secretary, on the basis of a standing order that the document was not before the House of Lords. In fact, the desert journals of both Palmer and Gill have never been made available to the public. Their whereabouts are unknown. They may still be in the hands of the descendants of these men, or they may have been lost or destroyed. All we have are the extracts quoted by Sir Henry Yule in his obituary of William Gill and by Blunt in his *Secret History of the British Occupation of Egypt*.

The Daily News had mentioned on 16 March that Walter Besant's memoir of Professor Palmer was soon to be published and that it would contain extracts from the private letters and journals of Palmer and Gill by way of refutation of Blunt's version. *The Times* reviewed Besant's book on 29 May, claiming that it 'throws a flood of light on much that has been obscure in connexion with the objects and fate of the Palmer Expedition.' *The Times* picked up on a long passage in the book on the character of Palmer's mission. In that passage, in accordance with Northbrook's spoken instructions (related to Besant on the eve of Palmer's departure):

[Palmer] undertook to attempt the detachment of the whole of the tribes if he could from the Egyptian cause, and in order to effect this he was to make arrangements with the Sheikhs; he was to find out on what terms each would consent to make his people sit down in peace, or, if necessary, join and fight with the British forces, or act in any other way, for our interests which might seem best. He was, if possible, to agree to terms, and his promise would be regarded as binding ... As to the Canal ... he was to take whatever steps he thought best for an effective guard of the banks of the Canal, in case Arabi should attempt its destruction. Indeed, before he left England, he had submitted to the Government careful estimates in detail of the probable cost of preventing the destruction of the Canal, or repairing it if damaged in any place.[40]

The reviewer for *The Times* noted: 'This account of the matter, of course, differs from that hitherto given by the government.' Although *The Times* regretted that Besant had not quoted more passages from Palmer's official report (dated 1 August 1882) of his negotiations with the Bedouin, there was enough to indict the government. The reviewer noted that Palmer had informed Hewett at Suez that 'I have obtained from the most influential men in the country [the paramount sheikhs] promises of support for our cause ... [The] task was a delicate one, and I have had to give exorbitant sums in baksheesh payment for escorts, etc. I think from £20,000 to £30,000 would secure the whole of the tribes ... I can call a meeting of the Sheikhs within a fortnight and lay the case before them.' The reviewer thought that 'there is reason to believe that, though the scheme was at the last moment limited in its scope by Lord Northbrook, it was to attend this meeting that Palmer, with Captain Gill ... started on 9th August from the Wells of Moses on his last ill-starred journey'.[41] After the release in June of another Blue Book of Supplementary Correspondence (C.3761) that comprised Palmer's report of 1 August 1882 (delivered to the Admiralty by Seymour on his return to the UK in March) and Colonel Warren's last despatches, further attempts by the newspapers and MPs to investigate this matter came to nought. There was no public appetite for such an investigation, especially after the funeral of the murdered men and their consecration as national heroes. The publication of Warren's definitive report on the fate of the Palmer expedition put to rest any doubts about the circumstances of the party's murder:

> The chief men all through the affair were Salim es Sheikh, Salim ibn Subheh, Hassan ibn Murched, Salem abu Telhaideh, and Said el Ourdeh, and these agreed together that the five must be killed, and then put it to the vote of the Bedouin who also agreed ... The preliminary arrangements having been made the five prisoners were driven in front of the Bedouin over some rough ground for about a mile to the ravine of Wady Sadr. This appears to have occurred during the heat of an August day, and as none of the prisoners had on their hats, it seems likely that by the time they arrived at the place selected for the murder they were almost unconscious. The Bedouin have been unwilling to state whether they used violence in driving the prisoners down, but the probabilities are that they were subjected to very rough treatment.
>
> Professor Palmer is reported to have repeatedly said that he would give all the money if their lives were spared, and referred to

Meter, but as the latter had refused to give up anything the Bedouin would not listen.

On arrival at the Wady they were obliged to climb down some steep cliff in order to arrive at the plateau overlooking the gulley into which they were to be cast; this being accomplished they were placed in a row facing the gulley with five Bedouin, one behind each, told off to shoot them at a given signal. They were then driven towards the edge of the gulley, but before the signal was given Merche el Rashdeh fired at Professor Palmer and killed him. Salem abu Telhaideh, who was standing near, was also supposed to have fired at the same time. The fall of Professor Palmer appears to have caused the others to realise their danger, and they made a dash forward, some for the bottom of the Wady, down a cliff about sixty feet deep, and one (Khalil Atik) ran down along the edge of the gulley and was overtaken and slain by Salameh abu Telhaideh and Sheikh Salem. The others were shot in endeavouring to get down the cliff by Teyeid el Ourdeh, Harash and Ali Showeiyer. Several now descended to the bottom, and not only despatched those who still breathed, but appeared to have thrust their swords through each of the party. Captain Gill only is said to have been taken alive when they got down to the bottom of the Wady [he was then killed].[42]

The remains of Professor Palmer, Captain Gill and Lt. Charrington, and their servants, contained in a lead-lined box, were carried back to England in the P&O steamer *Nepaul*, which had been used as a transport during the Egyptian campaign. The panelled coffin of plain English oak made in Portsmouth dockyard bore a plate with the inscribed names of the three Britons and the fact that they had been 'killed August 11th 1882'. The coffin was conveyed from Waterloo Station to St Paul's Cathedral on 5 April 1883. Northbrook had arranged with the dean and chapter for the three men to be interred in the crypt, on the naval side, near Admiral Lord Nelson's sarcophagus. It was testimony to the strong feelings evoked in Britain by the story of the Palmer expedition that some five hundred people attended the funeral the next day. Many officers of the Royal Engineers and the Navy were present, including those who had been most involved: Lord Northbrook, Lord Alcester (Seymour), Colonel Warren and Admiral Hoskins. The pathos of the occasion was symbolized by the attendance of the actor-manager Henry Irving, who was a long-standing friend of Palmer. Palmer's widow was too ill to attend and was represented by her step-daughter, family friends and Walter Besant. The Gill and Charrington families were present in strength (though Mrs Charrington had died in February, possibly of grief at her son's death). At noon on 6 April the mourners assembled in the crypt and formed a procession, the latecomers lining the walls back to the chancel chapel. They followed the coffin, bedecked with a Union Jack; the procession was led by Dean Canon Liddon, the chapter and the boys' choir to a catafalque in front of the altar table. As the mourners moved to their seats, they placed wreaths on the coffin. Canon Liddon read the lesson, and then the procession reformed, and the coffin was borne to the grave. There was a great crush of mourners seeking to take part in the final ceremony. As Palmer's old paper, *The Standard*, described it:

> After the opening service at the grave side, the choir sang the hymn, 'Thy will be done,' the voices having a specially solemn effect in the semi-darkness and confined space in which the ceremony took

place ... At the conclusion of the service, Hymn No. 140 was sung – 'Jesus lives, no longer now.' When the mourners had taken their last look and departed, the visitors pressed forward, and it was some time before the crypt was restored to its ordinary solitude.[43]

A slab of Aberdeen granite with their initials carved into it was placed over the interred coffin containing the remains of Palmer, Gill and Charrington. A brass memorial plaque was installed on a nearby wall with a dedication to the men written by Gill's friend and fellow Sapper officer, Colonel Sir Henry Yule.[44] It reads:

In Memory of Three Brave Men. Professor Edward Henry Palmer, Fellow of St John's College Cambridge, Lord Almoner's Reader [sic] in Arabic and a Scholar and Linguist of Rare Genius. Captain William John Gill, R.E. An Ardent and Accomplished Soldier And A Distinguished Explorer. Lieutenant Harold Charrington, R.N. of H.M.S. *Euralyus*, A Young Officer of High Promise.

Who When Travelling on Public Duty in the Sinai Desert Were Treacherously and Cruelly Slain in the Wadi Sadr. August 11th MDCCCLXXXII.

Their Remains After the Lapse of Many Weeks, Having Been Partially Recovered And Brought To England, Were Deposited Here With Christian Rites, April 6th MDCCCLXXXIII.

This Tablet Has been Erected By The Country In Whose Service They Perished To Commemorate Their Names, Their Worth And Their Fate.

That Tragic Fate Was Shared By Two Faithful Attendants, The Syrian Khalil Atik And the Hebrew Bakhor Hassun, Whose Remains Lie With Theirs.

'Our Bones Lie Scattered before the Pit, as when one breatheth and cleaveth Wood upon the Earth, but our eyes look unto Thee O Lord God!'[45]

Yule was also instrumental in arranging for the establishment of a memorial medal in Gill's name; it was funded by the family and to be awarded by the Royal Geographical Society (of which Gill was a fellow) for recent services to exploration.

After the funeral there was some discussion in the Admiralty about despatching Lt. Burton, who had returned to Egypt, to cut an inscription on a rock overlooking the spot at which the three men and their Arab servants had been murdered in Wadi Sadr. However, the deteriorating security situation in Egypt and the Sinai as a result of the Mahdist revolt prevented this from happening. On the recommendation of Prime Minister William Ewart Gladstone, Queen Victoria granted Mrs Palmer an annual pension from the Civil List of £200, in recognition of the services her late husband had rendered to the country. Moreover, Parliament agreed to a credit on the Egypt vote to set up a £6,000 trust (with Besant as one of the trustees) to provide for the education of the Palmers' children. Warren urged the Foreign Office and the Admiralty to make claims against the Egyptian government for some £3,000 for the loss of equipment by Palmer's expedition, which would help in paying compensation to the impoverished mothers and widows of Palmer's Arab servants. But the bureaucrats dismissed this on the grounds that it was not comparable to the losses to persons and property which had occurred as a result of the riots in Alexandria, after Seymour's bombardment, the recompense for which they were pressing upon the Egyptian government. The personal effects of the Bedouin murderers of Palmer's party had been sold at Suez but had only fetched 10,000 piastres (or £100). This was a long way short of the £2,000 still owing to the British government for the lost gold. Warren believed that the Shedides had probably extorted most of the money from the sons of the murderers, who were well-off. Warren suggested that the Admiralty and the Foreign Office make a claim on the Egyptian government, which was bound to reclaim the funds from the Bedouin. Warren was tenacious in his quest for justice right to the end, even offering to return to Egypt to search for Palmer's body.[46]

8

A modern-day Moses

Warren's services in the Sinai were recognized by a grateful British government, which, on the recommendation of Foreign Secretary Lord Granville to Queen Victoria, awarded him a Knight Commandership of the Order of St. Michael and St. George (KCMG) in May 1883. The Khedive conferred Egyptian decorations on Warren, Lt. Haynes and Lt. Burton. Warren's achievements were considerable. He had taken a small party of Sapper officers along all the Exodus routes in search of Palmer's party. He had then extricated them safely and intact. He had discovered what had happened to Palmer and his companions. He had achieved all this through patient and effective cross-examination of witnesses and suspects, which enabled him to reconstruct with painstaking precision the sequence of events leading to the violent deaths of the Britons. With his politicking at Cairo, Suez and Zagazig as well as at Tor, Akabah, Nakhl and El Arish he had forced the Bedouin sheikhs not only to cooperate in the manhunt but also to participate actively in it. This was more difficult than it looked because the Shedides and others obstructed him at every turn. Warren managed to track down many but not all of the killers (the guilty Terebin eluded him). He supplied the commission at Zagazig with the key evidence, but he was disappointed by the early executions of the murderers since this effectively curtailed the manhunt. Lastly, Kitchener said that Warren's actions had created a deep impression in Sinai and made the region safer for foreign travellers. Presumably this was because the Bedouin would now think twice about killing Europeans. As Kitchener put it, Warren had single-handedly managed to 'pacificate' the desert.[1]

The one question, however, to which Warren's enquiry did not provide a conclusive answer is why Palmer, Gill, Charrington and their two servants were murdered. This is a matter Haynes in his later account of the manhunt came to consider. He cited a story his fellow Sapper officer Horatio Herbert Kitchener had been told by a Hawetat tribesman at Wadi Sadr in November 1883:

Arabi Pasha, directed by the Evil One—may he never rest in peace! —sent to his lordship the Governor of Nakhl to tell him that he had utterly destroyed all the Christian ships of war at Alexandria and Suez; also that he destroyed their houses in the same places, and that the Governor of Nakhl was to take care if he saw any Christians running about in his country, like rats with no holes, that the Arabs were to finish them at once. On hearing this news, a party of Arabs started to loot 'Ayun Musa and Suez. Coming down Wadi Sudur they met the great sheikh Abdullah [Palmer] and his party; they thought they were the Christians spoken of by Arabi Pasha, running away, so they surrounded them in the wady; all night they stopped around them, but did not dare to take them till just at dawn, when they made a rush on them from every side and seized them all.

The Arab Sheikh, who had come with the party, ran away with the money. The Arabs did not know Sheikh Abdullah, and did not believe his statement, and when he offered money, his own Sheikh would not give it, so they believed that the party was running away from Suez, and they finished them there. Afterwards the great colonel came and caught them, and they were finished at Zag ez Zig. May their graves be defiled![2]

Based on this evidence, Haynes deduced three possible reasons why Palmer and his companions were murdered. First, it is possible that the Bedouin did not believe what Palmer told them and thought he and his party were in flight from Suez. Second, perhaps Palmer had offered the Bedouin money, but Meter Abu Sofieh would not hand it over. Third, it is possible that the murder occurred as a result of Arabi's order to the governor of Nakhl. Haynes dismissed the first reason because the Bedouin had followed Palmer since the moment he left Suez and were aware of the situation there. The second reason had been substantiated by the findings of Warren in the desert. As to the third reason, Haynes admitted that this was hard to prove. By finding and punishing the individuals responsible for the murders, as was the British way of justice, Warren and his fellow Sappers had allowed the Bedouin, who were under the control of their sheikhs, to withhold

all information concerning the attitude of their leaders during the war, and [they] only told us those incidents that tended to their credit. Thus we were constantly informed that Shedid[e] had sent word to the desert that any Christians captured were to be sent to

Cairo unhurt. This feature of the evidence was perhaps consequent on our employment of the sheikhs in the search for, and arrest of, the guilty parties; but that it is probable that if we had succeeded further in our enquiry, and had succeeded in arresting the Terabin culprits, we should then have obtained the evidence of men removed from the Shedid[e]s, and doubtless mutual recriminations would have followed and have led to important results.[3]

Reflecting on the murders ten years later, Haynes concluded that the account offered by Warren's enquiry was incomplete. It did not give sufficient weight to three facts. First, it did not consider that the Towarah had opposed Palmer's return to the desert on the grounds that it was not safe to travel. Second, it did not take into account that the way that the Bedouin treated Palmer and his companions, stripping them of their clothes and manhandling them, indicated that they intended to kill them. Third, Warren's account failed to realize that the Bedouin did not seem to be inclined to ransom their captives. Given these facts, Haynes discounted Warren's conclusions that the circumstances surrounding the capture of Palmer's party and the escape of Meter Abu Sofieh with the gold were the real reasons for the murders. Haynes believed that there were 'weightier and more deep-seated reasons'.[4] He blamed Arabi Pasha and his immediate circle for declaring a jihad, which led to the murder of Christians in the Sinai by the Bedouin. It should be noted that the Bedouin had raided Ayun Musa and Tor intent on the murder of Christians and in search of loot. Palmer and his men were the next targets. It is likely that a combination of God and gold lay behind their murder.

As for Palmer's suitability for his dangerous mission among the Bedouin, Haynes, like Besant, had his doubts. He blamed Gill for an 'error of judgment' in choosing Palmer for a task that was a job for a soldier rather than for an academic. Richard Burton would have been the more appropriate choice. Palmer was too trusting of the Bedouin whom he had befriended, which led him to the erroneous conclusion that he had won them over to the British cause. Both Palmer and Gill seem to have read more into Lord Northbrook's instructions to 'obtain information' about the Bedouin in relation to possibly having to defend the Suez Canal. Palmer persuaded himself and then Gill that the wholesale disbursement of gold sovereigns (to the tune of £20,000) among the Bedouin would secure their allegiance to Britain and induce them to act against Arabi's rebels. The critics of the Gladstone government's intervention in Egypt were to make much of this discrepancy, revealed to Parliament in 1883 in the published Blue Book correspondence. Haynes believed that Palmer may have caught 'war-fever' in Egypt and wanted to 'do his bit' in the desert for his country. His major mistake was to ignore Moussa Nassier's warning not to enter the desert at such a dangerous time. Palmer compounded his mistake by not signing a contract with his escort to provide him with camels. This would have given him some sort of guarantee of their allegiance. Warren was not to make this mistake, which helps explain his success in travelling in the Sinai during his enquiry. But Warren had also co-opted the paramount sheikhs in Cairo to ensure some cooperation from the tribes not only in providing escorts but also in helping to track down the murderers. This highlighted that the mission to the Bedouin should have been entrusted to a practical soldier rather than to an idealistic professor. Warren's experience as a surveyor and archaeologist in Palestine stood him in good stead in pursuing his manhunt in the Sinai. He was to try to put these talents to later use as commissioner of the Metropolitan Police during the investigation of the Jack the Ripper murders. Unfortunately, he fell foul of a Conservative home secretary who hated Warren's liberal politics and a cabal of careerist senior police officers who resented having a soldier as commissioner. It was also ironic that these policemen should also be millennialists, something about which Warren was sceptical, given his Jerusalem background. Unable to do his job, Warren had no choice but to resign. We will never know whether, with his proven detective skills, Warren would have found Jack the Ripper as he did the perpetrators of the Palmer murders. The stews of Whitechapel were *terra incognita* for Warren, but he had shown in Jerusalem and the Sinai a doggedness in the pursuit of the truth against official obstruction and intractable locals which would have stood him in good stead in London. Alas, he was not to have the chance. He had shown that the Sappers knew how to perform their designated tasks in the desert and could survive to bring home key intelligence. This lay at the heart of their success in gathering intelligence for Britain in the Sinai and Palestine, usually working undercover as archaeologists, map surveyors and even detectives, as they sought to safeguard the routes to India against the machinations of rival European powers, especially France and Russia.

Palmer proved remarkably robust during his successive missions in Sinai and Palestine, but his overweening desire to empathize with his Bedouin interlocutors warped his judgement as to what was possible in the summer of 1882. It is interesting that another well-known Orientalist, Arminius Vambery, was scathing in his condemnation of the Gladstone government for believing there was any chance of winning over the Bedouin to the British cause. This criticism raises the question as to the extent to which Palmer romanticized the Bedouin, the 'sons of the desert', and whether this blinded him to their true motives for their actions and ultimately led him to overestimate his ability to influence them to his way of thinking. The evidence for this is contradictory. On the one hand, Palmer had in the past condemned the Bedouin for their nomadic habits, which he regarded as being destructive of the environment. On the other hand, he revelled in his encounters with the Bedouin, convincing himself that he was one of them, the great Sheikh Abdullah! Throughout his life, Palmer had a strong tendency to assume the colour of his surroundings and his companions; he relished role-playing, whether with gypsies, sailors, academics, journalists, soldiers or cameleers. His last role, on Her Majesty's Secret Service in the Sinai, proved to be beyond his talents. If Blunt is to be believed, Palmer was also driven by poverty as a jobbing academic and journalist to risk his life in the Sinai in order to support his new wife and children in London. The entries in his desert diary show that he was thrilled by the prospect of earning serious money from the British government for his mission to the Bedouin.

As for Captain Gill, his superior in the War Office Intelligence Department, Colonel East, had no doubt that it would be 'no easy matter to replace him'. Due to 'the confidential nature of the work on which he was employed, it is not possible, that the great value of the information he has at various times, and at great risks, collected, can ever be known to the public, but it has been fully appreciated by those for whom he worked so zealously.'[5] This was not true at the time and has not been so since. The Blue Books and Besant's biography of

Palmer contained much information for the public on Gill's mission to Egypt. Later generations have been able to access Gill's surviving diaries and the records of the Admiralty, War Office and Foreign Office for more detail on Gill's remarkable adventures. In the six years that Gill worked as an intelligence officer for the War Office, he undertook missions to northwest China, Burma, Persia, Afghanistan, Tripoli and Egypt. He was a restless individual who craved the excitement of adventure on the frontiers of the British Empire. He courted an early death as a hero rather than die an old man in his bed. His wish came true in Wadi Sadr. Was he beaten to death with his walking stick, as was reported by the BBC in 2010? Warren's final report on the Palmer mission gives a detailed account of the murders and the weapons used, namely, rifles and swords. There is no mention of a walking stick nor was one listed on the manifest of the personal effects of Palmer and his companions which were repatriated to England. The question arises as to whether Gill would need a walking stick in the desert, especially as the item in question seems to have been a Malacca cane. It is hardly an essential item of desert kit. It could be that the walking stick belonged to Gill and was found among his personal effects in England and handed down in the family together with the story that it had belonged to the man who had been murdered in the Sinai while 'spying' for England. Such are the tales that families tell themselves and anyone who will listen in order to try and make sense of their histories. Such stories are also good selling points when putting family heirlooms up for auction. The real question is, what happened to the final desert letters and diaries of Gill and Palmer? They were last used by Wilfrid Scawen Blunt for his newspaper campaign against the Gladstone government over the Egyptian campaign and by Colonel

Sir Henry Yule for his obituary of Gill. There seems to be no trace of them in either Blunt's or Yule's private papers. The diaries and letters should have been returned to the families of Gill and Palmer, but again they were not found among the papers these men left behind. Until these diaries and letters are discovered, perhaps among some unsorted family papers, we will not have the full, final, unadorned words of Gill and Palmer on the eve of their rendezvous with death in the desert.

APPENDIX: DRAMATIS PERSONAE

The murdered

Captain William Gill (RE): a skilled surveyor of the Corps of Royal Engineers, with a passion for exploration from China to North Africa. Killed while on Secret Service duty in the Sinai, August 1882.

Professor Edward Henry Palmer: Lord Almoner's Professor of Arabic at Cambridge University and an expert on the Bedouin of the Sinai, who knew him as Sheikh Abdullah. Killed while on Secret Service duty in the Sinai, August 1882.

Lieutenant Harold Charrington (RN): flag lieutenant to Admiral William Hewett, commander-in-chief, East Indies Station, HMS *Euralyus* at Suez in August 1882. Killed while on Secret Service duty in the Sinai, August 1882.

Khalil Atik: Syrian Christian dragoman for Gill. Killed at Wadi Sadr, August 1882.

Bakhor Hassun, Jewish servant of Palmer. Killed at Wadi Sadr, August 1882.

The killers

Sheikh Salem, Salami Abu Telhaideh, Salem Abu Telhaideh, Ali Shwair, Merceh el Rashdeh—all executed by hanging near Zagazig in 1883.

Salami ibn Aid, Muhammad Arthun, Murshed ibn Said, Aid ibn
Salem M'Haisen, Salami Abu Owardeh, Aid Abu Rigal, Salim Sulman
and Ali Effendi, ex-governor of Nakhl—all sentenced to various terms
of imprisonment in Alexandria in 1883.

For the sheikhs, see appendix 'Principal tribes of the Sinai'.

The manhunters

Lt.-Colonel Sir Charles Warren (RE): experienced surveyor of
Jerusalem and Palestine, led the hunt for the killers in the Sinai.
Knighted for his efforts. Later chief commissioner of the London
Metropolitan Police during the investigation of the Jack the Ripper
murders. He was assisted by Lt. Haynes (RE), Lt. Burton (RE), and
Quartermaster Sergeant Kennedy (RE).

Captain Sir Richard Burton: famous explorer of Africa and Asia.
British consul-general in Trieste who helped search for Palmer.

The intelligencers

Major General Sir Charles Wilson (RE): surveyor of Palestine and
the Sinai. Founder of the Intelligence Department of the War Office.
Served as intelligence chief in Turkey and Egypt. Blamed for failing
to save Major General Charles Gordon (RE) at Khartoum in 1885.

Captain Horatio Herbert Kitchener (RE): surveyor of Palestine and
Cyprus. Succeeded Wilson as intelligence officer in Egypt and Sudan
in 1885. Later avenged the death of Gordon by conquering Sudan in
1898. British warlord in the Boer War and First World War.

The Palestine Exploration Fund

The founders of the Palestine Exploration Fund (PEF): James Fergusson, indigo trader, architectural historian and archaeologist; George Grove, lighthouse engineer and musician. Both ran the Crystal Palace as an attraction.

Walter Besant: best-selling novelist, author of biography of Palmer and secretary of PEF in succession to Grove.

The consuls

Noel Temple Moore: British consul, Jerusalem.

Rev. William Schapira: British consul, Jaffa.

George West: British consul, Suez.

Edward Malet: British consul-general, Cairo.

Mitzakis: Greek consul, Suez.

The sailors

Admiral Sir William Hewett: commander-in-chief, East Indies Station.

Admiral Sir Frederick Beauchamp Paget Seymour (Lord Alcester): commander-in-chief, Mediterranean Fleet.

Admiral Anthony Hoskins: second in command, Mediterranean Fleet.

Captain Grenfell: HMS *Cockatrice*.

Captain Stephenson: HMS *Carysfort*, senior naval officer, Suez.

Egyptian officials

Raoulfs Pasha: governor of Suez.

Osman Bey Rafat: Aide-de-Camp (ADC) to the Khedive.

Riaz Pasha: Minister of the Interior.

Ali Effendi: Arabist governor of Nakhl.

Said Effendi: Arabist governor of El Arish.

Mustapha Mamnoon: tyrannical governor of El Arish.

Bekka Effendi: successor to Mustapha Mamnoon as governor of El Arish.

Hassan Effendi: newly appointed governor of Nakhl.

The politicians

Lord Northbrook: First Lord of the Admiralty.

Lord Granville: Secretary of State for Foreign Affairs.

Lord Hartington: Secretary of State for India.

Hugh Childers: Secretary of State for War.

William Ewart Gladstone: Prime Minister.

APPENDIX: PRINCIPAL TRIBES OF THE SINAI

The interlaced connections between the Bedouin tribes of the Sinai were hard one it was hard for Europeans to grasp as they seemed contrary to their view of traditional Bedouin life as one of 'sons of the desert' living separately from the *fellahin* (peasants) cultivators of 'the sown'. All the Sinai Bedouin had relatives and allies among the Bedouin and *fellahin* of Egypt and Palestine.

The Teyahah: a powerful and warlike tribe who roamed the central part of the desert of Tih and the 'south country', or Negeb, the semi-fertile areas at the southern end of Palestine. They were in some cases well-disposed to the Franks, or European Christians. They subsisted by providing camels for the *haj* caravans from Egypt to Akabah and thence to Mecca or for travellers taking the long desert route to Palestine from Nakhl to Gaza. Palmer dealt with Sheikh Misleh and his brother Sulaiman, of the Sagairat branch of the tribe.

The Lewehat, the Amarin, and the Azazimeh also inhabited the south country, in Turkish territory. The Lewehat were not a formidable tribe. Meter Abu Sofieh was of this tribe but had ceased to live among them, instead decamping to the Sofieh near Wadi Sadr. The Azazimeh were always at war with their neighbours.

The M'said were a branch of the Lewehat. They were a poor tribe straddling the banks of the Suez Canal near Kantara.

The Tumeilat, the Maasi, Bili Ben Ali and the Ayeidi lived west of the Suez Canal. The latter three tribes had been pushed out of the land between Jabal Maghara and Ismailia by the Terebin, with whom they had a blood feud.

The Souwaki: a powerful but poor tribe around El Arish. At war with the Terebin, with whom they had a blood feud.

The Terebin: a number of large and powerful tribes, who could put some 2,000 fighting men into the field. They lived mainly around Gaza, but there were also detached minor tribes near the Suez Canal and an important one at Gizeh, near Cairo. Although the Egyptian Terebin had become mainly sedentary *fellahin*, they retained close connections with the Sinai or Syrian Terebin around Gaza. The latter had an unenviable reputation for being fanatically anti-Christian, untrustworthy and deceitful. Some of their sheikhs were kept as hostages in prison by the Ottoman Turks to compel the tribes to good behaviour. It did not seem to alter their behaviour, however, as Turkish tax-collecting expeditions beyond Gaza were often driven out. Three of the killers of Palmer and his party were Terebin.

The Hawetat (or Haiwatat): a number of tribes to the east of the Gulf of Akabah and in the Wadi Arabah (where they went under the name of Alawin). They had detachments between Akabah and Suez. They were to be found in strength between Suez and Cairo and at Zagazig. They took their lead from the wealthy family of Sheikh ibn Shedide, who lived near Cairo and had influence with the Egyptian government as well as over the Sinai Bedouin. Two of the killers of Palmer and his party were from the Debour branch of the Hawetat.

The Towarah, divided into a number of minor tribes, inhabited the desert of the Sinai Peninsula. They kept themselves apart from the other Bedouin tribes. Moussa Nassier was the hereditary chief of the Sowahili branch but not sheikh of all the Towarah since there was none. According to Palmer, the Towarah had some 4,000 fighting men and 8,000 camels under Hasan ibn Ahmar, sheikh of the Walad Said branch, and Eid, sheikh of the Jabaliya branch. These figures seem rather high. Palmer and Gill over-estimated the number of fighting men the Sinai Bedouin could deploy (50,000), whereas the actual number was more like 10,000. The Nofiat, near Zagazig, were connected to the Towarah. Anxious to deflect attention from the Hawetat, the Shedides falsely accused the Aligat section of the Towarah, led by Sheikh Ode Ismaili, of the murders of Palmer and his party.

NOTES

1 Captain Gill's walking stick

1 www.bbc.co.uk/news/uk-scotland-edinburgh-east-fife-11418672. Accessed 26 January 2018, 2019.

2 Recovering Jerusalem

1 Charles Warren, *Underground Jerusalem* (London, 1876), pp. 40–1.

2 Britons in the nineteenth century usually referred to this region as 'the Near East' but the current term 'Middle East', with which readers will be more familiar, will be used in this book.

3 Robinson and his fellow missionary, Eli Smith, published their findings in the three-volume *Biblical Researches on Palestine, Sinai, Arabia Petraea and Adjacent Regions* in 1841. This earned Robinson the gold medal of the Royal Geographical Society and the opprobrium of the Rev. George Williams (former chaplain to the protestant bishop of Jerusalem) in his *The Holy City* (1849). The latter volume included as an appendix the British military map of Jerusalem.

4 Naomi Shepherd, *The Zealous Intruders. The Western Rediscovery of Palestine* (London: Harpercollins, 1987), p. 76.

5 The French archaeologist Marquis Melchior de Vogues used Pierotti's data as the basis of his own map, with modifications, published in 1864 in *Le Temple de Jerusalem*.

6 Whereas Grove had travelled to the Levant and seen Jerusalem in 1858–9, Fergusson had not.

7 In a letter to *The Times* dated 17 March 1864 Grove, supported by Fergusson, accused Pierotti of 'inaccuracies, discrepancies and plagiarisms, as must go far to destroy all confidence in the book and its author unless they can

be satisfactorily explained'. Pierotti, supported by George Williams, denied the charges. But the British Architects' council, upon consideration of the evidence, found in favour of Grove. Pierotti had been cashiered from the Royal Corps of Military Engineers in Piedmont in 1849 for deserting with his unit's funds (Grove obtained a copy of the judgment of the military court). Pierotti's later career involved organizing package tours to Palestine from Paris.

8 C. W. Wilson, *Ordnance Survey of Jerusalem Made in the Years 1864 to 1865* (Southampton, 1866), p. 86.

9 Whitworth Porter, *History of the Corps of Royal Engineers*, Vol. II (London, 1889), p. 269.

10 Mark Twain had a similar first reaction to Palestine, which he regarded as arid, squalid, boring and depressing (see his *Innocents Abroad*, 1867).

11 The British ambassador in St Petersburg, Lord Wodehouse, secured 'from a very secret source', namely, an agent in the Russian government, a copy of Masurov's report and forwarded it to London. See TNA, FO 65/517, Wodehouse to Malmesbury, No. 29, 27 March 1858. The British consul in Jerusalem, James Finn, also reported on Grand Duke Konstantin's visit to the Holy City, which for the duration became 'a Russian city', complete with Russian sailors uniformed in white. See FO 181/361, Malmesbury to Crampton, No. 229, with three encls., 16 June 1859.

12 See Rachel Hewitt, *Map of a Nation. The Biography of the Ordnance Survey* (Cambridge, 2010), p. 303; Wilson, *Ordnance Survey of Jerusalem*, Fardreezhi's notes of 6 and 15 May 1865.

13 Porter, *History of the Corps*, p. 269.

14 Wilson, *Ordnance Survey of Jerusalem*, p. 45. Wilson discovered that some of Pierotti's plans bore little relation to reality and raised the question as to whether he had, indeed, visited some of the cisterns.

15 Ibid.

16 Wilson, *Ordnance Survey of Jerusalem*, p. 84.

17 See PEF/JER/33/1-3, Notes on Jerusalem Water Supply, by Major F. W. Stephen, 20 July 1918, and JER/35, C.W. Wilson, 'The Water Supply of Jerusalem', Address at AGM of the Victoria Institute, 26 May 1902.

18 According to Sir Henry James, Wilson learnt from the Bedouin and some European residents of Palestine that in the early summer the level of the Dead Sea fell 'at least 6 ft. below the level at which it stood on the day that

the levelling was taken, which would make the depression 1298 feet, and we may conclude that the maximum depression at no time exceeds 1300 feet'. James was 'certain that the levels have been obtained with absolute accuracy to within 3 or 4 inches'. PEF/JER/WIL/20, Colonel Sir Henry James, 'Report on the Levelling from the Mediterranean to the Dead Sea'. Paper read to the Royal Society, 3 May 1866, published in the *Proceedings of the Royal Society*, Vol. 15, No. 84 (1866-7).

19 *PEF, Proceedings and Notes, 1865–1869*, Report of the Proceedings at a Public Meeting, 22 June 1865, p. 4.

20 See *Palestine Exploration Quarterly*, Vol. 19, No. 1 (January 1887), p. 12; Haim Goren, 'Scientific Organisations as Agents of Change: The Palestine Exploration Fund, the *Deutsche Vereinzur Erforschung Palästinas* and Nineteenth Century Palestine', *Journal of Historical Geography*, Vol. 27, No. 2 (2001), pp. 153–65 and 'Sacred but Not Surveyed: Nineteenth-Century Surveys of Palestine', *Imago Mundi*, Vol. 54 (2002), pp. 87–100.

21 Grove letter to *The Times*, 17 January 1866.

22 British Library, Add. Ms. 38991, Layard Papers, Vol. LXI, f.352, Grove to Layard, 11 August 1865.

23 In a series of letters to *The Times* (for 12 and 21 February, 3, 9 and 23 April and 21 May 1866), Grove relayed the progress of Wilson's survey in order to drum up interest and support, in particular urgently needed funds, from the public for the PEF.

24 Bangor Cathedral was restored by Sir George Gilbert Scott between 1870 and 1880. Scott was a supporter of the PEF.

25 Watkin W. Williams, *The Life of General Sir Charles Warren* (Oxford: Blackwell, 1941), p. 20.

26 W. Bro. Colin Neil Macdonald, *Warren! The Bond of Brotherhood* (Singapore, 2007), p. 52.

27 Ibid., p. 14. Warren, along with the novelist Sir Henry Besant, Edward Henry Palmer, the Cambridge Lord Almoner Professor of Arabic (who will feature later in this book), and the artist William Simpson set up the Masonic Archaeological Research Institute (MAI). Besant was honorary secretary of the MAI and gave his address as 9 Pall Mall East, London, SW, the address of the PEF, of which he was to become the secretary in 1868. The object of the MAI was to 'promote the interests and elevate the study of Freemasonry, by systematic and scientific meaning of masonic symbols, rites and traditions.' In the first season of the MAI in 1871, Simpson read a paper on 'Phallic

Worship', Palmer spoke on 'the Secret Sects of Syria', Warren submitted but did not read a paper on 'Moorish Architecture', and Besant held forth on the 'Secret Religions of the Middle East' and 'The Excavations in Jerusalem'. The MAI had a short life, but the drive by Irwin and Warren for a higher knowledge of Freemasonry led to the establishment in 1884 of the *Quatuor Coranati* Lodge No. 2076, of which Warren became Worshipful Master. Irwin later played a prominent role in the Golden Dawn, the Rosicrucians, the Order of the Brothers of the Swastika and the rite of Swedenborg.

28 The Grand Lodge alone in 1868 contributed £105 to the costs of Warren's work in Jerusalem, and a similar amount came from other Masonic lodges in Britain. That represented about a twelfth of Warren's agreed annual PEF allowance from late 1868, or, to put it another way, it funded one month's digging in Jerusalem. *PEF Proceedings and Notes*, Statement of Progress, 1868, p. 25.

29 *PEF Proceedings and Notes*, 1865–1869, Extracts from Report of Public Meeting of 11 June 1868, p. 6.

30 Ibid.

31 *PEQ, Quarterly Statement*, New Series, 1871, Vol. 3, No. 2, p. 90.

32 *PEF, Proceedings and Notes*, 1865–1869, Reports from Lieutenant Charles Warren, Royal Engineers, to George Grove, Esq., Hon. Secretary, VII, 1 October 1867, p.18. See also Jeffrey A. Blakely, Yaakov Huster and Felicity Cobbing, 'Charles Warren's Survey of the Plain of Philistia: Geographic Notes on the Hesi Region', *PEQ*, Vol. 146, No. 3 (2014), pp. 198–204.

33 C. Warren, 'On the Reconnaissance of a New or Partially Known Country', *Proceedings of the Royal Geographical Society of London*, Vol. 19, No. 2 (1874–5), p. 164.

34 Ibid., p. 157.

35 Ibid., p. 164.

36 Ibid., p. 165.

37 Ibid., pp. 165–6.

38 Ibid., p. 166.

39 Ibid., p. 167.

40 Watkin W. Williams, *The Life of General Sir Charles Warren* (Oxford, 1941), pp. 61–3.

41 Ibid.

42 Fergusson refused to accept Warren's conclusions, disparaging them and apparently misrepresenting Wilson's views in his *The Temples of the Jews and the Other Buildings in the Haram Area at Jerusalem* (London, 1878). A furious Warren later adduced forty-three arguments refuting Fergusson's theory. See C. Warren, *The Temple or the Tomb; Giving Further Evidence in Favour of the Authenticity of the Present Site of the Holy Sepulchre, and Pointing Out Some of the Principal Misconceptions Contained in Fergusson's 'Holy Sepulchre' and 'The Temples of the Jews'* (London, 1880). The PEF committee found in favour of Warren. However, by his own admission, Wilson was 'quite unprejudiced as regards the Sepulchre'. He had 'always seen the difficulties attending Fergusson's theory. I believe however that the question can only be settled by excavation. No one has yet met Fergusson's architectural argument as regards the Dome of the Rock [that it was Constantinian] or explained its presence in the Haram. I cannot believe it was built by the Arabs.' PEF/WIL/15/142, Wilson to Besant, 13 October 1877. It was, indeed, built in 691 AD on the order of the Umayyad Caliph Abd el-Malik, but its architecture and mosaics were copied from nearby Byzantine Christian churches and palaces. This curious mix of styles might explain Wilson's erroneous belief about its origin. Wilson seems to have shared Fergusson's 'strictures' with regard to the necessarily incomplete way Warren had presented his work to the public in his progress reports to the PEF, printed in its 'Quarterly Statements' and in his popular editions, *The Recovery of Jerusalem* and *Underground Jerusalem*. The problem really lay in PEF's delayed publication, until 1884, of Warren's full plans of his excavations. PEF/JER/WAR/53/2, Wilson memo, 11 August 1880 and Executive Committee report.

43 Wynn, *Warren*, p. 66.

44 PEF/JER/201, Morrison to Besant, 30 December 1869; Warren, *Underground Jerusalem*, p. 337.

45 A perusal of the pages of the *PEF Proceedings and Notes* for 1865–9, and the PEF *Quarterly Statements* from 1869 to 1879 gives no indication of Warren's discontent over the behaviour of Groves, which would have embarrassed the latter, and over his handling of the allocation of the limited funds available from public subscription. One has to look instead at Warren's *Underground Jerusalem,* which contains terse comments and correspondence not to be found in the PEF archives, whether in the Grove or Besant papers. These were heavily weeded by Warren and Wilson after the death of Grove, presumably to spare all concerned and the PEF from any further embarrassment. Given the subsequent destruction of the private papers of both Wilson and Warren, we have only the surviving evidence in *Underground Jerusalem*, which they could not destroy.

46 Simpson made a number of drawings of the shafts and cisterns under the Haram, which were exhibited at the Pall Mall gallery in 1872. Some of these watercolours were donated to the PEF, of which Simpson became a committee member.

47 On the initiative of Morris, a Royal Solomon Mother Lodge was set up in Jerusalem, and at its first meeting on 7 May 1873, Bro. C. F. Tyrwhitt-Drake was present as acting secretary. As we shall see, Tyrwhitt-Drake was Palmer's constant companion in their journey across Sinai, Syria and Palestine.

48 In 1899 another Middle Bronze Age channel leading from the Gihon Spring to the Siloam Pool area was discovered. This was replaced by King Hezekiah's Tunnel, a 533-metre-long aqueduct, which was intended to provide Jerusalem with a secure water supply during the Assyrian siege, which took place about 701 BC.

49 Warren's work was included in a revised version of the OS map of the Haram (1876) and in a detailed study of the walls of the Haram by Wilson in 1880 (see PEFQSt, 9–65) and by Warren, *Plans, Elevations and sections, etc, shewing the Results of the Excavations of Jerusalem, 1867–70* (London, 1884), aka 'Warren's Atlas'. The works of Wilson and Warren are still in use today since it has been very difficult for modern archaeologists to conduct any further work within the Haram because of religious sensibilities.

50 Warren, *Underground Jerusalem*, p. 82.

51 Prussian interest and influence surged after the pilgrimage to Jerusalem by Crown Prince Frederick in 1869.

52 For an informative and entertaining account of 'The Affair of the Moabite Stone' see chapter 11 of Neil Asher Silberman, *Digging for God and Country. Exploration, Archaeology and the Secret Struggle for the Holy Land, 1799–1917* (New York, 1982), pp. 100–12.

53 See Warren, 'On the Reconnaissance', pp. 155–69.

54 See *Survey of Western Palestine*. Introduction to the Palestine Exploration Fund Explorations at Jerusalem, 1867–70, by David M. Jacobsen (Archive Editions, PEF, 1999), p. 26.

55 Macdonald, *The Bond of Brotherhood*, p. 52.

56 Quoted in ibid., p. 52.

3 In the Desert of the Exodus

1 E. H. Palmer, *The Desert of the Exodus. Journeys on Foot in the Wilderness of the Forty Years' Wanderings* (Cambridge, 1871), Pt. 1, p. 1, quoting Arthur Penhryn Stanley, *Sinai and Palestine. In Connection with Their History* (London, new edition, 1868), pp. xiv–xv.

2 There is some fragmentary evidence to suggest that, as part of this survey, Capt. Felix Jones had accompanied the traveller Welbey across the Sinai in 1830 and had fixed the trigonometrical and astronomical points of the principal mountains. But as he explained at a Royal Geographical Society meeting in 1869, the survey notes had been lost by the departments concerned in Whitehall, presumably the Admiralty and the India Office. See F. W. Holland, 'Recent Explorations in the Peninsula of the Sinai', *Proceedings of the Royal Geographical Society of London*, Vol. 13, No. 3 (1868–9), pp. 204–19.

3 Palmer, *Exodus*, p. 2.

4 *The Times*, 26 September 1872.

5 Ibid.

6 See TNA, OS/1/12/3 for correspondence on the organization of the Sinai Survey.

7 Walter Besant, *The Life and Achievement of Edward Henry Palmer* (London, 1883), pp. 11–12; see David Sunderland, *These Chivalrous Brothers* (Alresford, 2016), Chapter 5, *passim*, for an entertaining account of Palmer's colourful background.

8 Palmer, *Exodus*, p. 11.

9 Ibid. For the debate over the possible routes taken by the Israelites across Sinai, see G. I. Davies, *The Way of the Wilderness* (Cambridge, 1979), Chapter 8, *passim*.

10 *The Times*, 26 September 1872.

11 Holland, 'Recent Explorations', pp. 208–9.

12 Ibid., p. 212.

13 R. Lepsius, *A Tour from Thebes to the Peninsula of Sinai* (London, 1845), p. 65 and *Briefe aus Aegypten* (Berlin, 1852), pp. 345–54, 447–51.

14 In this the survey was following in the footsteps of J. L. Burckhardt, *Travels in Syria and the Holy Land* (London, 1882), p. 609 and E. Robinson, *Biblical*

Researches in Palestine, Mount Sinai and Arabia Petraea, Vol. 1 (London, 1841), pp. 140–1.

15 *The Times*, 26 September 1872.

16 C. W. Wilson, *Ordnance Survey of the Peninsula of Sinai* (Southampton, 1869), p. 113.

17 *The Times*, 26 September 1872.

18 As for other sites for Mt. Sinai, a contemporary explorer, Charles Beke, preferred an extinct volcano in the Land of Midian, northwest Arabia though he later opted for a mountain near Akabah, as did others. See his *Mount Sinai a Volcano* (London, 1873) and *Discoveries of Sinai in Arabia* (London, 1878). Others sought a suitable mountain near Kadesh or southeast of Suez. Some have suspended judgement on the issue. See Davies, *Way of the Wilderness*, pp. 63, 109–10.

19 Holland, 'Recent Explorations', p. 214.

20 Besant, *Palmer*, p.84. For Palmer's notebooks recording the Sinaitic inscriptions, see St John's College, Cambridge, W14 (James 610) and PEF Archive, PEF/SIN/1–13. Professor Davies thinks it 'more likely that first personal disappointment and then the heavy burden of university teaching which he undertook distracted him from the task, and his early death in 1882 did not allow him the leisure of later years in which to return to it.' See Graham Davies, 'E.H. Palmer's copies of the Nabataean Inscriptions in the Sinai Peninsula.' Paper given at a symposium on the work of German epigrapher Julius Euting, Tübingen, July 1999. Professor Davies informs me that an expanded version of this paper will be published in a forthcoming *Festschrift*.

21 Ibid.

22 Sinai Survey, p. 54; Palmer, *Exodus*, p. 81.

23 Palmer, *Exodus*, p. 46.

24 Ibid., p. 65.

25 Colonel Sir Charles Watson, *The Life of Major-General Sir Charles Wilson* (London, 1909), p. 71.

26 J. Bury, *The Cambridge Ancient History*, Vol. II (Cambridge, 1924), p. 358.

27 See Israel Finkelstein and Neil Asher Silberman, *The Bible Unearthed* (New York, 2002), Chapter 2, *passim*.

28 Palmer, *Exodus*, Pt. 2, p. 284.

29 Ibid., p. 529.

30 Richard Burton, 'The Late E. H. Palmer', *The Academy Magazine*, No. 574, 5 May 1883.

31 Palmer, *Exodus*, Pt. 2, p. 291.

32 Besant, *Palmer*, pp. 97–8.

33 Palmer, *Exodus*, Pt. 2, pp. 297–9.

34 Ibid., pp. 325–6.

35 Ibid., pp. 330–4.

36 Palmer made his own contribution to the heated debate about the location of the Holy Sepulchre when he copied and translated the Cufic inscriptions around the Dome of the Rock and pronounced them to indicate that it had been built by Abd el-Melik and not Constantine. This confirmed the findings of the Rev. Williams and Warren rather than those of Fergusson. See Besant, *Palmer*, pp. 111–24.

37 See Andrew Vincent, 'The Jew, the Gipsy and el-Islam: An Examination of Richard Burton's Consulship in Damascus and his premature recall, 1868–1871', *Journal of the Royal Asiatic Society of Great Britain and Ireland*, No.2, 1985; Richard Burton, entry in *DNB*; R. Burton and C. Tyrwhitt-Drake, *Unexplored Syria. Visits to the Libanus, the Tulul el Safa, the Anti-Libanus, the Northern Libanus and the 'Alah* (London, 1872); Fawn Brodie, *The Devil Drives* (New York, 1967), pp. 281–3; Jon R. Godsall, *The Tangled Web: A Life of Sir Richard Burton* (Leicester, 2008), pp. 284–300, 328–50.

38 Burton was condescendingly critical of Palmer's popular account of his wanderings in the desert of the Exodus on the grounds that Palmer had not then learnt that 'Sinai' was simply a modern forgery, dating from after 200 AD; that the Jewish nation never knew the location of 'the Mountain of the Law'; that the first Mt. Sinai (Jebel Serbal) was invented by the Copts; the second (Jebel Musa) by the Greeks; the third (also Jebel Musa) by the Muslims, and the fourth (Jebel Safsafeh) by the American Dr Robinson. According to Burton, the 'Exodists' would have travelled by the existing haj highway from Suez to Akabah and learned Jews were inclined to believe that 'the real Tor Sinai' lay somewhere in the Tih desert north of the great pilgrimage line. Palmer insisted on translating the vulgar 'Tih' as the 'Wilderness of *the* Wanderings', but Burton said it meant a wilderness where man wanders. According to Burton, he had a friendly banter with Palmer about this. And the latter finally 'seemed to agree in opinion with me'. See Burton's obituary of Palmer in *The Academy Magazine*, no. 574, 5 May 1883. A modern assessment of Palmer's oriental scholarship (in the *DNB*) regards it to be of varying quality. His *Concise Dictionary of the Persian Language* (1876; 2nd ed, 1884) was at the time a useful work for beginners, but it has largely been superseded. Palmer was the first to translate the entire works of an Arab poet, *Beha ed-din Zoheir of Egypt* (1876-7), though he made free with the verse. His literal translation of *The Koran* (1880) was hastily done but has its admirers. His *Arabic Grammar* (1874) was the first European attempt to explain and illustrate Arabic inflexion, syntax and prosody as used by the Arabs. He produced a *Grammar of Hindustani, Persian and Arabic* (1882; 2nd ed., 1885) and revised the New Testament in Persian for the Bible Society, among other works. Palmer was Lord Almoner's Professor of Arabic at Cambridge University from 1871. After the death of his first wife in 1878 and his remarriage the following year, he grew disenchanted with university life and became a journalist for the London *Standard* newspaper, writing on a variety of subjects, including French slang, Dick Whittington, Indian magic and trained elephants.

39 The site of Kadesh has long been in dispute among scholars. In the early decades of the nineteenth century, Karl von Raumer and Edward Robinson believed Kadesh lay in the Aravah, the Great Rift Valley running from the southern end of the Dead Sea to the Red Sea. But John Rowlands ventured to 'Ain Kadis in 1842 and pronounced it to be Kadesh, a claim that was later supported by Keil and Delitzsch in 1867, Palmer in 1871 and Henry Clay Trumbull in 1881. Dean Stanley in 1856 preferred Petra, as do some modern biblical scholars.

40 TNA, FO 78/2191, Moore to FO, 18 December 1871.

41 John James Moscrop, *Measuring Jerusalem. The Palestine Exploration Fund and British Interests in the Holy Land* (Leicester, 2000), p. 118.

42 WO 33/30/640, Report on Egypt by the D.Q.M.G., War Office, 1876. After Russia's declaration of war on the Ottoman Empire on 24 April 1877, there seems to have been an attempt by an Armenian or Maltese to blow up the banks of the canal with dynamite. See D. A. Farnie, *East and West of Suez. The Suez Canal in History, 1854-1956* (Oxford, 1969), pp. 261, 266. Major Alexander Bruce Tulloch was en-route to reconnoitre Crete and joined MacDougall in Egypt and drew up a plan for military operations from the canal to Cairo. See Major-General Sir Alexander Bruce Tulloch, *Recollections of Forty Years' Service* (Edinburgh, 1903), pp. 213–14.

43 See Tulloch, *Recollections*, pp. 244–57; James Exelby, 'The Secret Service Major and the Invasion of Egypt', *History Today*, November 2006, pp. 40–1.

44 *The Royal Engineers Journal*, 1 December 1882, obituary of Captain William John Gill.

45 Gill had a family connection with the moving spirits behind the PEF and the surveys of Jerusalem, Palestine and the Sinai. His father, Robert, an officer in the Madras Native Infantry, was commissioned by the East India Company to paint copies of the Buddhist murals at Ajanta, Maharashtra, 'before decay and the recklessness of Tourists had entirely obliterated them' (quoted in Tony Hadland, *Glimpses of a Victorian Hero: Captain William Gill, Explorer and Spy* (2002), p. 3). Gill's photographs of these murals were later published in London, with descriptions by James Fergusson (*One Hundred Stereoscopic Illustrations of Architecture and Natural History* [1864] and *Western India and Rock-Cut Temples of India* [1864]). Moreover, Gill's paintings of the Ajanta frescoes were exhibited at the Indian Court of the Crystal Palace at Sydenham (at the behest of Fergusson and George Grove) and were destroyed by fire in the late 1860s.

46 He published the scientific results in 'Travels in Western China and on the Eastern Borders of Tibet', *Proceedings of the Royal Geographical Society*, Vol. 22, No. 4 (1877–8), pp. 255–71, and his travel diaries in two volumes as *The River of Golden Sand* (London, 1880). He made a traverse survey and very complete maps of his route, in forty-two sheets on a scale of 2 miles to the inch.

47 Whitworth Porter, *History of the Royal Corps of Engineers*, Vol. 2 (London, 1889), p. 375.

48 RGS Archive, WJG4, Tripoli Diary, entry for 15 March 1882.

49 Ibid., entry for 7 April 1882.

4 On secret service in the Sinai

1 For the debate on who was really responsible for this massacre (Arabi, Tewfik or the mob), see M. E. Chamberlain, 'The Alexandria Massacre of 11 June 1882 and the British Occupation of Egypt', *Middle Eastern Studies*, Vol. 13, No. 1, (January 1977), pp. 14–39. She establishes that the *mustafazin*, the gendarmerie, played an active role in the killing of Europeans, but she

does not follow up her statement (p. 23) that they were under the command of the Minister of War, namely Arabi. She makes more of their usual function as a police force normally under the control of the civil authorities.

2 Ronald Robinson and John Gallagher, with Alice Denny, *Africa and the Victorians: The Climax of Imperialism in the Dark Continent* (New York, 1961), entitled their chapter on the British intervention in Egypt in 1882: 'The Suez Crisis', partly reflecting the publication of their book in the wake of the 1956 crisis.

3 Hampshire Record Office, Northbrook Papers, 92M95/NP6/4/2, Diary for 1882, entry for 23 June 1882, tel. no.78, 23 June. D. A. Farnie, *East and West of Suez*, p.287, says that 'Arabi reportedly considered sending cannon to the banks of the Canal as well as powder-laden barges into the fairway but took neither course of action.' His source is a letter from Gladstone to Granville of 24 June 1882 (in A. Ramm, *The Political Correspondence of Mr. Gladstone and Lord Granville, 1876–1886*, Vol. 1 (Oxford, 1962), p. 381), but Gladstone's information must have come from Tulloch who states that the barges were already anchored in the fairway. Tulloch asked for and received permission from the War Office to 'employ confidential agents' for intelligence gathering. See Northbrook diary entries for 24 and 26 June 1882.

4 Northbrook Papers, 92M95/NP6/4/3/5A, Confidential Print (CP), Pt. 2, Correspondence between Northbrook and Seymour, No. 41, 22 and 23 June 1882.

5 Ibid., No. 46, Northbrook to Seymour, 30 June 1882, encl. 'Notes on the Bedouins in the Vicinity of the Suez Canal'. See 92M95/NP6/4/2/2 for Egypt. Confidential Memorandum for the accompanying sketch map by Gill 'showing the positions of some of the Bedawi Tribes near the Suez Canal'. See also copy on TNA, WO 33/39.

6 Ibid.

7 Ibid.

8 Ibid.

9 Besant, *Palmer*, pp. 253–4.

10 Northbrook Papers, 92M95/NP6/4/2/4, Northbrook note for his journal of 29 June 1882, on back of Gill's 'Notes on the Bedawin in the vicinity of the Suez Canal'.

11 Wilfrid Scawen Blunt, *Secret History of the British Occupation of Egypt: Being a Personal Narrative of Events* (New York, 1922), pp. 303–4.

12 Ibid., p. 306.

13 Besant, *Palmer*, pp. 253–4. This would seem to indicate that Palmer had far more latitude to carry out his instructions than David Sunderland has allowed. See the latter's *These Chivalrous Brothers*, pp. 18–21.

14 Ibid.

15 Ibid.

16 Blunt, *Secret History*, p. 304.

17 Besant, *Palmer*, pp. 255–7.

18 Northbrook Papers, 92M95/NP6/4/3/5A, No. 47, Seymour to Northbrook, 1 July 1882.

19 Parliamentary Papers (PP), C.3494. Correspondence respecting the murder of Professor E.H. Palmer, Captain W.M. Gill, RE, and Lieutenant Harold Charrington, RN, p. 1, Adm. To Seymour, tel., 5 July 1882.

20 Besant, *Palmer*, p. 258.

21 Northbrook Papers, 92M95/NP6/4/35A, No.50, Seymour to Northbrook, 8 July 1882.

22 Blunt, *Secret History*, p.304. Mrs Palmer later allowed Blunt to see Palmer's desert journal and letters, from which Blunt took notes, which he later used as the basis of his attack on the British government for sending the Palmer expedition to Egypt. Palmer's desert journal cannot be traced, but extracts from it can be found in Besant's biography of Palmer and Blunt's *Secret History*.

23 Besant, *Palmer*, pp. 258–60.

24 Blunt, *Secret History*, p. 305.

25 Besant, *Palmer*, p. 260.

26 Ibid., p. 261.

27 PP, C-3761, Supplementary Correspondence Respecting the Murder of Professor E.H. Palmer, Captain W. M. Gill, RE, and Lieutenant Harold Charrington, RN, 1883, p. A2, Palmer to Seymour, 15 July 1882.

28 For the debate on the bombardment of Alexandria, see Robinson et al., *Africa*, pp. 110–13; Farnie, *East and West of Suez*, pp. 288–9; C. L. Seymour, 'The Bombardment of Alexandria: A Note', *The English Historical Review*, Vol. 87, No. 345 (October 1972), pp. 790–4; Colin S. White, 'The Bombardment of Alexandria, 1882', *Mariner's Mirror*, Vol. 66 (1980), pp. 31–50.

29 Besant, *Palmer*, p. 266.

30 Ibid., p. 267.

31 Ibid.

32 Ibid., p. 268.

33 Blunt, *Secret History*, p. 305.

34 Besant, *Palmer*, pp. 268–9.

35 Ibid., p. 275.

36 Ibid., p. 272.

37 Ibid., p. 270.

38 Ibid., p. 273. Emphasis in original.

39 Blunt, *Secret History*, p. 307. Based on an investigation of Palmer's financial affairs, David Sunderland (*These Chivalrous Brothers*, pp. 206–14) has concluded that Palmer was effectively bankrupt and that it was to help recoup his fortunes that he accepted the dangerous mission to the Sinai Bedouin.

40 Besant, *Palmer*, p. 279.

41 Ibid., p. 281.

42 Ibid., p. 282.

43 Northbrook Papers, 92M95/NP6//4/35A, No. 61, Northbrook to Seymour, 3 August 1882.

44 Farnie, *East and West of Suez*, p. 291.

45 Caird Library, National Maritime Museum Greenwich, Alcester Papers, SCL 1, Hewett to Sec. of Admiralty, No. 78, 1 August 1882.

46 Ibid., p. 297.

47 Northbrook Papers, 92M95/NP6//4/35A, No.65, Northbrook to Seymour, 10 August 1882. Northbrook had made a similar point to Queen Victoria; see 92M95/NP6/4/2/9, Northbrook to the Queen, 1 August 1882.

48 Palmer continued in his erroneous belief that the Lewehat (a minor branch of the M'said) were an 'important tribe', spoke of Sheikh Meter Abu Sofieh as 'his friend', and that he had arranged to meet him at the Ayun Musa in twelve days' time.

49 PP, C-3761, pp.4–7, Palmer to Hewett, 1 August, 1882.After reading Palmer's report, Gill said that if the British delayed dealing with the 50,000 Bedouin they would join Arabi. Gill thought £25,000 not too much to pay for 50,000 men. The matter of the sheikhs imprisoned at Jerusalem could be coordinated by letter. But it was 'of the utmost urgency' to give Palmer definite instructions and the authority to proceed. Gill's comments were excised from C-3761, probably because they would have revived the criticism in Parliament of the Palmer Expedition. See Chapter 6 and ADM 116/45.

50 Caird Library, Alcester Papers, SCL 1, Hewett to Sec. of Admiralty, No. 78, 1 August 1882.

51 Besant, *Palmer*, p.282.

52 Northbrook Papers, 92M95/NP6//4/35A, No.61, Northbrook to Seymour, 3 August 1882.

53 The Blue Book of Supplementary Correspondence on the Sinai Murders (C-3761), published in 1883. See ADM 16/45.

54 See Chapter 6.

55 PP, C-3494, Admiralty to Hewett, 6 August 1882.

56 Blunt, *Secret History*, p. 308.

57 In Pickard's report of 25 September Sheikh Salamen was confused with both Meter Abu Sofieh and Sheikh Suleiman of the Teyahah. Warren pointed out that this led to the initial supposition that Meter Abu Sofieh had not betrayed the party. See C-3761, p.8, Warren to Admiralty, 21 February 1883.

58 Ibid., p. 9; TNA, FO 78/3416, Moore to Granville, No. 19, 13 September 1882.

59 Besant, *Palmer*, pp. 282–3.

60 PP, C-3493, p. 9.

61 Northbrook Papers, 92M95/NP6//4/35A, No. 55, Northbrook to Seymour, 20 July 1882.

62 Northbrook Papers, 92M95/NP6//4/35A, Confidential Correspondence between Northbrook and Hoskins, No. 2, 21 July 1882.

63 Royal Geographical Society (RGS), William Gill Papers, Vol. 3, Obituary Notice for Gill in *Royal Engineers Journal*, 1 December 1882, quoted in Tony Hadland, *Glimpses of a Victorian Hero: Captain William Gill, Explorer and Spy* (Coventry, 2002), p. 74.

64 ADM 116/44 Pt. 1, Blue Book draft 'A', p. 3, minute for Northbrook, 16 January 1883, Hoskins to Seymour, 1882.

65 RGS, Gill Papers, REJ obit. Notice, quoted in Hadland, *Gill*, p. 75.

66 Ibid.

67 Blunt, *Secret History*, p. 308.

68 Besant, *Palmer*, p. 284.

5 Manhunt in the desert

1 TNA, ADM 116/44, Part 1, Blue Book draft 'A', p.3, minute for Northbrook, 16 January 1883, Hoskins to Seymour, 8 August, 1882, Hoskins to Admiralty, 14 and 17 August 1882, Hoskins to Seymour, 20 September, 1882, encl. Pickard to Hoskins, 19 September 1882. Pickard's name was deleted from the published Blue Book (C3494) in order to preserve his anonymity and safety from possible Egyptian reprisals.

2 PEF, PAL. (II), 12–29, *The Standard*, 16 August 1882.

3 PEF, PAL. (II), 12–29, *The Standard*, 19 August 1882; RGS, Gill Papers, Vol. 3, Newspaper cuttings, *Leeds Mercury*, 19 August 1882.

4 ADM 116/44, Part 1, Blue Book draft 'A', Hewett to Admiralty, 3 September 1882, encl. Hewett to Seymour, 1 September 1882.

5 Northbrook Papers, 92M95/NP6/4/3/5A, Northbrook to Seymour, 25 August. Private; 92M95/NP6/4/3/5B, Northbrook to Hewett, 18 August 1882.

6 ADM 116/44, Part 1, Blue Book draft 'A', Admiralty to Seymour, 22 August 1882, Hoskins to Admiralty, 23 August 1882, Hewett to Admiralty, 22 August 1882, Hewett to Northbrook, 26 August 1882, Hoskins to Northbrook, 27 August 1882.

7 RGS, Gill Papers, Vol.3, Newspaper Cuttings, *The Standard*, 29 August 1882, *The Globe*, 29 August 1882.

8 ADM 116/44, Part 1, Blue Book draft 'A', Hewett to Admiralty, 3 September 1882, encl. Hewett to Seymour, 1 September 1882.

9 A.E.Haynes, *Man-Hunting in the Desert* (London, 1894), p. 9.

10 Ibid., p. 284.

11 Ibid., pp. 7–8. Warren seems to have later edited this report and published it as 'Notes on Arabia Petraea and the Country Lying between Egypt and Palestine', *PEQ*, Vol. 19, No. 1 (January 1887), pp. 38–46.

12 PP, C-3761, p. 17.

13 Ibid., p. 16. Captain Foote had filled one of the Suez dry docks with freshwater as a last reserve for the townspeople.

14 Ibid., p. 14; Cd 3494, Hewett to Seymour, 7 and 16 September 1882.

15 Northbrook Papers, 92M95/NP6/4/3/5B, Hewett to Northbrook, 4 September 1882.

16 Haynes, *Man-Hunting*, p. 18.

17 Haynes, *Man-Hunting*, p. 20.

18 See RGS, Gill Papers, Vol. 3, Newspaper Cuttings, *The Globe*, *The Daily News*, 13 September 1882 and *The Standard*, 26 September 1882.

19 Ibid., p. 24.

20 C.3494, p. 17, Hewett to Seymour, 16 September 1882, encl. Warren to Hewett, 8 September 1882.

21 Ibid., p. 27.

22 Ibid., pp. 26–8, based on Cd. 3494, pp. 16–18, Warren to Hewett, 8 September 1882.

23 C.3494, p. 21, Hewett to Seymour, 16 September 1882, encl. Warren to Hewett, 10 September 1882.

24 Haynes, *Man-Hunting*, pp. 30–1.

25 C.3494, pp. 23–5, Hewett to Seymour, 27 September 1882, encl. Warren to Hewett, 24 September 1882.

26 ADM 116/44, Part 1, Blue Book draft 'A', Hewett to Seymour, 27 September 1882, encl. Warren to Hewett, 24 September 1882, encl. 3, Warren to Moussa Nassier, 16 September 1882.

27 C.3761, p. 17, Warren to Admiralty, 10 April 1883.

28 Haynes, *Man-Hunting*, p. 45.

29 C. 3494, pp. 23–5, Hewett to Seymour, 27 September 1882, encl. Warren to Hewett, 24 September 1882.

30 C.3761, p. 17, Warren to Admiralty, 10 April 1883; Haynes, *Man-Hunting*, p. 47.

31 C.3494, p. 27, Hewett to Admiralty, 8 October 1882, encl. Warren to Hewett, 4 October 1882.

32 Haynes, *Man-Hunting*, p. 52.

33 Ibid., p. 53.

34 C.3494, p. 12, Hewett to Admiralty, 17 September 1882.

35 C.3494, p. 27, Hewett to Admiralty, 8 October 1882, encl. Warren to Hewett, 4 October 1882.

36 Haynes, *Man-Hunting*, p. 56.

37 Ibid., pp. 56–7.

38 The three sheikhs were Ibrahim Monsoorah and the brothers Mabarah and Mabrook Abu Atwa.

39 C.3494, p. 27, Hewett to Admiralty, 8 October 1882, encl. Warren to Hewett, 4 October 1882.

40 Haynes, *Man-Hunting*, p. 58.

41 Ibid., p. 61.

42 Ibid.

43 Ibid.

44 Ibid.

45 Present at this meeting were three representatives from the Shehide family from Cairo, who were of the Hawetat tribe, Ibrahim Mansoorah and seven followers from the Towarah/Aligat tribe and Hassan Shaiyr of the Sawalhah. Sheikh Hassan of the Terebin was missing and required.

46 Haynes, *Man-Hunting*, p. 68.

47 Ibid., p. 71.

48 Ibid., pp. 71–2.

49 Ibid., p. 74.

50 Ibid., p. 75.

51 Ibid., p. 77.

52 Ibid., pp. 77–8.

53 Ibid., p. 80.

54 Ibid., pp. 81–2.

55 Ibid., pp. 83–4.

56 Ibid., p. 88.

57 C.3494, p. 15, SNO, Suez, to Admiralty, 17 October 1882.

6 Warren and the Bedouin

1 Haynes, *Man-Hunting*, p. 93.

2 Ibid.

3 C-3494, p. 39, Warren to Seymour, 20 October 1882.

4 Ibid., p. 95.

5 C-3494, p. 40, Warren to Seymour, 20 October 1882.

6 Ibid, p. 97. *The Times* later claimed (2 March 1883) that Palmer and his companions were all shot and that none leapt off the cliff. See Chapter 6 for the definitive version of their deaths.

7 Ibid., p. 99.

8 Haynes, *Man-Hunting*, p. 104.

9 Ibid., p. 107.

10 Ibid., p. 108.

11 *The Times*, 17 October 1882.

12 C-3494, pp. 31–2, Gill to Northbrook, 23 October 1882.

13 See ADM 116/44, Part 1, minute for Northbrook, 16 January 1883, Blue Book draft 'A', pp. 32–3.

14 Haynes, *Man-Hunting*, p. 108.

15 Ibid., pp. 112–13.

16 Ibid., p. 114.

17 Ibid., p. 116.

18 Ibid., p. 118.

19 Ibid., p. 18.

20 ADM 116/44, Part 1, minute for Northbrook, 16 January 1883, Blue Book draft 'A', p. 57.

21 Ibid., p. 58.

22 *The Times*, 6 November 1882.

23 Northbrook Papers, 92M95/NP6/4/3/5A, No 90, Northbrook to Seymour, 27 October 1882.

24 Ibid., No. 91, Seymour to Northbrook, 28 October 1882.

25 C-3494, p. 85, Moore to FO, 24 November 1882.

26 Haynes, *Man-Hunting*, p. 122.

27 Ibid., p. 130. Emphasis in original.

28 Ibid., p. 133.

29 C-3494, p. 64, Warren to Seymour, 14 November 1882.

30 Haynes, *Man-Hunting*, p. 162.

31 Ibid., pp. 163–4.

32 C-3494, p. 91, Warren to Alcester, 25 December 1882.

33 ADM 116/44, Part 2, minute for Northbrook, 16 January 1883, Blue Book draft 'A', pp. 84–5, Burton to FO, 16 November 1882.

34 C-3494, p. 84, Moore to Granville, 31 October 1882.

35 C-3494, p. 78, Warren to Admiralty, 3 December 1882.

36 ADM 116/44, Pt. 2, Blue Book draft 'A', p. 62, Warren to Northbrook, 27 November 1882.

37 Haynes, *Man-Hunting*, p. 187.

38 Ibid., p. 193. In contradistinction to Wilson and Palmer, Haynes agreed with Burton that Jebel Musa was not Mt. Sinai. Burton and Haynes preferred a site in the group of mountains in the Tih, north of the haj route from Suez to Akabah, about midway between these two places.

39 Gill's notebook has gone missing, although his earlier travel notebooks and papers, were later donated by his family to the Royal Geographical Society and can be found in the latter's archive. The fragments from Palmer's notebooks can be found in the Palestine Exploration Fund archive.

40 Haynes, *Man-Hunting*, p. 223. Haynes did not reveal the serious tensions between the Charringtons and the Sapper officers with regard to the conduct of the manhunt and the journey to Wadi Sadr. See Sunderland (*These Chivalrous Brothers*, Chapter 15, *passim*) for details, based on Lt. Burton's diary.

41 Northbrook Papers, 92M95/NP6/4/3/5A, No. 96, Seymour to Northbrook, 16 November 1882 and No. 107, Seymour to Northbrook, 14 January 1882.

7 The final judgement

1 Haynes, *Man-Hunting*, p. 228.

2 Ibid., p. 231.

3 ADM 116/45, Pt.IV, Supplementary Correspondence, Warren to Alcester, 18 February 1883.

4 Haynes, *Man-Hunting*, p. 232.

5 Ibid., p. 235.

6 ADM 116/45, Pt.IV, Supplementary Correspondence, Fitzroy to Alcester, 18 February 1883.

7 Haynes, *Man-Hunting*, p. 243.

8 Ibid., p. 246.

9 Ibid., p. 247.

10 Ibid., p. 249.

11 Ibid., pp. 256–8.

12 Ibid., p. 259.

13 Ibid., p. 260.

14 See House of Commons Parliamentary Papers, C.3494 and C.3761, 1883.

15 *The Times*, 2 March 1883.

16 Blunt, *Secret History*, p. 303.

17 Ibid.

18 *The Times*, 2 March 1883.

19 For a comparison, see C.3494, pp. 23–5, Hewett to Seymour, 27 September 1882, encl. Warren to Hewett, 24 September 1882, and ADM 116/44, Part 1, Blue Book draft 'A', Hewett to Seymour, 27 September 1882, encl. Warren to Hewett, 24 September 1882, encl. 3, Warren to Moussa Nassier, 16 September 1882. Campbell-Bannerman informed the House of Commons on 5 March 1883 that only four people besides the 'Heads of the Admiralty' had seen the confidential papers, namely, the draft and the final version. 'One of those four persons was allowed to see the actual Papers, and the others were furnished with copies in the strictest confidence.' Hansard, HC Deb, 5 March 1883, vol. 276, cc 1438–509.

20 This censure on West by *The Times* indicates that the editors must have seen the entire original draft of the Blue Book since West's passage on the hazards of interviewing the Bedouin was excised from the final, published Blue Book. For the different versions of West to the FO, 20 November 1882, compare C.3494, p. 50 with ADM 116/44 Pt. 2, p. 85.

21 Hansard, HC Deb, 5 March 1883, Vol. 276, cc1438–509.

22 Ibid.

23 C.3494, p. 2, Seymour to Admiralty, 6 August 1882.

24 Hansard, HC Deb, 5 March 1883, Vol. 276, cc1438–509.

25 Ibid.

26 Ibid.

27 Haynes, *Man-Hunting*, p. 268.

28 *The Times*, 10 March 1883.

29 Ibid.

30 HC Deb 12 March 1883, Vol. 277, cc210–12.

31 Ibid.

32 HL Deb 16 March 1883, Vol. 277, cc672–83.

33 Blunt, *Secret History*, p. 31.

34 HL Deb 16 March 1883, Vol. 277, cc672–83.

35 Ibid. Wentworth's quoted extracts were rough versions of the originals, but they conveyed the correct gist.

36 HL Deb 16 March 1883, Vol. 277, cc672–83.

37 Ibid. (italics mine)

38 Ibid. Northbrook confirmed this in a letter to Hewett dated 21 March 1883 in reply to Hewett's explanation of his conduct of 1 December 1882, when he said that: 'I should not have hesitated if it had been necessary, but it did not seem to be required at the time, so I instructed you to hold on by my telegram of the 6th of August.' Northbrook Papers, 92M95/NP6/4/3/58, Northbrook to Hewett, 21 March 1882.

39 Ibid.

40 *The Times*, 29 May 1883.

41 All quoted passages from *The Times*, 29 May 1883.

42 C.3761, p. 16, Colonel Warren, History of the Expedition of Professor Palmer, 21 February 1883.

43 *The Standard*, 7 April 1883.

44 There are also memorials to Lt. Charrington in Holy Trinity Church, Barkingside, London, near the family brewery and in the parish church at Hunsdon, Hertfordshire, where the family had a house.

45 The Crypt, St. Paul's Cathedral, London.

46 Warren's behaviour would seem to discount Sunderland's suggestion (see *These Chivalrous Brothers*, p. 214) that the bankrupt Palmer had himself embezzled the £2,000 in gold sovereigns, burying it in the desert for later collection or having a P&O ship's captain smuggle it back to England for delivery to Mrs Palmer.

8 A modern-day Moses

1 Haynes, *Man-Hunting*, p. 335.

2 PEQ, Vol. 16, No. 4 (October 1884), Major Kitchener's Report, pp. 202–3. Haynes, *Man-Hunting*, pp. 272–3 has a shortened version of the quotation from Kitchener's Report.

3 Haynes, *Man-Hunting*, pp. 274–5.

4 Ibid., p. 275.

5 *The Royal Engineers Journal*, 1 December 1882.

BIBLIOGRAPHY

Manuscript Sources

British Library

Add.Ms.38991, Layard Papers.

Caird Library, National Maritime Museum, Greenwich

Alcester Papers.

Hewett Papers.

Hampshire Records Office

Northbrook Papers.

St. John's College, Cambridge

Palmer notebooks and scrap book.

National Archives, Kew, London

ADM 116: Admiralty: Record Office: Cases.

FO 65: Foreign Office, General correspondence before 1906. Russian Empire.

FO 78: Foreign Office: General correspondence before 1906, Ottoman Empire.

FO 181: Foreign Office: Embassy and Consulates, USSR (formerly Russian Empire), General correspondence.

OS/1: Ordnance Survey, Central Registry, Registered Files, Special Maps and Surveys.

WO 33: War Office. Reports. Memoranda and Papers (O&A Series).

Palestine Exploration Fund, Marylebone, London

PEF/JER Jerusalem Water Supply.

PEF/JER/WIL Wilson's Surveys of Jerusalem.

PEF/JER/War Warren's Survey of Jerusalem.

PEF/WAR Warren's Miscellaneous Letters, 1876–1880.

PEF/WIL/LET Wilson's Miscellaneous Letters.

PEF/SYR Syrian Improvement Committee.

PEF/SIN Sinai Survey, 1868–9.

PEF/PAL Expedition to the Desert of the Exodus (Tih), 1869–70; Expedition to Gaza and Death of Professor Palmer, 1882–3.

PEF/ARA Survey of Wadi Arabah.

PEF, Proceedings and Notes, 1865–1869; Quarterly Statements, New Series, 1869–1879; Palestine Exploration Quarterly (PEQ).

Survey of Western Palestine (Archive Editions, PEF, 1999).

The Royal Geographical Society, London

The William Gill Papers, Tripoli Diary.

Newspapers

The Daily News.

The Globe.

The Standard.

The Times.

Official Records (Printed)

Hansard, House of Commons and House of Lords Debates, 1882–3.

Parliamentary Papers, C.3494.Correspondence respecting the murder of Professor E.H. Palmer, Captain W.M. Gill, R.E., and Lieutenant Harold Charrington, R.N.; C.3761. Supplementary correspondence respecting … Professor Palmer, Etc (London, 1883).

Wilson, C.W. *Ordnance Survey of Jerusalem Made in the Years 1864 to 1865* (Southampton, 1866).

Wilson, C. W. *Ordnance Survey of the Peninsula of Sinai* (Southampton, 1869).

Other Printed Sources

Barber, M. *The New Knighthood. A History of the Order of the Temple* (Cambridge: Cambridge University Press, 2010).

Beadnell, H.J.L. 'Central Sinai', *Geographical Journal*, Vol. 67, No. 5 (May 1926), pp. 385–98

Beaver III, W. *Under Every Leaf: How Britain played the Great Game from Afghanistan to Africa* (London: Biteback, 2012).

Beke, C. *Discoveries of Sinai in Arabia* (London, 1878).

Beke, C. *Mount Sinai a Volcano* (London, 1873).

Ben-Arieh, Y. 'The Geographical Exploration of the Holy Land', *PEQ*, Vol. 104, No. 2 (1972), pp. 81–92.

Besant, W. *The Life and Achievements of Edward Henry Palmer* (London, 1883).

Bidwell, R. L. 'Edward Henry Palmer', *Bulletin (British Society for Middle Eastern Studies)*, Vol. 13, No. 1 (1986), pp. 45–50.

Blakely, J. A.,Y. Huster and F. Cobbing, 'Charles Warren's Survey of the Plain of Philistia: Geographic Notes on the Hesi Region', *PEQ*, Vol. 146, No. 3 (2014), pp. 198–204.

Blunt, W. S. *Secret History of the British Occupation of Egypt* (New York, 1922).

Brodie, F. *The Devil Drives* (New York: Norton, 1967).

Burkhardt, J. L. *Travels in Syria and the Holy Land* (London, 1882).

Burrows, M. ' "Mission Civilisatrice": French Cultural Policy in the Middle East, 1860–1914', *The Historical Journal*, Vol. 29, No. 1 (March 1986), pp. 109–35.

Burton, R. 'The Late E.H. Palmer', *Academy Magazine*, No. 574 (5 May 1883).

Burton, R. and C. Tyrwhitt-Drake. *Unexplored Syria* (London, 1872).

Bury, J. *The Cambridge Ancient History*, Vol. 2 (Cambridge: Cambridge University Press, 1924).

Chamberlain, M. E.'The Alexandria Massacres of 11 June 1882 and the British Occupation of Egypt', *Middle Eastern Studies*, Vol. 13, No. 1 (January 1977), pp. 14–39.

Chamberlain, M. E. 'Sir Charles Dilke and the British Intervention in Egypt, 1882', *British Journal of International Studies*, Vol. 2, No. 3 (October 1976), pp. 231–45.

Cox, F. 'Khedive Ismail and Panslavism', *Slavonic and East European Review*, Vol. 32 (1953/1954), pp. 115–32.

Davies, G. I. *The Way of the Wilderness* (Cambridge: Cambridge University Press, 1979).

Davies, G. I. 'E.H. Palmer's copies of the Nabataean Inscriptions in the Sinai Peninsula', unpublished conference paper, July 1999.

De Vogues, M. *Le Temple de Jerusalem* (Paris, 1864).

Emerit, M. 'La Crise Syrienne et l'Expansion Economique Francaise en 1860', *Revue Historique*, T207, Fasc. 2 (1952), pp. 211–32.

Exelby, J. 'The Secret Service Major and the Invasion of Egypt', *History Today*, November 2006.

Farnie, D. A. *East and West of Suez. The Suez Canal in History, 1854–1956* (Oxford: Clarendon Press, 1969).

Fergusson, J. *The Temples of the Jews and the Other Buildings in the Haram area at Jerusalem* (London, 1878).

Finkelstein I. and N. A. Silberman. *The Bible Unearthed* (New York: Free Press, 2002).

Gavish, D. 'French Cartography of the Holy Land in the Nineteenth Century', *PEQ*, Vol. 126, No. 1 (1994), pp. 24–30.

Gibson S. D. M. Jacobson. *Below the Temple Mount in Jerusalem* (Oxford: Tempus Repartum, 1996).

Gill, W. 'Travels in Western China and on the Eastern Borders of Tibet',
    Proceedings of the Royal Geographical Society of London, Vol. 22, No. 4 (1877–
    8), pp. 255–71.

Gill, W. *The River of Golden Sand* (London, 1880).

Godsall, J. R. *The Tangled Web. A Life of Sir Richard Burton* (Leicester:
    Matador, 2008).

Goren, H. *Dead Sea Level* (London: I. B. Tauris, 2011).

Goren, H. 'Scientific Organisations as agents of change: the Palestine
    Exploration Fund. The *Deutsche Verein zur Erforschung Palastinas* and
    nineteenth century Palestine', *Journal of Historical Geography*, Vol. 27, No. 2
    (2001), pp. 153–65.

Goren, H. 'Sacred but not Surveyed: Nineteenth Century Surveys of Palestine',
    Imago Mundi, Vol. 54 (2002), pp. 87–100.

Haag, M. *The Templars. History and Myth* (London: Profile Books, 2008)

Hadland, T. *Glimpses of a Victorian Hero* (Coventry, 2002).

Hamblin W. T. and D. R. Seely. *Solomon's Temple. Myth and History*
    (London: Thames and Hudson, 2007).

Haynes, A. E. *Man-hunting in the Desert* (London, 1894).

Hewitt, R. *Map of a Nation. The Biography of the Ordnance Survey*
    (Cambridge: Granta Books, 2010).

Holland, F. W. 'Recent Explorations in the Peninsula of the Sinai', *Proceedings
    of the Royal Geographical Society of London*, Vol. 13, No. 3 (1868–9),
    pp. 204–19.

Holland, R. *Blue Water Empire. The British in the Mediterranean since 1800*
    (London: Penguin, 2012).

Hopkins, A. G. 'The Victorians and Africa: A Reconsideration of the
    Occupation of Egypt, 1882', *Journal of African History*, Vol. 27, No. 2 (1986),
    pp. 363–91.

Hopwood, D. *The Russian Presence in Syria and Palestine, 1843–1914*
    (Oxford: Clarendon Press, 1969).

Howe, K. S. 'Mapping a Sacred Geography. Photographic Surveys by the
    Royal Engineers in the Holy Land, 1864–68', in J. M. Schwartz and J. R.
    Ryan (eds), *Picturing Place. Photography and the Geographical Imagination*
    (London: I. B. Tauris, 2003).

Howe, K. S. *Revealing the Holy Land. The Photographic Exploration of Palestine*
    (Santa Barbara: University of California Press, 1997).

Iseminger, G. L. 'The Old Turkish Hands; the British Levantine Consuls, 1856–
    1876', *Middle East Journal*, Vol. 22, No. 3 (1968), pp. 297–316.

Jarvis, C. S. *Yesterday and Today in Sinai* (London: Edinburgh, W. Blackwood,
    1931).

Jones, Y. 'British Military Surveys of Palestine and Syria, 1840–1841',
    Cartographic Journal, Vol. 10, No. 1 (June 1973), pp. 29–31.
Lipman, D. 'The Origins of the Palestine Exploration Fund', *PEQ*, Vol. 120, No. 1
    (1988), pp. 46–54.
Lepsius, R. *A Tour from Thebes to the Peninsula of Sinai* (London, 1845).
Lepsius, R. *Briefe ans Aegyten* (Berlin, 1852).
Macdonald, C. N. *Warren! The Bond of Brotherhood* (Singapore, 2007).
MacHaffie, B. Z. '"Monument Facts and Higher Critical Fancies": Archaeology
    and the Popularization of Old Testament Criticism in Nineteenth Century
    Britain', *Church History*, Vol. 50, No. 3 (September 1981), pp. 316–28.
Marlowe, J. *The Making of the Suez Canal* (London: Cresset Press, 1964).
Mange, A. E. *The Near Eastern Policy of Napoleon III* (Urbana: University of
    Illinois Press, 1940).
Miller, W. *The Ottoman Empire and its Successors, 1801–1923* (London: Frank
    Cass, 1966).
Montefiore, S. S. *Jerusalem. The Biography* (London: Weidenfeld &
    Nicolson, 2011).
Moscrop, J. *Measuring Jerusalem* (London: Leicester University Press, 2000).
Mosse, W. E. 'Russia and the Levant, 1856–1862, Grand Duke Constantine
    Nicolaevich and the Russian Steam navigation Company', *Journal of Modern
    History*, Vol. 26, No. 1 (March 1954), pp. 39–48.
Musgrave, M. (ed.) *George Grove. Music and Victorian Culture* (London:
    Palgrave Macmillan, 2003).
Ohne, E. *Photographic Heritage of the Holy Land, 1839–1914*
    (Manchester: Institute of Advanced Studies, Manchester Polytechnic, 1980).
Palmer, E. H. *The Desert of the Exodus* (Cambridge, 1871).
Pierotti, E. *Jerusalem Explored* (London, 1864).
Porter, W. *History of the Corps of Royal Engineers*, Vol. 2 (London, 1889).
Ramm, A. *The Political Correspondence of Mr. Gladstone and Lord Granville,
    1876–1886*, Vol. 1 (Oxford, London: Offices of the Royal Historical
    Society, 1962).
Ritmeyer, L. *The Quest. Revealing the Temple Mount in Jerusalem*
    (Jerusalem: Carta Jerusalem, 2006).
Robinson E. and E. Smith. *Biblical Researches on Palestine, Sinai, Arabia Petraea
    and Adjacent Regions* (1841, reprinted Cambridge, 2015).
Robinson, R J. Gallagher and A. Denny. *Africa and the Victorians* (New York: St.
    Martin's Press, 1961).
Rodogno, D. '"The Principles of Humanity", and the European Powers.
    Intervention in Ottoman Lebanon and Syria in 1860–1861', in B. Simms
    and D. J. B. Trim (eds) *Humanitarian Intervention. A History* (Cambridge:
    Cambridge University Press, 2011).

Ryan, J. B. *Picturing Empire. Photography and the Visualization of the British Empire* (London: University of Chicago Press, 1997).

Sandes, E. W. C. *The Royal Engineers in Egypt and the Sudan* (Chatham: Institution of Royal Engineers, 1937).

Scherer, P. 'Partner or Puppet? Lord John Russell at the Foreign Office, 1859–1865', *Albion*, Vol. 19, No. 3 (1987), pp. 347–71.

Scholch, A. 'The "Men on the Spot" and the English Occupation of Egypt in 1882', *Historical Journal*, Vol. 19, No. 3 (September 1976), pp. 773–85.

Seymour, C. L. 'The Bombardment of Alexandria: A Note', *English Historical Review*, Vol. 87, No. 345 (October 1972), pp. 790–4.

Shanks, H. *Jerusalem. An Archaeological Biography* (New York: Random House, 1995).

Shanks, H. *Jerusalem's Temple Mount* (London: Continuum, 2007).

Shepherd, N. *The Zealous Intruders. The Western Rediscovery of Palestine* (London: Collins, 1987).

Silberman, N. *Digging for God and Country* (New York: Knopf, 1982).

Smith, W. (ed.) *A Dictionary of the Bible* (London, 1863).

Smithers, A.J. *Honourable Conquests* (London: Pen & Sword, 1991).

Stanley, A. P. *Sinai and Palestine in Connexion with their History* (London, 1856).

Sumner, B. H. 'Ignatyev at Constantinople I', *Slavonic and East European Review*, Vol. 11 (1932/1933), pp. 341–53.

Sunderland, D. *These Chivalrous Brothers* (Winchester: Chronos Books, 2016).

Thornton, A.P. 'Imperial Frontiers in the Levant, 1870–1900', in his *File on Empire* (London: Macmillan, 1968), pp. 221–51.

Tibawi, A. L. *British Interests in Palestine* (London: Oxford University Press, 1961)

Todd G.E. (ed.) *The Autobiography of William Simpson* (London: T. Fisher Unwin, 1903).

Tulloch, A. B. *Recollections of Forty Years' Service* (Edinburgh: W. Blackwood, 1903).

Vincent, A. 'The Jew, the Gipsy and el-Islam'. An Examination of Richard Burton's Consulship in Damascus and his premature recall, 1868–1871', *Journal of the Royal Asiatic Society of Great Britain and Ireland*, No. 2, 1985, 155–73.

Wade, S. *Spies in the Empire* (London: Anthem Press, 2007).

Ward, A. W. and G. P. Gooch. *The Cambridge History of British Foreign Policy, 1783–1919* (Cambridge: Cambridge University Press, 1923).

Warren, C., 'On the Reconnaissance of a New or Partially Known Country', *Proceedings of the Royal Geographical Society of London*, Vol. 19, No. 2 (1874–5), pp. 155–69.

Warren, C. *Plans, Elevations and sections, etc., shewing the Results of the Excavations of Jerusalem, 1867–70* (London, 1884).

Warren, C., *The Temple of the Tomb* (London, 1880).

Warren, C. *Underground Jerusalem* (London, 1876).

Watson, C. *The Life of Major-General Sir Charles William Wilson* (London: John Murray, 1909).

White, C. S. 'The Bombardment of Alexandria, 1882', *Mariner's Mirror*, Vol. 66 (1980), pp. 31–50.

Whitty, J.I. 'The Water Supply of Jerusalem, Ancient and Modern', *Journal of Sacred Literature* (April 1864), pp. 133–57.

Williams, G. *The Holy City* (London, 1849).

Williams, W. W. *The Life of Sir Charles Warren* (Oxford: Blackwell, 1941).

Wilson, C. W. 'Recent Surveys in Sinai and Palestine', *Journal of the Royal Geographical Society*, Vol. 43 (1873), pp. 206–49.

Wilson C. W. and C. Warren. *The Recovery of Jerusalem* (London, 1871).

Young, P. *George Grove, 1820–1900. A Biography* (London: Macmillan, 1980).

Yule, H. 'Obituary of Captain William John Gill', *Royal Engineers Journal*, 1 (December 1882).

Zachs, F. 'Novice or Heaven-Born Diplomat? Lord Dufferin's Plan for a Province of Syria, 1860–1', *Middle Eastern Studies*, Vol. 36, No. 3, pp. 160–76.

INDEX